HOSPITAL SOCIAL WORK

The Interface of Medicine and Caring

Joan Beder

Routledge
Taylor & Francis Group
New York   London

Published in 2006 by
Routledge
Taylor & Francis Group
270 Madison Avenue
New York, NY 10016

Published in Great Britain by
Routledge
Taylor & Francis Group
2 Park Square
Milton Park, Abingdon
Oxon OX14 4RN

International Standard Book Number-10: 0-415-95067-8 (Softcover)
International Standard Book Number-13: 978-0-415-95067-1 (Softcover)
Library of Congress Card Number 2005016922

Library of Congress Cataloging-in-Publication Data

Beder, Joan, 1944-
   Hospital social work : the interface of medicine and caring / Joan Beder.
        p. ; cm.
   Includes bibliographical references and index.
   ISBN 0-415-95067-8 (pb : alk. paper)
   1. Medical social work. [DNLM: 1. Social Work Department, Hospital. W 322 B411h 2005] I. Title.

HV687.B43 2005
362.1'0425--dc22   2005016922

Taylor & Francis Group
is the Academic Division of Informa plc.

Visit the Taylor & Francis Web site at
http://www.taylorandfrancis.com

and the Routledge Web site at
http://www.routledge-ny.com

HOSPITAL SOCIAL WORK

To the many, so busy social workers who let me ask my questions; to my colleagues and friends for their support; to my family and loved ones who take an active interest in what I find compelling; and to you, Matthew, who makes it all worthwhile and especially sweet.

CONTENTS

FOREWORD

Hospital Social Work: The Interface of Medicine and Caring is a comprehensive review of the many aspects of hospital social work. Joan Beder has skillfully blended descriptions of key health issues and family and patient perspectives with the roles that social workers play in all facets of hospital life. Written with an original yet experienced approach, the book addresses what hospital social workers do, where they do it, how, and why. Easy to read and informative, this is the most current treatment of issues impacting social workers in hospitals today.

Highlights:

Each area of hospital social work practice is reviewed, humanizing the academic aspects as well as providing concrete examples.

Summaries of interviews with real-life social workers provide detailed insights into each area (e.g., oncology) at the end of each chapter.

The most up-to-date information regarding new health care organizations and policies that impact hospital social work is included.

More than 130 social workers at more than 20 urban and rural hospitals were interviewed in the writing of this book. They represented burn units, critical care areas, intensive care units, pediatric settings, emergency rooms, dialysis units, surgical units, and general medical floors. Numerous department heads and administrators were consulted by the author. The caring, frustrations, and satisfactions associated with hospital social work are illustrated as well as the benefits of helping those who are ill and their caregivers.

Students of social work studying health care and social work practice are the main beneficiaries of this text. The reader will learn about various medical conditions and what is involved in the care of the patient as well as understand the family members' and caretaker's experiences. The reader will hear the voices of the social workers, see how and where they work, and "feel" the atmosphere of the hospital.

Each chapter is organized to first educate about a certain medical condition, based on research and the latest medical information. Illnesses are viewed from the perspective of the patients and their caregivers. Next the roles of new or aspiring social workers are explored, amplified by concluding comments of social workers addressing the following questions:

What does a social worker actually do?

How do social workers define their roles and functions in a particular unit?

What are the expectations of a social worker in a defined hospital unit?

More specific questions are answered in each chapter.

Social workers and related health care professionals will find this book of interest as it highlights the interactions of the medical world and those who deal directly with the patients and caregivers.

The dedication and struggles of all involved in caring for the sick, comes forth in the comments and observations of those interviewed. If you are considering social work, especially social work in a hospital, this book will educate and hopefully inspire.

ABOUT THE AUTHOR

I love the profession of social work; I love that there are so many ways to be a good social worker and so many places that the individual interests of the social worker can be realized. I marvel that one social worker can be working in a senior center with a geriatric population whereas another can be counseling children, using play therapy as a medium of helping. Another social worker can be working in city government developing programs for the homeless while his or her counterpart does individual psychotherapy with a depressed client. So many different expressions of helping, building on the motivation of individuals who want to help others as their life's work.

My own journey in social work has taken many twists and turns, but for the most part, I have been involved in the medical end of the profession, counseling oncology and AIDS patients and family members, while developing an expertise in grief and bereavement. Although I have been teaching at Yeshiva University, Wurzweiler School of Social Work for more than 15 years, I have continued to be immersed in the world of medicine, continuing my work and research in oncology, AIDS, and nephrology.

I teach students how to be good social workers; social workers who can listen, be empathic, and combine their skill and passion in a helping relationship. I teach from a systems perspective, helping the student see that many influences and individuals create a given moment and that the greatest flaw in a social worker is taking a one-dimensional view of any given situation. This perspective is utilized and applied in medical social work and forms the basis for assessment and intervention in many situations. This orientation seems to be the key to being able to understand and assist those who are hospitalized.

I thank each social worker who spent time with me, and I hope that this volume acknowledges the wonderful work you do. If we can motivate a new student or a social worker who is not certain what aspect of social work to embrace and is drawn toward hospital social work, our efforts will have been well served.

I applaud my social work colleagues and celebrate them through this volume.

Finally, I wish to thank the following reviewers for their contributions to this edition: Vikki L. Vandiver, Shantih Clemens, Kathleen M. Wade, Ken Feifer, and Barry Rock.

Joan Beder, DSW

1

ABOUT MEDICAL SOCIAL WORK

This chapter introduces the reader to various aspects of the social work profession as it has developed in hospitals. It explores the history of medical social work, the theoretical perspectives that guide social work practice in the medical setting, the nature of collaboration with other health care professionals within the hospital, and the meaning and impact of managed care on the delivery of social work services.

HISTORY OF MEDICAL SOCIAL WORK

Social work in health care began in the United States at Massachusetts General Hospital (MGH) in the early 1900s. At the turn of the century, a steady progression away from home care for the sick had begun; hospitals were slowly replacing the home as the locus of medical treatment in the United States. Concurrent with this shifting venue of care, physicians were beginning to realize that the living conditions and personal problems of patients were a factor in their illness and recovery. In 1889, the Johns Hopkins Hospital, for example, had begun a home visiting program for medical students to learn about their patients and how they live. However, it took the forward vision of Dr. Richard C. Cabot, chief of medicine at MGH, to see the necessity of creating the position of social worker.

Part of the motivation to initiate social work services at the turn of the century was the proliferation of certain medical conditions in the United States. Tuberculosis was prevalent in many cities, fueled by the deplorable conditions in factories and workshops. Syphilis was also quite common. Both conditions required long hospitalizations and aftercare with extended separation from the patient's family. Polio and the pregnancies of unmarried women were also concerns of these early health care workers. Dr. Cabot conceived the idea of introducing a nonmedical presence into the hospital. As a physician, Cabot realized that he and his colleagues were cut off from direct observation of patients and were unable to assess the impact of their home life, their family relationships, and their work as factors in their illness. "As a physician caring for clinic patients at the MGH, Cabot became increasingly concerned that his patients were blocked in carrying out medical treatment by their many individual and family problems. ... He decided to bring social workers into the MGH to work with physicians on the patients' social problems as related to the medical treatment" (Bartlett, 1975, p. 212). Cabot also envisioned that social workers would help patients adjust to their hospitalization by having social workers provide information and reassurance to patients and their family members. It would be the task of the social worker to explain the impact of the illness and detail what the hospital stay would entail.

In 1905, Cabot appointed Garnet I. Pelton, a nurse, to fill the first hospital social work position in the United States. She was to report to the doctors on the domestic and social conditions of the patients, help patients fulfill doctors' orders, and provide a link between the hospital and community agencies and organizations. In 1906, Ida Cannon succeeded Mrs. Pelton. Within a few years, social work positions had been established at Bellevue Hospital and Johns Hopkins, and other hospitals had begun exploring the possibility of establishing such a position (Nacman, 1990).

Ida Cannon was well suited for medical social work. She had years of nursing experience and had studied psychology and sociology as part of her university training. She had worked for years doing home visits with poor families in Minnesota and had developed a first-hand understanding of the relationship between social problems and illness. Initially, the hospital's board of trustees was ambivalent about establishing a social work program, as evidenced by the fact that the program was not considered an official department of the hospital and funds to support the department were solicited from personal friends of Dr. Cabot and later from other contributors. But, by 1914, the hospital officially recognized social work activity on the wards, and Ida Cannon was given the title "chief of social services." And in 1919 the trustees of MGH voted to make the Social Services Department an integral part of the hospital (Nacman, 1990).

Cannon became a spokesperson for social workers in hospitals. Her leadership in the profession rested on three essential ideas: (1) she kept the individual patient and his or her needs in central focus; (2) she identified and continually interpreted the basic concept of the social aspects of illness and of good patient care; and (3) she emphasized the teamwork of the professions — medicine, nursing, social work, and others (Bartlett, 1975). In short, Cabot expected the role of the social worker to revolve around bridging the gap between the hospital environment and the patients' usual social environment in order to remove barriers to effective medical treatment. Social workers were also expected to work toward modifying any social, environmental, or emotional problems that could impact the patients' health condition (Cowles, 2000).

The implication of the shift from using volunteers to assist families outside of the hospital to employing social workers to perform this function meant that professional schools of social work began to grow as the need for trained social work staff took hold. It also signaled the beginning of collaboration, albeit tentatively in the beginning, among social workers, nurses, and physicians.

It was from these beginnings that social work became established in hospitals and has grown over the decades to become a vital and necessary part of how hospitals care for patients. From one social worker in 1905, social work departments had begun in 100 hospitals in 1913 and 400 hospitals in 1923. In 2002, more than one quarter of the 477,000 social workers in the United States were working in and for hospitals (Cowles, 2003). Although a number of changes have occurred over the years, the basic orientation to the work, as envisioned by Dr. Cabot and articulated by Ida Cannon and others, has endured. What remains of their pioneer work is the need to see the patients as part of interlocking systems that include their immediate family and widen to include their community and the larger political community, which dictates care and entitlements. What has changed is that social workers are no longer seen as handmaidens of the doctors. "Theirs is a new relationship within the institution and with other health care providers as they initiate and implement social-health services. They emphasize their professional independence while they enter into sound collaborative and team relationships" (Rehr, 1998, p. 18).

SOCIAL WORK PRACTICE IN HOSPITALS — THEORETICAL PERSPECTIVES

Today, the role of the social worker is clearly established; social workers are found in every area of the health care delivery system (Dziegielewski,

2004). Although practice venues differ (small or large hospital, urban or rural setting) and organizational constraints pull social workers one way or another, core concepts bind the practice of social work in all hospitals. These concepts serve as the foundation upon which social work services are based. "The unifying theoretical perspective ... is the view that people can best be understood and helped in the context of the conditions and resources of their social environment. Social environment refers to the quality and characteristics of one's life situation, including interpersonal relationships, resources for one's needs, and one's position, roles, and participation in society" (Cowles, 2000, p. 10). This orientation, known as the person-in-environment, was what motivated Dr. Cabot and Ida Cannon to establish social work in their hospital, so that the physicians could enhance their healing potential by having a greater understanding of what their patients had to deal with when they left the hospital. Did patients have people in their immediate environment who could care for them? What supports existed and what needed to be enhanced? Were there community resources that could be brought to patients to help them recover? The centrality of understanding people as they relate to their environment, and the reciprocal relationship of people to their environment, goes beyond medical and hospital social work and is the core of all social work practice.

Specific to the hospital social worker is the biopsychosocial approach to practice. "Social work's biopsychosocial approach provides a carefully balanced perspective, which takes into account the entire person in his or her environment and helps social workers in screening and assessing the needs of an individual from a multidimensional point of view" (Berkman & Volland, 1997, p. 143). The biopsychosocial approach considers three overlapping aspects of the patient's functioning: "bio" refers to the biological and medical aspects of the patient's health and well-being; "psycho" refers to the patient's self-worth, self-esteem, and emotional resources as they relate to the medical condition; and "social" refers to the social environment that surrounds and influences the patient. It behooves the social worker to assess each of these domains to gain a full understanding of the patient (Rock, 2002). This view of practice is also referred to as a holistic view because it seeks to encompass the whole picture of the individual and places the individual in a context that informs social work intervention.

To best serve their patients, social workers need special skills and levels of knowledge. Consistent with and within the context of the person-in-environment and biopsychosocial orientations to practice, schools of social work prepare social workers, stressing the need for the medical social worker to understand the patient population and their health problems, the organizational setting, the community, intervention modalities, and methods of research and program evaluation.

Understanding the patient population and health problems includes being familiar with the usual path, treatment, and management of a particular illness. This knowledge facilitates the engagement, assessment, planning, cooperation, and overall communication with the patient and family members. In addition, it allows the social worker to knowledgeably interact with the other health care professionals with whom it is necessary to communicate on behalf of the patient. An understanding of the organizational setting facilitates interdisciplinary teamwork and informal advocacy on behalf of the patient. Knowledge of the community allows the social worker ease in linking patients to resources and facilitating referrals to other health-related programs that will aid the patient. Understanding of specific treatment modalities and intervention approaches allows the social worker to meaningfully interact with patients and family members in the role of counselor and confidante. This skill enables the social worker to connect with the patient or family member to address emotional concerns and help the patient resolve problems as they relate to the medical condition. Social workers are trained to be able to do research in any work setting. The social worker's ability to design and conduct research keeps social work vital and responsive to patient needs while documenting new areas of knowledge and understanding. Research on existing programs, especially those that reinforce interdisciplinary cooperation, is vital to serving patients' and family members' needs (Cowles, 2000).

COLLABORATION: THE INTERDISCIPLINARY TEAM

Collaboration is a complex and dynamic process that occurs when two or more health care providers cooperate and assist one another in the service of a patient or family member. Collaboration takes place between and among the various components of the health care team, also called the interdisciplinary team. The rationale for collaboration and interdisciplinary teamwork is that multiple kinds of knowledge and skill need to be involved and applied to best service the patient and family.

Members of the interdisciplinary team can include physicians, nurses, social workers, physical therapists, psychiatrists, nutritionists, and others who may be providing care to the patient. The particular unit or service within the hospital dictates the exact makeup of the interdisciplinary team. The functions of such teams include shared assessment of patient problems and needs, exchange of relevant information, team teaching of staff, development of intervention plans, ethical decision making, delegation of tasks and responsibilities, and evaluation of outcome (Cowles, 2000).

Collaboration of this type requires a high degree of cooperation to be successful, with each participant knowing that he or she has something to contribute and that the contribution will be recognized in the decision making about the patient. Collaboration has the potential to work well on a medical unit, but it is not without potential difficulties. Because the goal is to bring together different professions to address the needs of one patient, it is acknowledged that different professions bring different attitudes, values, skills, and service orientations to the deliberations regarding what may be best for the patient (Rehr, Blumenfield, & Rosenberg, 1998).

The social workers interviewed for this volume were asked whether their unit worked collaboratively and whether they felt valued as part of their unit's interdisciplinary team. Almost every social worker functioned as part of a team; a large percentage of these workers felt they were a valued member of their team. In some settings, social workers were less valued than some of the other professionals on the team, but generally, collaboration of the various disciplines was supported.

MANAGED CARE

In the latter part of the 1980s it became clear that the cost of health care delivery had skyrocketed to crisis proportions in the United States. The causes for this are many, including the aging population, the ascendancy of the "baby boomers," remarkable advances in technology, and the rise in the cost of services. In addition, the insurance industry had been faltering and hospital costs were escalating, causing smaller hospitals to either close or merge in order to be sustained. Managed care was born out of the need to control the costs of health and mental health care; managed care has become the main mechanism for cost containment in the last decade or so. Managed care may be seen as a market-driven arrangement for health services that is pervasive in the United States (Rock, 2002). It is important to note, "Managed care is not about the consumer (patient). It is not about quality. It is, however, about cost and the perceived need on the part of government and the insurance industry to control it" (Gibelman, 2002, p. 17).

Managed care involves the administration and oversight of health and mental health services by someone other than the patient and provider. The goal of managed care is control over the service delivery system of health care as well as regulation of the actual services, all efforts focused on cost containment (Corcoran, 1997). Managed care plans are designed to reduce medical costs by discouraging unnecessary services, by setting limits of duration and types of service, and by providing market inducements for providers to limit the services made available to patients (Edinburg & Cottler, 1997). This is accomplished through a mix of health insurance, government assistance, and payment programs that seek to retain quality and access while controlling the cost of services (Lohmann, 1997).

Within the health care arena, managed care has affected the practice of social workers in numerous ways. It has provoked ethical issues, has changed the nature of practice, and has moved the focus of social work services to greater accountability with a focus on evidence-based practice. In the area of ethical issues, when managed care companies demand access to client records or detailed information related to the patient and the treatment, they potentially compromise patient confidentiality, a primary arena for ethical violation. In addition, managed care companies can place limits on treatment that may well run counter to professional assessment, creating an ethical dilemma for the social worker. This is seen especially in hospitals when patients are discharged before the social worker believes they are ready for and capable of managing outside of the hospital. The nature of practice has also been deeply eroded in that managed care companies now dictate the limits on reimbursable care, duration of treatment, and some medication choices. Finally, managed care has refocused service with high demands on accountability and the need to document outcomes. The social worker is required to document that services provided result in achievement of the goals of their stated service plan. Vigilance in creating a service plan as well as conscientious tracking are now demanded of the social worker (Gibelman, 2002).

Not all the changes wrought by managed care are seen as negative. Many people support the tighter control of costs and treatment initiated by the managed care organizations. The accountability demanded by managed care has strengthened some services within the medical and hospital arena. For social workers, it has shifted many of them away from bedside relationships with patients; paperwork demands and shortened stays have decreased the interpersonal nature of their work. Physicians have their own distress with managed care, more focused on fee structures and permissible procedures as well as length of stays, and so forth. It behooves social workers to find their niche within the managed care structure and maximize their relationships with colleagues and with patients and their families.

SUMMARY

The practice of hospital social work in the 21st century dates to the turn of the last century when Dr. Richard Cabot and Ida Cannon gave voice and form to a new type of social work, one in which the social worker became an active participant in the management and care of sick people. Working with the hospital physicians, the social workers were able to add dimension and breadth to the understanding of the "surround" of the patient as it influenced health outcomes. This partnership has expanded over the many decades since the pioneering work of Ida Cannon at Massachusetts General Hospital.

The current hospital social worker works from a biopsychosocial approach, taking into consideration the person-in-environment. This sound theoretical base facilitates the efforts of the social worker who participates in an interdisciplinary environment to best meet the needs of the patient with a broad-based understanding of the family and community influences. Modern hospital social work is practiced in an environment of managed care, which has shaped medical and mental health services in the United States for the last decade. Managed care has brought to the practice of social work and medicine sweeping changes, some welcomed and seen as improvements over non–managed care and some that have been described as severely limiting. Regardless of the views about managed care, it likely will dominate and dictate medical treatment, in some form or another, for years to come. Hospital social workers have and will continue to adapt and function in this milieu and offer fully professional services to those who are ill.

2

GENERAL MEDICAL SOCIAL WORK

WHAT SERVICES ARE INCLUDED?

Modern hospitals offer medical care on numerous units, sometimes delineated by floors. The units this chapter will focus on include orthopedics, obstetrics/gynecology, neurology, surgery, and gerontology. Each unit presents similar situations for patients and staff: patients are admitted and have a rapid turnaround time, and for the most part, social work services are similar from unit to unit. Many of the functions described in this chapter are performed by social workers throughout a hospital, specifically case management, utilization review, and discharge planning.

Case Management and Utilization Review

Case management is grounded in federal legislation involving Medicare reimbursement. In 1983, the U.S. government altered the reimbursement system for Medicare recipients from one in which hospitals determined the cost of care to one in which the government dictated reimbursement rates based on the severity and kind of diagnosis. These diagnostic-related groups (DRGs), as they were called, comprised distinct categories of illnesses, and the government determined standard reimbursement rates for hospital services related to each specific illness. Under this system of reimbursement, for example, if a patient came to the hospital for a hernia operation, the government would set a reimbursement rate of $5,000 for all hospital services rendered. If the hospital incurred greater expense than the preset rate, the hospital would have to absorb the overage. In reaction to the DRGs and other concerns about payment through third-party insurers, most hospitals have initiated a monitoring system called utilization review, which tracks services and utilization of hospital resources, including length of stay and appropriateness of admissions. Through utilization review, all hospital services fall under a level of scrutiny that is responsive to cost, with the goal of offering medical services at the least expense to the hospital. Social workers have a role in utilization review because they are involved in discharging of patients on schedules mandated by the DRGs and enforced by the individual hospital (Hammer & Kerson, 1997). In many instances, these policies result in shorter hospital stays, reduction of in-hospital services, and decision making that may not always be in the best interest of the patient but provide a cost benefit to the hospital.

Discharge Planning

In 1986, federal legislation in the form of the Omnibus Budget Reconciliation Act mandated that every hospital have a process for planning patient discharges. According to the Omnibus Budget Reconciliation Act, a discharge plan must be included in the patient's medical record and discussed with the patient or patient representative. The underlying purpose of this law was to facilitate speedy discharge of patients (Sharpe, 1991). As a result, the role of discharge planner is now firmly established and integrated into the structure of the contemporary hospital (Iglehart, 1990). The Omnibus Budget Reconciliation Act and the Medicare reimbursement legislation of 1983 ushered in the concept of medical care known as managed care. Managed care is designed to control access to and the cost of health care, also referred to as medical cost containment.

Every social worker interviewed for this volume identified discharge planning as a defining task of their work in the hospital. "Implementing discharge planning activities, and their coordination, are central functions of the hospital-based social worker. Today's social workers monitor comprehensive discharge planning services in a case management context" (Blumenfield, Bennett, & Rehr, 1998, p. 83). Discharge planning must be done to enable the purpose and survival of the hospital as a financially stable institution.

The American Hospital Association (1984) defines discharge planning as an interdisciplinary process guided by the following essential elements:

1. Early identification of patients likely to need complex posthospital care
2. Indication of patient preferences for posthospital care

3. Patient and family education
4. Patient and family assessment and counseling
5. Planning, development, and coordination of community resources needed to ensure continuity of care after discharge
6. Postdischarge follow-up to ensure services and plan outcome

In most hospitals these activities fall within the realm of the social work department, although nursing departments are also involved in this work. From the viewpoint of social work, discharge planning is an aspect of professional activity that helps patients cope with their illness and its effects, move through the hospital system, and eventually return to their home with all the necessary supports to sustain their health. This service encompasses assessment of individual needs, formulation of an adequate and safe discharge plan, and implementation of the plan that ensures the safety and well-being of the patient in a timely manner (Davidson, 1990).

Upon patient admission in most hospital and general medical units, social workers are expected to begin the work of patient needs identification and assessment to begin the discharge process. "Social workers' skills, values, and resources make them able to act as discharge planners because they advocate for clients; understand policy constraints and organizational ethics; ensure continuity of care through knowledge of relationship building, organizational dynamics, and community resources; and monitor the costs and duplication of services within their respective health care institutions" (Hammer & Kerson, 1997, p. 239). The central goal of discharge planning is for the social worker to fully address the highly individualized needs of each patient and provide safeguards at home for his or her care. In general, it requires the social worker to have psychological knowledge applying a bio-psychosocial approach to care that addresses a wide range of patient and family needs and incorporates the skills and orientation of the medical and other health care professionals. The social worker must also have a network of and knowledge of community-based services and an understanding of how these services can best be accessed in the service of the patient upon discharge (Blumenfield et al., 1998).

The question of what social workers actually do within the task of discharge planning was answered by Kadushin and Kulys (1993) in research with 80 social workers in 36 hospitals. Their findings showed that the provision of concrete services after discharge was the most basic, essential component and primary focus of discharge planning. Such service arrangements may include home health care, medical equipment, transportation, or delivery of medical supplies and medication. The severity of need of the patient and family may make the acquisition of concrete services either all consuming or only a small part of the work of creating the discharge plan. In hospitals with a needier patient profile, social workers spend many hours attempting to link the patient with necessary resources. Counseling around discharge and the experience of illness did not take up much of the time of the social workers in the study; the counseling that was enacted focused on engaging patients and family members in decision making to enable them to have some level of control over discharge disposition. Other activities by the social workers related to discharge planning included assessment of financial, social, and psychological resources available to the patient and family; coordination with other medical staff to facilitate the discharge plan; documentation to produce a written record of what has been and needs to be done for the patient; and linkage activities focused on obtaining services for patients and families after discharge (Dziegielewski & Kalinoski, 2004; Kadushin & Kulys, 1993).

SOCIAL WORK SERVICES ON SPECIFIC UNITS
Social Work on the Orthopedics Unit

Patients are admitted to the orthopedic unit of a hospital for various reasons, including bones broken from trauma, elective orthopedic surgery to repair broken bones, and bone injury as a result of an accident. Traumatized or accident victims who sustain serious orthopedic injury face problems such as depression, isolation, chronic pain, anger, and guilt (Bradford, 1999).

In an effort to understand the scope of the social worker's role in an orthopedic unit, I interviewed four social workers. Caseloads varied from 18 to 24 patients on each unit. Length of stay on the unit was short, between 2 to 5 days depending on the severity of the injury. Many of the injured patients had had surgical intervention; others had broken a bone or bones and were on the unit for casting and stabilization before being discharged. The stay on the unit was described by one of the social workers as a stage experience: admission, surgery, rehabilitation, and discharge. Upon patient admission, the social worker is responsible for assessment, which, because the turnaround for most patients is so brief, is focused on the resources in the home to support that patient and his or her ability to function after hospitalization. Almost every patient receives physical therapy while on the unit and has posthospital physical therapy requirements. Because of the follow-up needs and as per hospital requirements, discharge planning begins upon admission.

For some patients, discharge to their home is not possible, because their care needs are too great. For these patients, many of whom are elderly, the social worker arranges rehabilitation or nursing home placement. Some patients need acute rehabilitation to reach a level at which they can function independently. Sometimes the placement decision revolves around whether the patient is oriented and alert; those who are severely disoriented will be placed in a longer-term nursing care facility for rehabilitation. Families are often central to the discharge disposition, because they are involved in providing the care needed by the recovering patient.

The initial reaction of both patient and family to an accident or trauma often is disbelief. The social workers who were interviewed considered crisis intervention a necessary skill for being able to deal with families and patients. The overall goal of social worker intervention was to educate both patient and family toward restoring function and independence for the injured person. The social workers found themselves initially trying to put the medical episode into perspective for all concerned: What does this medical situation mean for now and what does it mean for the long run? "Initially, the situation can be catastrophic to the family, but we always have options," said one social worker. She added, "We do the work for them to get them where they need to be, both literally and emotionally."

Due to the quick turnaround of the unit, the social workers were limited in terms of their ability to really connect with either patients or family members, and a common lament was that there was never enough time to address the multiplicity of needs each case presented. The team approach was described by all the social workers as generally working well except for the occasions "when the placement has not been fully arranged and the medical staff is rushing to move the patient out. In these cases, I have to intervene with the doctors and sometimes plead for one more day. It can be frustrating, especially as there are not that many places for patients to go for good rehab."

One of the often-mentioned approaches to working with those seriously injured was to empower the patient toward greater functionality. "Being supportive and universalizing their situation is often helpful, as most patients are eager to hear success stories," explained one worker. She added, "You have to be truthful, however, and try to bring the patient to an understanding of their injury."

Social Work in the Obstetrics/Gynecology Unit

The obstetrical unit in the hospital treats women who are giving birth. If a woman has a vaginal delivery that is without incident, she will be in and out of the hospital in 48 hours. If the delivery is by cesarean section, she will be sent home in 3 days. Seven social workers in four different hospitals were interviewed; the number of patients for whom the social workers were responsible ranged from 15 to 40. Discharge planning for a routine delivery was described as relatively easy unless there were issues of poverty or it was deemed that the mother was not able to adequately care for the newborn. In these cases, the social worker arranges for aides and financial entitlement assistance to help the new mother. One social worker remarked, "Time drives all the work; getting the patient stabilized and out of the hospital as soon as is feasible is what it is about. But, within that we make every effort to send the patient and her baby home to the best environment possible."

It is not unusual for a woman on the obstetrical unit to give birth to an infant who is very ill or is premature, and the infant will remain in the hospital when the mother leaves. This is usually a difficult time for a new mother, especially if the infant is seriously ill. The social worker will be drawn into such circumstances, offering support and problem solving as needed. However, once the woman leaves the obstetrical services, the social worker is no longer involved with the mother; their relationship ends and the case is turned over to the staff of the neonatal unit.

In some instances, when the pregnancy is considered high risk, the pregnant woman will be in and out of the hospital during the tenure of her pregnancy. In these cases, the social worker has a greater opportunity to provide supportive counseling and to get to know the patient and her family and their individual needs.

More serious and challenging for the social worker are situations in which the newborn dies while the mother is in the hospital or the mother miscarries. In these cases — in one hospital there were as many as two or three per week — social workers may conduct a burial ceremony or mass for the infant. They prepare a viewing room for the parents; they dress the infant, make prints of the baby's footprint, and take photographs for the parents. The parents are encouraged to spend as much time as they want with the deceased infant. The social workers also help with funeral arrangements and provide bereavement counseling for the family. Social workers identified this situation as very difficult. "I find myself in each of the women and, as I am close in age to many of them, and have had a miscarriage myself, I have to be so careful of boundaries or I will lose it altogether," lamented one of the interviewees.

A particularly difficult area of the work, identified by several of the social workers, is preparing a discharge plan for a mother who the social worker does not feel is going to be "a fit mother." "It is very hard when you don't want to discharge the baby to the mother. It just doesn't feel right and you only have your intuition to go on and no concrete evidence to prevent the mother from leaving the hospital with her baby. What I have learned," she continued, "is to trust my intuition and try to arrange for additional services in these situations and hope that it all turns out well." Another social worker stated, "The most troubling aspect of my job is when I know the mother to be 'unfit' and I have to struggle with whether the baby is going to be safe. And, there is nothing I really can do."

Equally difficult is when a mother does not want to be pregnant nor does she really want the newborn. In one case, a woman who was 36 weeks pregnant came into the hospital in active labor. She told the social worker that she did not want the baby. The social worker began making arrangements for the baby to be adopted, but before all the arrangements were completed, the mother eloped from the hospital, leaving the baby in the hospital. Upon admission, she had given a false name and address, making follow-up impossible, so the baby was released to an agency to be adopted. These types of situations — described by social workers as frustrating and provocative — are not all that frequent but make the work challenging when they occur.

Generally, obstetrical social workers describe themselves as content with their work and drawn to the aspect of regeneration. As stated by one worker, "I see so much new life on this unit. It is stimulating, and while every day is different, and each case is different, seeing the newborns is always a thrill. I am still in awe of new life."

In the gynecological unit, female patients present with a wide range of medical concerns relating to reproductive functions or diseased parts of the pelvic region or illness related to a sexually transmitted disease. Some of the women on this unit will have had a hysterectomy, will be suffering from a gynecological cancer, or will have had complications related to a pregnancy or abortion. Depending on the reason for admission, the social worker performs assessment and evaluation and begins discharge planning early in the patient's hospitalization (MacLean-Brine, 1994). In many instances, the social workers felt that one of their main responsibilities was to "translate the language of the doctors to the patient and family members. This often involves education of the patients as to their diagnosis and what they can expect of their illness experience. In these interchanges, we try to be supportive and caring and offer emotional support."

In two of the city hospitals, the social workers identified the difficulty for some minority patients to access services. For socioeconomically more affluent patients, minority or not, there is time to focus on emotional concerns and help them return to their day-to-day level of functioning. But for those without insurance or resources of support, the work is more focused on concrete needs. As such, a large part of the work of these social workers is attempting to provide as much ancillary service for the patients as possible. This often causes social workers to feel overworked, because resources are frequently strained and hard to access for those who are most needy.

A theme that emerged from interviewing these social workers, all of whom were women, was their commitment to working with women — feeling a kinship to other women and wanting to work with and help especially women. One social worker said, "It is my calling to work with women; my mission; and I love my work."

Social Work on the Neurology Unit

Patients who are admitted to the neurology unit may have brain injuries from strokes, tumors, or seizure disorders or have problems related to brain functioning that have yet to be diagnosed. Four social workers, in two different hospitals, were interviewed about their work in the neurology unit. Both hospitals split the social worker responsibilities between neurosurgery and nonneurosurgery patients. The neurosurgery patients were described as those who have had brain or spinal surgery, many with benign brain tumors, who need physical therapy and rehabilitation. Most of these patients spend a few days in the hospital and either return home or are referred to a care facility for rehabilitation. Outcomes vary, however, and some patients may face a long and difficult recuperation as they struggle to regain full brain function.

Nonsurgery patients often are hospitalized for a stroke; outcomes for this illness vary, with some patients in the hospital for short stays whereas others are hospitalized for as long as 3 weeks and then go to a nursing home for rehabilitation or long-term placement.

The intensity of working with patients and family members on the neurology unit varies depending on the age of the patient and severity of illness. Regardless of whether the patient has had surgery, the younger patients pose more difficult struggles for the social workers, as do those patients who have been fully functional before their neurological condition and who now face limits on their capacity to think and function. The social workers defined their role and function on their unit to work with patient and family members through the initial crisis of the patient's diagnosis through to disposition of their case. Part of what the social worker does is assess the family and support resources for the patient, with greater effort and concern for the patient who is now incapacitated by their neurological condition. If extended care must be arranged for the patient, the task falls to the social worker; if home aides or equipment need to be secured, it falls to the social worker to arrange.

The team on the neurology unit consists of physicians, surgeons, physical therapists, dieticians, psychologists, and psychiatrists. The multidimensional team is more expanded than on most other hospital units. The patient's mental capacity is assessed by a psychologist or psychiatrist, with specific physical therapy needs addressed to help the patient move toward their prestroke level of function or to educate toward new ways of moving and managing self-care tasks. The four social workers each stated that they felt that they were an integral part of this expanded team and that their contribution to the team was highly valued.

When asked to describe a difficult case, one of the social workers related the case of a prominent newspaper reporter who had been hospitalized with a stroke. He had returned home and was back in the hospital within a few months with a second stroke. What made the case difficult was the fact that after the first stroke, the patient went home with a positive attitude and with most of his faculties intact, except for a slight limp. The second stroke had been devastating: He had no capacity to speak, he could not move his entire right side, and he was unable to walk. He had been estranged from his wife for many years, but when the second stroke occurred he asked the social worker to contact her. The social worker did as asked but the wife wanted nothing to do with him; the social worker had a very difficult time conveying this to the patient, who was emotionally shattered by the indifference of his wife. "It was difficult telling him about his wife and seeing his heart break in addition to all the other terrible things that were happening to him," explained the social worker. Ultimately, the patient died in the hospital. "He was very angry, bitter, and sad, and I am sure that this hastened his death."

What makes the work vital for the social workers is that "There is always something around the corner, something different and new. The pace is sometimes frantic, and keeping up with it is the greatest challenge. But seeing especially some of the stroke patients regain their abilities is testament to the resilience of the body and spirit."

Social Work on the Surgical Unit

Seven social workers from the surgical units of three hospitals were interviewed. In two of the hospitals, the surgical department was divided into general surgical procedures (operations that are not related to cardiac conditions, oncology, or gynecology) and vascular procedures (surgeries due to problems with blood circulation). When asked to define the role and function of the social worker on the surgical service, one social worker stated that, "Our job goes from soup to nuts. I do discharge planning from day one. I do counseling with the patient and family, arrange for home care and whatever services are needed. In addition, I find myself in the role of teacher with residents and attendants. I orient them to the culture of the unit. As I am in a teaching hospital, this is a part of my job."

On a surgical unit, the relationship between social worker and patient is usually short term and tends not to preexist from prior hospitalizations. As such, the narrow focus of social work intervention was explained by a social worker who stated that her goal is, "To help the patient adjust to their illness and life changes, address their fears in a nonjudgmental arena, and work with both patient and family to understand their diagnosis and surgical experience."

On the vascular side of the surgical unit, many of the patients are older, even elderly, and have been battling disabling conditions for a long time. People who have had diabetes for many years are prone to vascular deterioration, and many of these patients must undergo amputation due to their conditions. These patients require a longer hospitalization and greater aftercare arrangements. Some patients, because of cognitive impairments, are not fully able to understand the seriousness of their situations. In these situations, the level of family involvement and resources has to be assessed, and if the patient and family disagree, the role of the social worker is to work toward agreement on the discharge plan. As one social worker explained, "The family and patient are one unit to us; we are here for both of them, and we cannot release a patient until everybody understands the plan. We take the patient and family where they are and focus on the positive and realistic. Sometimes, the bigger problem is not the family but the disagreement between the doctor and the social worker. We know the patients and their family better than the doctor and know when the patient is really ready to go home. Sometimes it is medically feasible, but the patient is not emotionally ready, and we have to advocate for the patient."

In describing what they find satisfying about their work, the social workers felt that, although many of their patients are very ill and will be facing chronic and complex medical situations, the satisfaction comes from helping a patient feel hopeful about life. One social worker explained that, "Anyone who leaves here with a will to live is someone I feel a personal victory about, as I have helped motivate him or her to be able to face their life even as an ill person. So many people who are here are depressed and frightened and if I can impact that, I feel that I have done a good job."

Social Work on the Geriatric Unit

Seven social workers in three hospitals were interviewed about their work on the geriatric unit. All the social workers agreed that the main focus of their work and efforts is toward heightening and strengthening their patients' level of independence. Many work from a strengths perspective, which highlights the positive aspects of a person's life, skills, and abilities and functionality. Their views were summed up by one social worker who stated, "The need for seniors to be independent and to retain their sense of self is essential to healthy aging and surviving. For the seniors who come through our unit, the ones who are the strongest and do the best are those who have retained their independence and, thus, their zest and spirit for life. In my work, I try to have each patient exert their independence and urge their involvement in all decision making."

Patients are on the unit for a variety of reasons (e.g., dementia, falls, heart problems, circulatory problems), usually with a theme of physical decline. Some patients are sent directly to the geriatric unit, depending on bed space, and some are transferred from other areas of the hospital based on the nature of their condition: Does their condition result from an age-related physical decline or is it due to a more general medical condition? Social worker responsibility on the units varied from 25 to 40 patients. Often the family presented more of a challenge than the work with the patients. Several of the social workers recounted situations in which the family was resistant to accepting the patient situation or the level of decline described by the medical team or resisted placement recommendations. In these cases, the social worker has to educate and work as closely as possible with the family to ensure a smooth discharge.

Although there is a lot of death on this unit, the social workers often play an important role with both the patient and family in these situations and seem to accept this aspect of their role. One social worker described one case as particularly satisfying despite the fact that it ended with the patient's death. A 92-year-old man who had fallen at home was admitted to the unit with dementia. He lived alone, his judgment was impaired, and he appeared to be undernourished. His son lived in a distant state and had not seen or spoken to his father for several years. (The son blamed him for the death of his mother.) The patient did not want the social worker to contact his son, but through counseling and urging, he agreed. The son traveled to the hospital to see his father and they spent a few days together. The social worker was involved in their reconciliation and felt very good about this aspect of her work. As plans were being made for the father to go to an assisted living situation, he had a fatal heart attack. Although the son was not present when his father expired, they had reconciled their differences and had had quality time together.

Every social worker interviewed suggested, in one way or another, that they always found something unique in each of their patients. Whenever possible, they spent time just talking with a patient and, inevitably, explained one interviewee, "There was something special about the patient that was communicated. Perhaps it was a perspective on life or something unique about an experience that they had had, but I always find something I like in the older person. So many in our society just want to dump these older people and don't see them as people with a history and a perspective. I think I learn more from my patients than they ever learn from me."

Geriatric social workers seem to really want to work with elderly people. They tend to come to the work having had special relationships with grandparents or other elderly adults. In their comments, the social workers expressed a real affection for elderly people and wanted to offer them the respect and dignity society often takes away from them. As such, they have made a special effort to talk and interact with their patients. The theme of dignity permeated the work of those interviewed.

SUMMARY

The units described in this chapter represent a broad range of social work services in a hospital. The primary role of the social worker is to facilitate discharge and engage the patient and family in the task. However, beyond this mandate, social workers have numerous opportunities to interact with and influence the patient and family situation and to find fulfillment in the work done.

3

THE RENAL SOCIAL WORKER

ABOUT THE KIDNEYS AND DIALYSIS

End-stage renal disease (ESRD) is a life-threatening chronic illness in which the kidneys cease to function: they are unable to excrete wastes, concentrate urine, and regulate the electrolytes in the body. Humans have two kidneys that are each about the size of an adult fist and weigh about one third of a pound. These organs are located on either side of the spine. The kidneys work to keep the body free of waste. In addition, they regulate red blood cell production, regulate blood pressure, and control the body's chemical and fluid balance. When kidneys are functioning normally, blood flows from the heart to the kidneys and through the body. The kidneys filter out waste products that are excreted through the urine. These filtering machines (kidneys) also play a role in the formation of healthy bones, by regulating calcium and phosphate concentrations in the blood and red blood cell production by releasing a hormone that promotes bone marrow growth. In ESRD, the kidneys do not function adequately to sustain life and patients must undergo some form of renal replacement therapy, through either dialysis or transplantation, to restore the functions carried out by the failed kidneys.

ESRD is caused by illness or trauma that damages the kidneys and impairs their function. Even though there are two kidneys, it is possible to have adequate kidney function with just one kidney. When the kidneys function at about 30% of normal, the patient begins to show signs of uremia (poisoning), with symptoms including weakness, nausea, loss of appetite, fatigue, and a bitter taste in the mouth. During this stage, which precedes dialysis or transplantation, the patient is monitored and treated with a combination of medication and lifestyle changes. At 10 to 15% of functionality, ESRD occurs (the final stage of kidney disease) and the patient requires renal replacement therapy (Frank, Auslander, & Weissgarten, 2003).

In 2001, 392,023 people in the United States had ESRD requiring some form of treatment. Approximately 1 in 693 or 0.14% of the U.S. population has the disease; estimated number of new cases each year is 89,250. The primary causes of ESRD are diabetes, hypertension, or kidney disease. The cost of caring for those with ESRD was staggering: in 2001, $22.8 billion in public and private spending. Upwards of approximately 56,000 people in the United States are waiting for kidney transplants (United States Renal Data System 2003 Report).

The most common treatment for ESRD is hemodialysis. This lifesaving treatment was introduced in 1960 by Dr. Belding H. Scribner. Dialysis is administered in dialysis centers that are usually affiliated with a medical center or hospital. It can also be administered in freestanding dialysis units staffed by nurses, social workers, and nephrologists (physicians who specialize in kidney disease).

During hemodialysis, the patient reclines in a chair and is attached through plastic tubing to the dialysis machine. Nurses facilitate the treatment, hook up the patient to the machine, and monitor the 3- to 4-hour treatment. The patient is unable to leave the chair and must remain relatively still while the machine pumps their blood through the filters in the machine. Physicians prescribe treatment time and monitor progress as well.

What happens during dialysis is that the blood is circulated outside of the body into an artificial kidney machine through a link to the person's circulatory system. The blood flows into the dialysis machine, is cleansed, and then returns to the patient's body. The dialysis process is continual, with new blood circulating into the machine and waste products and excess fluids circulating out. The link to the circulatory system is usually accomplished by a graft or fistula (a small plastic tube that connects an artery and a vein under the skin and allows the flow of blood in and out of the circulatory system and to the artificial kidney, the dialysis machine) to an artery in the arm or neck of the patient. Like healthy kidneys, the dialysis machine keeps the body in balance by removing wastes, keeping a safe level of certain chemicals in the body, and controlling blood pressure. In the United States, treatment is carried out in a hospital or dialysis unit three times per week.

An alternative treatment mode is peritoneal dialysis, in which cleansing dialysis solution (dialysate) is introduced into the peritoneal or abdominal cavity. After a designated amount of time, the fluid is drained from the body and fresh dialysate is introduced. Tiny capillaries in the abdomen act as filters of waste material. Access for peritoneal dialysis is gained through a flexible hollow tube that is surgically implanted through the wall of the abdomen into the abdominal cavity. This procedure is repeated every 4 to 6 hours during the day, with each fluid exchange taking 40 minutes. The procedure can also be accomplished at night when the patient sleeps. Every evening, the patient is hooked up to an automatic cycling pump that makes the needed fluid exchanges while the patient sleeps.

It must be understood that neither approach — hemodialysis nor peritoneal dialysis — replaces or is as efficient as normal kidneys (National Kidney Foundation [NKF], 1997). The treatments are designed to sustain life, but as such, serious changes in lifestyle and personal independence occur. Whether dialysis is performed at a dialysis center three times a week or daily in the home with peritoneal dialysis, large segments of time are spent in dialysis treatment. Travel limitations exist because the patient must be in proximity of a dialysis center to maintain the treatment regimen. There are serious dietary and fluid restrictions: a person with healthy kidneys excretes wastes naturally through urine, but because the kidneys in a dialysis patient are not functioning, fluid intake must be curtailed so it does not build up in the body. Diet restriction of salt and spicy food is imposed to reduce fluid retention. In addition, most people who are on dialysis experience fatigue and physical limitations (Beder, 1999).

Whereas technology has worked in favor of people with ESRD and treatments have extended their life span, both the disease and its treatment usually have negative implications for quality of life. Quality of life is a subjective yet all-inclusive construct that emphasizes physical, social, and psychological variables. Numerous studies have confirmed that the quality of life of dialysis patients is lower than that of the general population, especially in areas of physical functioning and emotional well-being (DeOreo, 1997; Mingardi et al., 1999).

Kidney transplantation offers the patient with ESRD the most optimistic alternative to either form of dialysis treatment. In a kidney transplant operation, a person with a failed kidney receives a new kidney to take over the work of cleaning the blood. Not every patient is eligible for a transplant; the patient must be relatively healthy to be considered. Two types of transplantation can occur: kidneys from a living donor and kidneys from an unrelated donor who has died (cadaver donors). A living donor is usually someone in the patient's immediate family. The advantage of receiving a kidney from a living donor is that the average long-term success rates tend to be somewhat higher than with transplants from cadaver donors. Perhaps more important, the patient does not have to be put on a waiting list for a kidney to become available and the surgery can be done at the convenience of both patient and donor. The donor must be healthy, have the same blood type as the patient, and share other medical similarities with the recipient. Donating and receiving a kidney are major surgeries, taking approximately 3 hours. The donor is able to live and function well with only one kidney. After a transplant, the patient is maintained on numerous drugs that address possible complications of rejection of the implant.

In the absence of a related, living donor, cadaver kidneys are also used. Technical advances have resulted in very good success rates for kidney transplants from cadaver donors. However, cadaver kidneys are in short supply and the patient must be put on a waiting list until a suitably matched kidney becomes available. Thousands of people with ESRD await transplant and are on the transplant list. The most common complication that may occur after transplantation is rejection of the kidney. The body's immune system may not accept the foreign kidney and acts to reject it. Physically, the patient will begin to develop the same symptoms of kidney failure: lack of urine output, nausea, vomiting, itching, headaches, decreased sensation in the hands and feet, and a rise in blood pressure. Although medications can address the problem of rejection of a transplanted kidney, the medications have numerous side effects including high blood pressure, weight gain, and a susceptibility to infections and tumors. A variety of factors influences the success of the transplantation, but between 80 and 90% of kidney recipients will continue to function 1 year after the operation. In the event that the transplant fails, the patient is usually able to resume dialysis treatments, but the level of disappointment experienced by patients and their families is often shattering. Getting a working kidney relieves patients from the rigorous regimen of dialysis and moves them into being able to have a more "normal" life — to work, travel, and be unencumbered by the restrictions of dialysis. When the new kidney fails (is rejected), the patient must return to a life dominated by the demands of treatment (NKF, 1997).

ESRD affects people in many ways. It is the basis of major modifications in lifestyle, life goals, vocational choices, opportunities, recreational activities, interpersonal relationships, family roles, and family position. Beyond the necessity of daily or three-times-per-week dialysis, the patient must adhere to dietary restrictions and medications. They experience changes in body image and function, including the loss of the ability to urinate, loss of physical energy, loss or change in sexual functioning, changed appearance due to surgery, and other signs of physical deterioration (Berkow, 1987). Because of the physical demands of the disease, many people with ESRD are unable to work.

The emotional strain of the disease and treatment is often profound. Rosen (1999) lists the following as anticipated feelings or reactions of the patient: fear, feeling trapped while living with chronic illness, anger, and guilt about being a burden to others, hurt, shame, and depression. Psychosocial stresses are a fixed feature of the lives of dialysis patients, with depression occurring in a large majority of patients. A review of the literature reveals that the incidence and prevalence of depression among dialysis patients is estimated to vary from 20 to 100% (Kimmel et al., 1995; Lopes et al., 2004; Smith Hong, & Robinson, 1985; Stewart, 1983). In some, depression comes and goes with long periods of remission, a depression beginning when a medical event occurs that results in further physical deterioration. In others, depression is a constant, requiring pharmacological intervention. "Depression among end-stage renal disease patients is a serious medical condition, as important as anemia. Treating depression in most ESRD patients is not an event; it is a continuum" (Smirnow, 1998, p. 106).

It is not difficult to imagine why someone with ESRD may become depressed. In the majority of patients, pre-existing illnesses have caused their ESRD. As such, they have been ill for a period of time and have been informed of, and probably have mixed or not-good feelings about, being on dialysis. For them, it is the end of the road toward avoiding treatments. Thus, persons diagnosed with renal failure tend to experience a dramatic shift in lifestyle that may include impaired social and occupational functioning, possibly resulting in financial problems and a lower standard of living. Travel is limited by the need to be near a dialysis center. "Often there is frustration from the fundamental gratification offered by eating and drinking that is denied due to dietary and fluid intake restrictions" (Mazzella, 2004, p. 41).

Depression in people with ESRD can have serious implications and can sometimes be lethal. Hailey et al. (2001) reported that between 11 and 22% of patient deaths are caused by withdrawal from dialysis, which may be caused by depression. People on dialysis are not necessarily more suicidal than other people with chronic serious illnesses; but dialysis patients have ready access to the means to die through noncompliance with their treatment regimens, either by withdrawing from dialysis or through egregious dietary violations (Beder, 1997).

Clearly, the implications of depression in people with ESRD must be recognized and addressed as a major treatment concern. Adherence to treatment, closely linked to depression, is a major problem for the ESRD population. Data from the U.S. Renal Data (USRD) study of 1998 show that missing one or more treatments per month increases a patient's risk of death by 25% within the next 2 years. Shortening treatment — coming off the dialysis machine before the blood has been fully cleansed — is another area of concern. The data from the USRD study showed that shortening treatment more than three times per month resulted in a 20% increase in risk of death. Missing dialysis is a habit that usually forms in the first 6 months of a patient's course of treatment and must be addressed as soon as the trend emerges to forestall further health and emotional complications (McKinley, 2000). Missed treatments cause fluid and waste buildup, a rise in blood pressure, potential blood poisoning, and potentially serious complications as chemical balances begin to shift.

Certain variables seem to influence missed treatments: age (elderly patients are less likely to miss treatments), Medicare status and insurance and financial problems (patients with financial or insurance problems are more likely to miss treatments), work status (those who are working miss more treatments), and difficulty coping with ESRD as assessed by social work staff. Insurance and financial issues are significantly related to being taken off the dialysis machine early (Dobroff, Dolinko, Lichtiger, Uribarri, & Epstein, 2001). Missed or shortened treatments can profoundly impact patient well-being and can result in patient deterioration, eventual hospitalization, and protracted health problems.

THE PATIENT EXPERIENCE

To fully understand the patient who needs dialysis, it is helpful to view the experience in stages. This conceptualization is based on the work of Frank et al. (2003), who designate two stages on the ESRD continuum. The crisis stage is when the patient first becomes aware of his or her symptoms and when diagnosis, initial treatment, and follow-up begin. This is a time of stress, anxiety, and fear as the treatment options begin to unfold; at the same time, physical problems are present and adjustments to them are pressing on the patient. The chronic stage occurs after the initial diagnosis and treatment, once the patient and family have begun to come to terms with the reality that this is a long-term disease and that there will be many difficulties and adjustments they will have to make. This is concurrent with when dialysis begins. Initially, many patients report feeling dramatically better, with relief of some of their symptoms and improvement in both their physical and mental state. Some of this shift is because a machine has begun to do the work of the failed kidney, which addresses some of the physical symptoms of ESRD. It also must be acknowledged that many dialysis patients have pre-existing conditions, most notably diabetes and high blood pressure, two diseases that impact kidney functioning and in many cases cause complete kidney failure.

Most studies indicate that patients enjoy higher quality of life in the first few months of dialysis treatment, followed by a decline in attitude after a year or more of treatment (Klang, Bjorvell, Berglund, Sundstedt, & Clyne, 1998; Szromba, 1998). The first 3 months may pose some challenges as the patient acclimates to the dialysis routine (Beder, 1999), but in general, as patients feel better physically, their spirits lift and life becomes easier. After a while, however, comes the realization that dialysis is now a way of life and that, as a dialysis patient, his or her well-being will forever depend on a machine and the medical world. The limitations on independence and the restrictions that the regimen imposes become very stressful for many patients. The chronic nature of the disease, the impact on the patients' ability to function, and the impact on their ability to control their quality of life are continuing challenges for patients.

THE FAMILY/CAREGIVER EXPERIENCE

In general, caring for someone with a chronic illness extracts a great deal from the caregiver; the illness affects the caregiver's psychological and physical well-being. In the case of the ESRD caregiver, there is the predialysis (crisis stage) situation in which the patient suffers from one of several illnesses that affects kidney function. The level of fatigue and stress for the caregiver mirrors that for the patient and, in addition, requires that the caregiver carry additional responsibilities as the illness progresses and the patient is more debilitated by failed or failing kidneys. Unlike some other illnesses, the progression of kidney disease may be slow but it is insidious, as the kidneys become more and more compromised, causing a variety of debilitating symptoms for the patient.

Once dialysis begins, the caregiver must deal with the rigors of treatment: making sure the patient gets to the treatment, making the accommodations to diet and fluid restrictions, and dealing with other ongoing struggles because financial and emotional accommodations may have to be made. Schneider (2004) studied first-degree caregiver reactions with a variety of variables and isolated physical fatigue as the most prominent negative feature of caregiver quality of life.

Smith and Soliday (2001) explored the effect of parental chronic kidney disease on the family. In interviews with more than 120 families in which one parent was on dialysis, they found that the illness affected the family in four ways: financial difficulties were exacerbated, physical limitations prevailed, gender roles shifted, and family issues intensified. Treatment-related financial problems plagued many of the families because the invasive nature of the dialysis treatment erodes the capacity to work. These financial burdens, as expected, directly influenced the family. A major issue affecting family functioning was the extreme fatigue parents with kidney disease experience and the limitations this symptom imposes on all aspects of family activity. Gender-specific roles in a more traditional household were impacted because the ability of women to perform traditional female roles in the home and of men to be responsible for financial support of the family were altered by the kidney disease, resulting in loss of self-esteem, ongoing tension in the home, and levels of depression. Family issues included the struggle for parents because they could not spend as much time in family activities as they desired, were not as available as they would have wanted to be in activities of nurturing and parenting, and worried about the direct effect of their illness on their children. Parents specifically expressed concern that family members spent a great deal of time worrying about them; this caused stress and guilt for many parents interviewed. It is realistic to conclude that chronic disease and ESRD affect more than the parent; the entire family system is affected. One caveat to be acknowledged is that not all people with ESRD have the same struggles. Younger patients manage better and are more independent than older patients (over 55); but the more critical factor in how a patient fares is the level of medical problems that existed before kidney failure. Many patients can function independently, hold jobs, and are active.

Campbell (1998) summarized the most frequently mentioned outcomes of caregiving over a lengthy period of time: loneliness and isolation; depression; frustration; anger and guilt; loss of emotional closeness between caregiver and partner; loss of freedom and time for one's own interests and development; fatigue from added roles; burnout and being overwhelmed; negative effects on relationships with friends, relatives, and neighbors; restricted involvement in the community; and restricted involvement in church and spiritual activities. One of the major outcomes of caregiving for a dialysis patient is isolation and loneliness. Once the patient settles into the routine of dialysis, the friends and family members who rallied at the beginning of the illness begin to drift away, as the treatment becomes unremittingly chronic rather than acute and competing demands force them to return to their own agendas (Campbell, 1998).

Clearly, caregivers and family members need to be cared for and supported as they tend to the needs of a person with ESRD.

THE RENAL SOCIAL WORKER

Since 1976, the federal government has mandated social work services in dialysis units. Guidelines have been established to respond to the multiple needs for assessment, resource procurement, team planning, advocacy, referral, education, and the ability to monitor interventions. The Council of Nephrology Social Workers of the National Kidney Foundation (2002) describes the role of the nephrology social worker:

> Nephrology social work services support and maximize the psychosocial functioning and adjustment of chronic kidney disease patients and their families. These services are provided to improve social and emotional stresses, which result from physical, social, and psychological concomitants of chronic kidney disease. . . . The nephrology social worker is part of an interdisciplinary team and provides collaboration with other team members to help them in understanding the biopsychosocial factors that can have an impact on treatment outcome. (p. 8)

Social workers are positioned in a unique place in a patient's life: they are trained to view patients in their multiple social systems and function from a person-in-environment perspective. Because social workers do not provide direct medical treatment, they are often the team members best suited to provide consistent, ongoing contact with the patient and family struggling with diagnosis and treatment (Beder, 1999). For these reasons, social workers have long played an integral role in the dialysis treatment team (Furr, 1998).

Although dialysis treatment can succeed in stabilizing the patient physiologically, the disease impedes the patient's functional ability across all domains — physical, mental, and social. Clearly, treatment of the whole person, and not just the damaged organ, requires that outcomes be taken into consideration in the planning of patient care. Social workers have the knowledge and skills to assess these domains and intervene accordingly. In addition, social workers as community liaisons can engage community resources on behalf of the patient, thus easing the burden of living with dialysis and encouraging more independent functioning. These resource connections include financial support, transportation, and needed equipment (Frank et al., 2003).

Perhaps the most critical roles of the social worker are those of case manager and education provider for the patient and family. At each stage of the illness experience — crisis or chronic stage — the patient and family are challenged to understand and integrate what is occurring physically to the patient. Often the patient or caregiver is confused by medical terminology, is overwrought by anxiety and fear, and needs elucidation of the treatment plan. As case manager, the social worker frequently assesses the patient and caregivers while arranging services, monitoring problem areas, and counseling as needed to maximize and optimize patient functioning. The mandate of social work services is to help patients and families manage the intricate, demanding, and tedious treatment regimen while they adjust to potentially severe and dramatic lifestyle changes.

Typically, the social worker is assigned a caseload of patients to be seen on a regular basis during dialysis visits. The social worker can see the patient at any time during treatment because the patient remains in one place for the many hours of dialysis. During these times, the social worker can attempt to address the concrete and emotional needs of the patient and often will respond to specific needs that have emerged. Contact with families can also take place during this treatment time.

SOCIAL WORKER COMMENTS

Twelve nephrology social workers were interviewed. Each worker was based in a hospital or a dialysis unit auxiliary to the hospital. The same sentiment was echoed by each worker: What gives them the greatest satisfaction is that they are able to get to know their patients and their patients' families and spend, in many cases, years working with them. Dialysis is one of very few services in the hospital system where a patient is able to see the same staff and social workers consistently. Because patients are assigned specific times and days for their treatment, there is regularity to when they will be in treatment. Several of the social workers agreed with Dobroff et al. (2001), who stated, "What can be so rewarding for renal social workers — and so challenging — is intervening with patients where the physical, psychological, and socioeconomic impact[s] are so intertwined" (p. 125). One of the social workers I interviewed said the dialysis unit "is the cream of the crop of social work jobs!"

Time on the dialysis unit is spent counseling, arranging transportation and attending to other concrete needs, dealing with crises that emerge, and doing paperwork. Caseloads varied from unit to unit, from a low of 34 cases to a high of 90. Despite these high caseload numbers, the social workers generally presented themselves as relaxed and comfortable in their positions. Their general feeling was that their efforts on behalf of new patients are vital, and the need to educate both the patients and their families takes precedence over other needs.

The offering of emotional support was the most frequent task of the social workers. In-depth counseling was not included in their description of their role and function; in part, as was stated, "There are staff psychiatrists to whom we are expected to refer. Often a patient will need medication, and we are not able to prescribe, so we call psych to help. The psychiatrist is part of the team." In addition, there is "just not enough time to spend in-depth time with any patient unless in the most extreme circumstances."

"I try to be there for their feelings, especially the new patients," said one in-patient dialysis worker. "Also," she said, "the family sometimes needs more attention than the patient. It is a different type of need. The patient has their own struggles — many are in denial that they have to be on dialysis — while the family has to deal with major adjustments and sometimes anger and guilt toward the patient." In terms of approach, one of the workers explained that she is adamant that the patients begin to realize that "Life is not only about dialysis; there is life during dialysis and it is there to be lived and appreciated." "Our job is to try to help the patients and families 'normalize' their life around the dialysis regimen," said another.

Death is not a constant feature of the dialysis unit, but when it occurs, due to the long tenure of relationships — one worker had known a patient for 20 years — it is difficult, and it is often made more difficult because of the long-term relationships with the family. One patient, a long-timer on the unit, died rather unexpectedly, and "I kept his wheelchair in my office for 3 months. I could not let go of him," commented the social worker.

Two especially difficult areas of work were identified: dealing with issues regarding transplants and dealing with patients who decide they want to stop treatment. Dialysis patients who are eligible for transplant and are relying on a cadaver kidney may have to wait years until a kidney becomes available. During the waiting time, they may deteriorate physically and, in some cases, not be able to endure the surgical procedure. The disappointment that is generated is profound. However, for the patient who is able, the waiting period seems interminable, and the social work staff has to be attuned to this dynamic. Much more difficult, as noted by several of those interviewed, is the management of the returning patient when their transplant has failed. The average transplant lasts between 9 and 12 years, so it is not uncommon for a patient to return to the dialysis unit to receive treatment. It is equally upsetting when a transplant has been effected and the patient's body rejects the kidney after a period of time. Both situations are always a difficult transition for the patient and family, and social work staff are engaged — and have feelings of sadness, frustration, and disappointment — in this struggle with the patient.

The issue of withdrawing from treatment was felt keenly by all those interviewed. In essence, when patients decide to stop treatment, they are committing suicide: they will die within a week to 10 days from toxins in their blood that are normally filtered by the kidney or dialysis treatment. This frequently posed ethical dilemmas in terms of patient self-determination and personal beliefs of the social work staff. One social worker reframed the struggle in a unique way and candidly explained, "My dilemma with stopping treatment is complicated. Because the treatment is such a nightmare and the patients are usually multiply challenged with all kinds of illnesses, I sometimes want to urge them to stop treatment as an act of kindness toward them. I want to tell them that it is okay to give up." In general, the "erosion of dialysis" as it was called, was difficult for the social workers to witness.

One of the social workers described a particularly difficult case that involved a 40-year-old male patient who weighed more than 500 pounds. He could not walk or sit upright and was noncompliant with his treatment. The treatment procedure was a challenge because special machinery and equipment had to be used to hook up the dialysis machinery. He was verbally abusive to staff, making it even more difficult to manage his needs. The social worker handling the case struggled with levels of approach and avoidance with the patient. "It was very hard to be empathetic while having a reaction to the weight and demands of the patient, knowing that he was depressed, and struggling with his illness," she said.

The counseling on the unit, as described by the social workers, included individual, family, and group modalities. More than half of the social workers were running support groups in their units and found that to be a very satisfying aspect of their work. Because of the multimodal approach, the social workers felt they were making a substantial impact on the lives of their patients and their patients' families and that they were responsible for many positive changes and transitions in their lives.

One social worker who had been in dialysis work for many years said, "The patients are so unbelievably brave. I feel like such a wimp in comparison. I love this work!"

4

THE CARDIAC CARE SOCIAL WORKER

ABOUT CORONARY HEART DISEASE

Approximately 64,400,000 Americans have cardiovascular disease (CVD); of these, 25,300,000 are estimated to be age 65 and older. CVD covers a number of conditions affecting the structures or function of the heart, including coronary artery disease (including heart attack), abnormal heart rhythms, heart valve disease, congenital heart disease, heart muscle disease (cardiomyopathy), vascular disease, and pericardial disease. CVD is the leading cause of death for both men and women in the United States; it accounted for 38.5% of all deaths, or 1 for every 2.6 deaths, in 2002. Nearly 2,600 Americans die of CVD each day, an average of one death every 34 seconds. CVD claims more lives each year than the next five leading causes of death combined (cancer, respiratory disease, accidents, diabetes, and flu or pneumonia). The cost of treating CVD and stroke in the United States in 2004 was estimated at $368.4 billion. In all instances of coronary heart disease, people at highest risk included those with high blood pressure, those who smoked, and those who had high cholesterol. In each category, the risk increased if a person has a sedentary lifestyle (little or no exercise) and was overweight (American Heart Association, 2004).

Coronary artery disease (a.k.a. coronary heart disease) includes heart attack (myocardial infarction) and chest pain (angina pectoris). In 2004, over 700,000 Americans had a new coronary attack and 500,000 had a recurrent attack. The average age of a person having a first heart attack was 65.8 for men and 70.4 for women. About 340,000 people per year die of heart attacks in an emergency department or before reaching a hospital. In 2004, the estimated direct and indirect cost of coronary heart disease was $133.2 billion (American Heart Association, 2004). Heart disease will strike 6.9% of the men in the United States and 6% of the women. In particular, the most seriously affected ethnic group is Black women, of whom 9% will develop heart disease. This group seems to be the hardest hit because of diet, smoking, and lack of exercise.

A heart attack causes permanent damage to the heart muscle. The most frequent cause of a heart attack is narrowing of the arteries that supply the heart with blood. Plaque deposits, which build up in the arteries, become dislodged and form a blood clot. If the clot blocks the arteries to the heart, the heart muscle becomes starved for oxygen and begins to permanently deteriorate. The degree of damage to the heart muscle depends on the size of the area supplied by the blocked artery and the time between injury and treatment. Heart muscle typically begins to heal soon after a heart attack and takes about 8 weeks to repair. Although functional, the damaged heart muscle and tissue are usually weakened, compromising the heart's ability to pump effectively.

In some situations of heart attack and unstable angina (chest pain), the treatment requires coronary artery bypass graft surgery. During bypass surgery, blood flow is rerouted through a new artery or vein graft, bypassing diseased artery sections to increase the blood flow to the heart muscle and tissue. Known as coronary artery bypass grafting or surgery (CABG or CABS), the surgery requires that the chest be opened and that the patient be put on a heart–lung bypass machine. The vein graft that serves as the replacement for the diseased artery is removed from the leg or mammary artery of the patient and attached to the coronary artery. The blood flow is permanently rerouted past the blocked area or areas. Patients are hospitalized for a week to 10 days, and recovery at home takes between 6 and 8 weeks. Bypass surgery often relieves symptoms of chest pain (angina), improves exercise performance, and reduces the risk of a future heart attack (Gillinov, 2002).

Recovery from this surgery takes many weeks. The procedures require the surgeon to take veins or arteries from one part of the body and implant them in the circulatory system of the heart. This means that the patient has had open-heart surgery as well as surgery to access a vein or artery elsewhere in the body. As such, there are multiple sites of surgical intervention and thus multiple sites of healing. Recovery involves time initially and lifestyle changes in the long run to prevent recurrence of the condition. Assuming the surgical outcomes are positive, the patient faces a period of rehabilitation and convalescence during which the heart heals and the body recovers from the surgery.

HEART ATTACK (MYOCARDIAL INFARCTION) AND BYPASS SURGERY — THE PATIENT EXPERIENCE

Heart Attack

A heart attack is an acute, life-threatening episode with a high initial mortality rate. The physical experience of a heart attack often follows a course: the person complains of slight to moderate chest pain; the pain increases and radiates down the left side of the body, back, or jaw; the person has difficulty breathing and may feel nauseous, dizzy, weak, and short of breath, with rapid or irregular heartbeats. One must seek medical care as soon as possible, because the best time to treat a heart attack is within 1 to 2 hours of the onset of symptoms. Immediate treatment includes medication therapy to break up and prevent blood clots from gathering and damaging heart tissue. In some cases, angioplasty — the insertion of a balloon device that is designed to open arteries closed by blood clots — is performed and, if necessary, bypass surgery may be initiated. Under all circumstances, the illness is serious, life threatening, and, for most patients and their families, sure to alter both everyday life and lifestyle, initially and possibly forever.

The experience of a heart attack can be conceptualized as occurring in two stages: the acute or crisis stage, when the patient is in the hospital, and the recovery stage, usually after the hospitalization. During the crisis or acute stage of the medical experience, while in the hospital and being treated, the patient may not be able to understand and grasp the severity and potential impact of his or her situation. However, once stable, the patient potentially experiences severe emotional distress. Keller (1991) documented that after the acute episode, patients experienced pain and expressed a fear of dying. Emotions are heightened by a lack of information concerning their condition; deep emotional distress and anxiety are common reactions. Because anxiety fuels feelings of apprehension, dread, or uneasiness, it can also have a negative impact on the recovery; patients who reported higher levels of anxiety were 4.9 times more likely to have complications after their heart attack (Moser & Dracup, 1996). Studies of long-term outcomes indicate that 20 to 30% of those who survive the initial crisis suffer severe and long-term psychosocial problems (National Health Service, 1998), with an increased potential for posttraumatic stress disorder (Pederson, Middel, & Larsen, 2003).

During the recovery phase, patients must significantly change their lifestyle to decrease the risk of a subsequent heart attack. Changes may include a more conscientious monitoring of diet, initiation of an exercise program, cessation of smoking, and measures taken to decrease stress. Depending on the degree of damage to the heart from the heart attack, resuming normal life activity usually begins slowly, as the patient's heart strengthens as it overcomes the damage caused by the attack. During the recovery period, the major task for patients is to "come to terms" with the meaning of the event in their life. Patients must confront their perceptions of themselves and their roles within the family and society. They have to cope with their fears and the fears of those around them while making lifestyle changes related to cardiac risk modification. Patients may also struggle with self-esteem, anxiety, depression, reduced family functioning, delay in returning to work, and diminished health status (Horn, Fleury, & Moore, 2002). A variable noted in the literature on recovery was that unmarried, hospitalized heart attack patients had higher death rates than those who were married (Chandra, Szklo, Goldberg, & Tonascia, 1983). This suggests that, for patients without a spouse, care might not be as immediately available and social contacts may be less frequent, and that the motivating presence of a partner gives patients a stronger desire to be well and reengage with life.

Bypass Surgery

CABG is rapidly becoming a routine form of treatment for those who have heart attacks or angina (chest pain) from heart disease. It is considered a major operation in terms of prevalence and cost and in terms of physical severity and emotional toll on the patient and family. Indeed, patients' overall quality of life is often markedly worse for several months after surgery, with symptoms including fatigue, pain at the surgical incision sites, loss of appetite, loss of sleep, heart rhythm disturbances, anxiety, depression, and mood swings (Allen, 1990; Mahler & Kulik, 2002). However, in time, the surgery usually reduces symptoms and improves quality of life for many patients.

The literature documents certain noteworthy variables in recovery and adjustment from CABG. Kulik and Mahler (1993) studied the recovery of 85 male patients, noting that married men who underwent CABG showed an in-hospital recovery advantage over those who were unmarried if and only if they received hospital visits from their spouses. In most medical outcome studies, married people fare better than unmarried. This relates to the level of connection and care that potentially exists between partners; the bond creates a reason to live and the connection, assuming the strength of the relationship is sound, is empowering. In addition, many people who are in hospitals are victim to the shortage of nurses and other staff. Visiting partners are able to provide additional care, tend to nonnursing chores, keep the patient company, and lift the patient's spirits. This may be the critical factor in understanding the statistics of the Kulik and Mahler study.

In the long term, the CABG patients in the Kulik and Mahler (1993) study who received greater emotional support experienced less emotional distress, felt they had a better overall quality of life, and complied more with behavior recommendations (smoked less, walked more) than did patients who had less emotional support. Contrada et al. (2004) studied religious involvement in 142 patients after CABG. Results of the study indicated that religious involvement may influence adaptation to heart surgery. "Stronger religious beliefs were associated with fewer surgical complications and shorter hospital stays. . . . Effects of religious beliefs and attendance on length of hospital stay were stronger among women than among men" (p. 234). Interestingly, in this study, prayer did not correlate with either positive or negative recovery outcomes. In a study of female patients post-CABG, Ai et al. (1997) found that women were more likely than men to experience postoperative depression, anxiety, and sleeping disorders and that women with lower socioeconomic status and poor general health had a higher risk for depression and less satisfactory health change postoperatively. Education, in this study, was the only protective factor against depression. Education speaks to the ability to have one's mind challenged in certain ways, moving thinking away from the self to broader areas; it potentially facilitates diversion from corrosive thought patterns; and it allows patients to potentially understand the language of the medical staff and be able to follow and understand directions for their care.

Although statistically men have more heart attacks, women are close behind in frequency. The belief that being female provides protection against heart disease is "currently being debunked in the health care community" (Rankin, 2002, p. 399). Research focusing on women after a cardiac event suggests that their recovery experiences may be more difficult than those of men; women have more physical and emotional problems during recovery. In the process of healing from heart attack, female patients expressed greater feelings of diminished self-esteem and self-worth, dependence on others, a lack of support and communication, and ongoing anger than their male counterparts (Fleury, Kimbrell, & Kruszewski, 1995). As long as 1 year after heart attack or surgery, women reported more anxiety, depression, sleep disturbances, clinical symptoms, and functional disability than men. Because of home and family responsibilities, women were less likely than men to enroll in cardiac rehabilitation programs and, of those who enrolled, women had higher dropout rates than men (Oldridge, Radowski, & Gottleib, 1992).

THE FAMILY/CAREGIVER EXPERIENCE WITH HEART ATTACK AND CABG

Heart attack or heart disease necessitating CABG threatens the integrity of the family by potentially challenging financial stability and role articulation, raising levels of anxiety within the family, possibly worsening family relationships, and compromising social support over the long term. Dhooper (1990) studied 40 families of first-time heart attack patients who were 60 years or younger in an attempt to understand how families adjust to this critical event. The families were studied while in the hospital, at 1 month and 3 months postevent, to see the impact on family functioning. The immediate reactions of the spouses to the news of the heart attack were reported as shock, disbelief, fear of losing the spouse, anger, and helplessness. These spouses suffered sleeplessness, loss of appetite, headache, trembling, restlessness, shortness of breath, irritability, lack of concentration, and forgetfulness. When the patient was declared out of danger but remained in the hospital, the levels of family anxiety were still high. A month after the patient returned home, the impact of the crisis on the emotional health of the family had somewhat lessened, but spouses were still highly anxious. In half of the families studied, social life changes had occurred. In more than one fifth of the families, a member of the family had become ill, considered to be related to the emotional strain on the family of the cardiac episode. By 3 months, the lives of most families had returned to normal despite continued levels of anxiety on the part of spouses. Children were also studied and, although reactions varied with age, they generally mirrored those of the spouses, with initial anxiety, a slow resumption of normalcy by 1 month, and by 3 months, the children had resumed their social life and the family situation was unremarkable.

Studies of patients undergoing cardiac surgery have identified beneficial aspects of supportive relationships. Kulik and Mahler (1989) found that CABG patients receiving a high level of social support were discharged sooner than patients with lowered social support. Social support has been documented as an essential aspect of healing in many illness situations. The presence of social support connects the patient to the larger community, helps the patient feel cared for and cared about, and often is a motivating force in getting well. Social support can be manifested through visiting, providing tangible help with driving and providing necessary food and services, etc. While in the hospital, patients who have strong ties with others, who have sources of social support, can be diverted from their illnesses, brought back into the fold and familiarity of their lives, and can realize their connection to others. While this is an abstraction, the literal caring and good social support that caring friends and neighbors can provide can lift the spirits of an ailing person and facilitate discharge as noted by the research.

King, Reis, Porter, and Norsen (1993) demonstrated that support to the patient's spouse had a beneficial impact on the patient's recovery. Schott and Bandura (1988) found that among wives of patients with myocardial infarction, the quality of relationships with their children, family, and friends was positively related to less psychosocial stress after the heart attack. Perception of spouse and patient causes and consequences of the myocardial infarction were studied to determine if there was a relationship between the congruence or lack of congruence of the couple and illness adjustment. The patients from couples with similar views reported lower levels of disability, fewer sexual problems, higher vitality, and better psychosocial adjustment (Figueiras & Weinman, 2003; Thompson, Galbraith et al., 2002).

In general, families go through levels of upheaval after the crisis of the heart attack. Spouses are naturally most affected because of their dependency on and relationship with the patient. Depending on the severity of the heart attack or surgery and the level of limitation or disability that has resulted, life can resume within a period of months. Lifestyle changes may have to be initiated, which can affect the lifestyle and activity level of the family. Conversely, the event can be seen as a "wake up call" to alter a lifestyle for the whole family, to eat better, exercise more, stop smoking, etc. Patient limitation often predicts family recovery. If the patient is able, within a short period of time, to resume many activities and is able to demonstrate consistent progress, the mood of the household can remain optimistic and hopeful.

THE SOCIAL WORKER IN THE CARDIAC CARE UNIT

The social worker in the cardiac care unit interfaces with the patient and family members. Because short hospital stays are now the rule for heart attack, in many instances, the interaction is short and the discharge plan becomes the focus of interaction. According to the Harvard Heart Letter (Lee, 2004), after a heart attack, some people are now being sent home after 72 hours. In the late 1950s, the average hospital stay following a heart attack was about 50 days; now it hovers around 5. Much of this decline in length of stay is due to drug therapy, technology, surgery, pain control, and general hospital care. Another reason is economics. Gone are the days of enforced bed rest for the heart attack patient. In most hospitals, as soon as the patient is stable, he or she will be encouraged to sit up, walk to the bathroom, and stroll the halls. This progressive exercise helps prevent blood clots from forming while strengthening the heart. Because of the shortened stays, social worker involvement may be limited, especially for a patient who is progressing well. Surgical patients stay longer, from 1 to 2 weeks, and patients who are not recovering may stay even longer.

Perhaps unique to the cardiac patient, posthospital lifestyle changes are usually mandated by the medical condition (i.e., changes in diet, exercise, and smoking; reduction of stress and anxiety; and conscientious medical management). Although the hospital stay may be short, the social worker must develop interventions for the patient and family that will help the individual to consider initiating and changing toward heart-healthy habits and changing individual coping strategies. Recovery involves continuous adjustment by both patient and family members as they attempt to adapt to the uncertainties of coronary heart disease. Many cardiac patients have one episode, make needed lifestyle changes, and never have further problems. Others will have repeated episodes, will be hospitalized frequently, and, after the first heart attack or coronary episode, will never return to wellness. For some, the damage to their hearts is so pronounced that they may never return to work or they will not be allowed to engage in vigorous activity or interact as they had with family and friends for fear of causing further damage to their hearts. The social worker can be a motivating force in helping the patient and family make these needed lifestyle adjustments. Interventions with family members can assist them in effectively managing their own anxiety and sense of loss and facilitating their ability to support the cardiac patient's recovery and efforts to modify risk factors after the cardiac event (Horn et al., 2002).

In social worker meetings with family and patient, during the acute and recovery phase of the cardiac event, the two simultaneous goals are to reduce psychological distress caused by the event and to provide guidance to support the efforts of the family and patient toward recovery. While in the hospital, during the acute phase of the event, social worker interventions on a cognitive level include extensive education regarding symptoms, rehabilitation, expectations, and community resources. Even a single intervention session with a family can be helpful, but a structured educational program later in the recovery period may prove to be the most effective because family members will be more ready to be able to hear and absorb educational content. On an emotional level, social support, either individually or through support groups held in the hospital, is very helpful because patient and caregiver concerns are raised in an accepting environment.

Several studies have attempted to document the efficacy of social worker and nurse intervention strategies. Thompson and Meddis (1990) studied the impact of four 30-minute educational and psychological support sessions with spouses of heart attack patients, comparing levels of anxiety with a control group who did not receive the support session interventions. The anxiety levels of the support session group receiving the intervention were lowered significantly in comparison to the nontreatment group. Lynn-McHale, Corsetta, and Brady-Avis (1997) intervened with a group of spouses and patients scheduled for bypass surgery, presenting a scripted slide presentation of the procedure and a tour of the intensive care area where initial recovery takes place. Both patients and spouses experienced significant decreases in anxiety over the control group, who had received standard preoperative teaching. These studies support the social work role of educator for hospitalized patients on the cardiac unit.

During the rehabilitation phase, when patients are released from the hospital, a number of intervention strategies are considered useful and enhance the quality of life for the patient and family members: educational discussion groups, counseling sessions, physical conditioning groups, and general support and self-help groups for both patients and family members. The goal of these outpatient interventions is to support risk factor modification efforts for the patient and family and enhance coping strategies (Van Horn et al., 2002).

In general, social worker interventions have to account for the level of anxiety and pessimism generated by the medical condition. They must present credible and positive information about the patient's current condition and the short- and long-term ramifications of the diagnosis. Any efforts that can be used to strengthen the patient's sense of power, choice, and control are considered useful (Ben-Zur, Rappaport, Ammar, & Uretzky, 2000). As an emotional support, the social worker has a presence that can be soothing and reassuring, while addressing the anxiety and uncertainty of the moment.

SOCIAL WORKER COMMENTS

Almost all of the dozen social workers who were interviewed for this section divided their time between the cardiac coronary care unit (CCU) and the nonintensive cardiac care area of their hospital. Patients in the CCU were those who had just received surgical intervention and had been transferred from the intensive care unit to the CCU (considered a step-down unit) before being transferred to the regular cardiac area. In the CCU, there may also be patients who are awaiting a transplant and are too ill to be on the regular cardiac unit. Patient and social worker interaction on the CCU is limited because the postsurgical patients are sedated and still under the influence of anesthesia and other pain medications. Family contact with the social worker frequently occurs in this area, as anxious family members, constrained by the very limited visiting privileges, seek information and guidance from the social work staff. On the regular cardiac floor, social workers are in frequent contact with both patients and family members because patients who have had a heart attack, stroke, or other cardiac episode are in various phases of recovery. Caseloads on the cardiac floor range from 25 to 36 patients per social worker.

For the patients on the cardiac unit, social workers defined their role and function as offering both concrete services and emotional support to both patients and caregivers. In general, the comments of the social workers reflected the reality that patients are in a state of shock after a heart attack as they struggle to incorporate what has happened to them. Physically, during the acute phase of their illness, patients are medicated, which can distort meaningful discussion of their medical future. The family, though, is eager to initiate these discussions and, according to the comments of several of the workers, the family requires a great deal of social worker attention. The social work skills that were frequently mentioned as useful in the work included the ability to offer emotional support, helping and allowing the family to vent their upset and fears, to acknowledge the condition of both patient and family, and to help the family begin to adjust to what has happened to them. In some cases, the social workers noted that they will sit with seriously ill CCU patients and hold their hands as a sign of support. Patience was mentioned by one social worker as an essential component of her approach to patients and family members, noting that "Sometimes, it is shocking how little the patient knows about good nutrition, the risks of smoking, or being overweight. I struggle to not judge my patients and have to exercise a lot of tolerance for having almost created the situation the patient is in. I sometimes want to scold the family for letting this happen, but, of course, I keep quiet."

In the role of discharge planner, which was mentioned as part of the daily responsibilities by all those interviewed, the social worker is responsible for putting together the care plan for the patient when he or she leaves the hospital. Often, this means arranging for rehabilitation services, setting up sessions with a nutritionist, coordinating additional services the patient will need, and ordering equipment if needed. But the overriding discharge planning mandate is to make certain that the medical needs of the patient will be consistently met. Does the patient live alone? Does he or she have steps to climb? Will there be someone who will supply the patient with food? Is the patient expected to take care of someone else? Questions such as these and others have to be answered before the social worker is able to release the patient with a conscientious care plan in place.

All of the social workers in the various hospitals worked with a team consisting of doctors, nurses, nutritionists, and physical and occupational therapists. The continuum of care between the social worker and the other staff was reported to be very good in some hospitals to satisfactory in others.

The challenge of the work seemed to lie in being able to effect a meaningful relationship between the social worker and the patient and his or her family members. Because the patient is on the unit for such a limited time, and the impact of the heart incident is so huge, there does not seem to be enough time to initiate and empower patients and families to address the impact and lifestyle changes that need to be made. Another challenge mentioned by some of those interviewed was the difficulty for the patient who does not have an involved family or who has no family at all. In these cases, the social worker must develop a care plan that is much more inclusive and complex to arrange. And, because time is limited and there is a strong push to discharge patients, the social worker struggles to make the needed arrangements for home care or transfer to a care facility. Along these lines, a social worker described the case of a 40-year-old woman who came to the emergency room. She had been living in a shelter, had no insurance, and was having severe chest pain. She was quickly stabilized and the social worker "filled out reams of forms to have the woman transferred to a care facility, but there are so few resources for the indigent and I had no idea what I was going to do with this patient. Finally, I was able to get her into a rehab unit, but I am sure that she is either deceased or back in the shelter."

A different case disposition involved a 34-year-old terminal lung cancer patient who was on chemotherapy. One evening, she began experiencing chest pains, came to the hospital, and was admitted to the cardiac floor. She had no family. Hospice services were engaged and, as she deteriorated, the social worker was able to forge a connection with her and was there when she died. The social worker said, "While I was very sad, I knew that I had helped someone in the most extreme of all situations."

"The work is not for everyone," commented one social worker. "It is for those who have a lot of patience, who are nonjudgmental, as you see a lot of self-destructive behavior from the patients and the families, and you have to be open minded." Another worker noted that, "It is very scary here, as this stuff can happen to anyone if they don't take care of themselves."

"The work is so real," said a 24-year veteran social worker. "I am not trying to save the world; I just want to connect with people in an open and intimate way and help them get well. The work is honest and I get a lot out of it; it affects my personal journey." Personal impact on this unit seemed high, with each social worker seeming to make his or her own lifestyle changes toward better health. "I am in touch with my own mortality in a way I had never been before working in the cardiac area. It has taught me that life is ephemeral, and I value every minute."

5

THE HOSPICE SOCIAL WORKER

ABOUT HOSPICE CARE

The history of hospice as a way of caring for sick and terminally ill people has its roots in medieval times when a hospice referred to a place where travelers were offered rest, care, food, shelter, and comfort. Over the centuries, the term has shifted, and in 1967, physician Dame Cicely Saunders founded the first modern hospice — St. Christopher's Hospice — in a suburb of London. Saunders introduced the idea of specialized care to the United States in 1963 during a visit to Yale University, where she unveiled her conception of holistic hospice care to physicians, chaplains, social workers, and nurses. In 1974, with the opening of Hospice of Connecticut, hospice care in the United States became a viable alternative to and extension of traditional health care for terminally ill people (Richman, 1995). By 2001, there were more than 3,000 hospice and palliative care programs in the United States, ranging from home care services to hospital care and from professional, palliative care teams to lay and volunteer workers (Bennahum, 2003).

The concept of palliative care is often confused with hospice service. The goal of palliative care is similar to hospice — it treats the whole person for medical, emotional, spiritual, and other physical needs — but is not necessarily for those who are terminally ill. Palliative care implies efforts toward pain control and management of debilitating symptoms. Many of those who have had palliative care will improve and eventually be well. Hospice care acknowledges the reality of imminent death whereas palliative care may be for patients who are not terminal but who seek pain control and emotional and spiritual support.

Hospice care is unique. Hospice may not literally be a place or even a subset of service. Instead, it is a philosophy of care for terminally ill people and their families. The hospice orientation is grounded in the conviction that dying patients need not suffer alone or without respite. At the core of hospice care is the belief that each of us has the right to die pain free and with dignity and that our families are to be offered the necessary support to allow us to do so. Underlying the delivery of care is the understanding that the patient is terminally ill, that no cure is expected for the patient's illness, and that the patient is expected to die within a matter of days or weeks. Hospice includes medical care with an emphasis on pain management and symptom relief designed to keep the patient comfortable as he or she in the process of dying. In the hospice, the only treatment offered is palliative (Naierman, 2003). Advances in pain management and greater understanding of and techniques for symptom relief have facilitated hospice service.

Hospice care is perceived by many as the transition — the period of passing from the life of the terminally ill person and the family as it was, to life in the present, to life at its ending, to whatever follows the death of the patient. It is a period of passing from acute hospital care to hospice inpatient or home care to death (Rusnack, Schaefer, & Moxley, 1988).

Medicare certifies more than 90% of hospices in the United States, in part because the majority of people who are cared for in hospice are covered by Medicare. Initiated in 1983, Medicare's hospice benefit became law in 1986. Under the provision of this law, Medicare pays a Medicare-certified hospice a predetermined daily rate for the total management of hospice care, including the provision of all core hospice services (physician, nurse, social worker, counselor, clergy, volunteers) and all additional services (pharmacist, physical therapist, occupational therapist, home health aide) as well as drugs and medical equipment. A patient must be certified for hospice care; that is, the physician attests that the patient is terminally ill, with less than 6 months to live (Richman, 1995). An additional aspect of the law, and one that is particularly helpful to patients and family members, is the elimination of paperwork; families are not required to submit claims or pay bills for hospice services. These services are handled by the hospice staff with social worker input for assessment. For those who are not Medicare or Medicaid eligible or are without medical insurance, financial accommodations are usually made based on ability to pay (Naierman, 2003).

Under the Medicare law, hospice services can be offered in free-standing hospice centers, hospitals, nursing homes and other long-term care facilities, and the patient's home. About 80% of hospice care takes place in the home of the patient or family member (Naierman, 2003). All terminally ill patients, including children, and all illness categories are accepted under hospice care, although some hospice centers are disease specific.

Under Medicare regulations, the delivery of hospice care, whether in the hospital or home, is through an interdisciplinary team that consists of a physician, nurse, master's level social worker, clergy or spiritual advisor, and trained volunteers. The team uses an interdisciplinary rather than a multidisciplinary approach. This distinction implies an intentional blurring of roles rather than a specificity of roles, because services frequently overlap as the team considers the patient and family members' welfare their main concern (Richman, 1995). Since 1983, hospices have used social workers on a somewhat limited basis, in part because of the role blurring and in part as an effort to contain cost (Reese & Sontag, 2001). However, those social workers who work in a hospice setting bring to their tasks a particular mindset and value base that helps them define and articulate their role in the care of terminally ill people.

HOME CARE VERSUS HOSPITAL HOSPICE CARE

Home health care has been evolving as a form of medical service since the inception and cost containment efforts of managed care (Davitt & Kaye, 1996). Recent trends suggest that home care is one of the fastest growing segments of the health care delivery system. The growth is in response to pressures on hospitals to discharge patients more quickly, more liberal government reimbursements and licensing of home care agencies, numbers of elderly persons and children with chronic illnesses living into adulthood, limited access to nursing home beds, and sophisticated technology available outside of the hospital (Egan & Kadushin, 1999).

A family member, who assumes the role of primary caregiver, undertakes responsibility for care in the home of the patient. Collaborating with this individual, the social worker becomes familiar with the lifestyle of the family and the needs of the patient. Ongoing assessment of patient and family needs is a primary role for the social worker, as well as coordination of services and liaison with community resources. Counseling for the family and patient is frequently required as the trajectory of the illness and the needs of the patient increase. Because all hospice care, whether inpatient or home, falls under the umbrella of a Medicare-certified hospital, social workers are mandated to supply psychosocial support to patients and family members (Rusnack, Schaefer, & Moxley, 1991).

Hospice social workers employed in a hospital setting work with patients who need to have their acute symptoms (pain or decline of functioning) controlled as well as provide respite for the caregivers. Hospice care is traditionally offered either in a discrete part of a hospital where a designated number of beds have been assigned for hospice cases or in an independent hospice setting devoted only to hospice care. The role of the social worker for the inpatient is somewhat different from the home care hospice social worker. With inpatient services, often the patient is too ill to be part of the continuum of care, and much more of the work is devoted to family and caretaker concerns. In the event that a patient is articulate and able to relate to a social worker, intervention is devoted to keeping the patient as emotionally comfortable as possible and being available to provide whatever is needed for "safe passage."

One of the more noticeable aspects of inpatient hospice care is that there is a minimum of activity. Because no aggressive care is offered to the hospice patient other than palliative measures, and no treatments (e.g., chemotherapies) are offered, the usual hustle and bustle of a traditional hospital setting do not exist.

HOSPICE AND SOCIAL WORK
Social Worker as Part of the Interdisciplinary Team

The philosophy and value base of social work are embodied in hospice care. All professions have value preferences that give purpose and direction to practitioners (Hepworth, Rooney, & Larsen, 2002). A holistic, ecological perspective characterizes modern social work values that view people and the social environments they inhabit as constantly influencing one another. From this perspective, social workers consider the patient and family as one unit, as the unit of care in the hospice or in the home, and will attempt to address the multiple needs of both the patient and family. Also implicit in the values of social work is the belief that all people are to be treated with dignity and worth. Hospice care is instrumental in guaranteeing that dying patients are cared for in a dignified manner and in a way that is respectful of their personhood. Modern social work practice calls for the social worker to see the "whole person as a dynamic amalgam of interdependent spiritual, emotional, physical, and social needs" (MacDonald, 1991, p. 276). McDonnell (1986) described hospice as "the embodiment of social work values, principles, and practice" (p. 225). As such, the worker considers not only the needs of the terminally ill patient but the needs of the family or caregivers as well. From this vantage point, the unit of care shifts from patient to patient and family.

As defined by Rusnack et al. (1991), the social worker, as a member of the interdisciplinary team, anticipates the needs of the terminally ill patient and family; accompanies the patient, family, and significant others through a caring process in whatever venue (home or hospital) it takes place; and advocates for "safe passage" of the terminally ill person. Often work must begin with helping the patient and family accept the reality that death is near. In some cases, this is readily accepted and anticipated, but in others, the physician and social worker have to work with the family and patient to come to a level of acceptance of their situation. In advocating for safe passage, the objective is not only to prevent or reduce barriers to care, but also to promote conditions that enhance the fit between and among the terminally ill patient, the family, and professional or medical caregivers.

In addition, in many hospice settings, the social worker is the skilled practitioner who advises the staff on counseling matters, helping them understand some of the complexities of family dynamics and of people coping with terminal illness. The social worker is frequently involved in initiating and offering emotional support to staff members (Rusnack et al., 1988). Despite increasing clarity regarding the role of social workers within the interdisciplinary team, demands to reduce health care costs have resulted in competition among health care providers, specifically between social workers and nurses. Although the competition between nursing and social work is not new, it is especially prominent within hospice care because nurses assert that the overlap in responsibilities between nursing and social work could be filled by using only nurses to deal with patient and family concerns. It has been suggested that the convergence of roles between nursing and social work needs to be recognized as well as the divergence of roles. Nursing remains focused on the physical needs of the patient; social work focuses on the emotional needs. Although both professions are dedicated to the welfare of the patient, each profession needs to recognize the uniqueness it brings to the professional arena of hospice care, thus allowing the other to claim certain areas of expertise (Reese & Sontag, 2001).

The actual work of the hospice social worker consists of membership in the interdisciplinary team. As a team member, the social worker frequently identifies family needs and accesses community resources; is available to the family and patient to discuss financial concerns, including advance directives and psychosocial issues; provides support and direction to team members; and is responsible for ongoing assessment and strategy development of the care plan. These responsibilities vary from hospice to hospice and from state to state, as do needed licensure and certification. It usually falls to the social worker to facilitate insurance and entitlements (Medicare or Medicaid) to cover the costs of medical care. The social worker also connects with community resources and service providers on behalf of the patient.

In general, the qualifications for a social worker include a master's degree in social work, at least 1 to 3 years of supervised experience in the health care field, ability to work within and contribute to an interdisciplinary team, understanding and compassion toward patients and families, and knowledge of community resources available to patients and their families (Eustler & Martinez, 2003).

Family Support for Hospice Caregivers

Caring for a terminally ill family member can be overwhelming. The social worker's systems-oriented perspective strongly suggests that caring for a dying family member affects all members of the family and every dimension of family functioning. In the literature, major stressors identified by hospice caregivers included unmet needs for help with patient care, household assistance, assistance in legal and financial matters, inadequate communication with formal care providers, and difficulties managing the balance between patient care and the caregiver's personal needs. Other stressors frequently mentioned by caregivers included inadequate sleep; inadequate information on management of symptoms, medications, and physical needs of the patient; and lack of access to physicians. Studies of hospice and family caregiving almost uniformly identify social support from family and friends as critical in helping the primary caregiver cope with caring for the dying patient. Social workers involved in hospice work need to assess the family care system, both initially and periodically, to determine areas of need and to devise ways to ease the burden of caregiving while utilizing the inherent strengths within the family system. Brief family counseling may often be needed to enhance and mobilize the care network on behalf of the patient (Patterson & Dorfman, 2002).

SOCIAL WORKER COMMENTS

In an effort to more fully understand the challenges and rewards of hospice social work, I interviewed social workers involved in both in-hospital and home care hospice work in several different venues.

The prospect of working with a caseload of people who are dying, with families in grief, and with a decided level of sadness permeating the work would prove daunting to many social workers considering work options. To my surprise, of the 15 social workers interviewed, the majority felt they had been drawn to the work and found great satisfaction from their labors. Some workers had had family members who had died under hospice care; others felt the ability to influence a particularly difficult part of life was especially fulfilling, and this drew them to hospice service. One of the inpatient hospice social workers commented that what is most satisfying is her ability "to provide a level of dignity to the patients in the time that they have left." For another, there is the "recognition that the end of life is a particularly important time and that the ability to help people in different ways and in so many areas has been the most sustaining aspect of the work."

Most social workers defined their role and function as a helpmate to the patients and family members. Typical comments included:

"I see myself as a companion along the way for the patient."
"For the family, I serve as the emotional anchor, often just listening and validating feelings and concerns."
"I provide a presence; people find me calming and I can tolerate their stories. I take different strands of what people are saying and hold onto them. If you don't listen, you get nowhere."

The prominent use of crisis intervention techniques (especially when a patient has taken a turn for the worse), active listening, and the ability to be in someone's personal space were among the many social work skills used frequently by those interviewed. In addressing the multiplicity of demands of their clients, several social workers commented that they needed to prioritize the caregiver and patient needs and work on those that are most pressing in order to maintain the hospice philosophy of safe passage and comfort care for all. This implies that the social work value of respect and dignity for the patient takes prominence over the needs of the family members or others. Ideally, all needs are met, but sometimes there are opposing needs; for example, the patient needs quiet but the family needs to talk, or the family is not accepting of the patient's impending death whereas the patient has made peace with his or her fate.

The social workers offered several case examples that demonstrated the range of challenges of hospice work. In many instances, they defined the hardest cases as those involving young people — patients who would be considered in the prime of their life rather than in decline. In addition, when the relationship with the patient and family spanned several months, social workers often struggled to handled their emotions.

For example, an inpatient hospice worker described the case of a 25-year-old African American woman who was dying from a rare cancer and had been in and out of the hospital for more than 5 months. The social worker had been involved with the patient, who was lucid even though dulled by pain medication. There was minimal family involvement, and although the social worker was able to secure Medicaid for the patient to receive home care, it was only after an intense struggle. Ultimately, the patient died in the hospital. According to the social worker, "The patient died very young and I did not see the end coming as fast as it actually did. Everyone on the unit was attached to her and she had made bonds with each of us. When you connect to situations it is difficult, but I feel that I did some amazing work with her for her to be able to accept her death."

Another difficult case was a 33-year-old man, with no family or friends, who was dying from cancer. The social worker stated, "This patient was extremely angry and yelled at staff constantly. He was angry at the world and the fate that had befallen him. His anger was taken out on everyone. I was able to tolerate his anger as long as I told myself that the anger was provoked by his illness. I had to meet with other staff to try to help them manage their anger at the patient."

Another social worker related the story of a survivor of the World Trade Center bombing who was subsequently diagnosed with cancer. The patient was 30 years old and his wife was having an extremely difficult time with his impending death. She felt strongly that she wanted him to die at home. According to the social worker, "I was able to facilitate that wish and felt a great sense of satisfaction that I could make that happen for this family. Nevertheless, I was deeply saddened to learn of his death 3 days later."

These examples illustrate the range of challenges faced by the social workers. Bearing witness to struggles with death and dying can become emotionally taxing for even the most trained social workers. Many of those interviewed stressed their need for reflection and diversion from the intensity of their work.

Often cultural issues emerge in the work, with different ethnic groups having death rituals the hospice worker must understand and respect. This situation was described most frequently by the home hospice workers because they were immersed in the home of the patient and were witness to many such moments. Consider the case of the 44-year-old man in an Asian family who spoke little English. The social worker had to negotiate the family needs through one of the older children who spoke English and had to be oriented to the use of candles and incense designed to help the patient pass on to another life. In addition, the social worker, realizing that the family did not have enough money to provide for funeral services for the patient, had to engage the Buddhist community to provide for his cremation. Culture evidences in other ways, including levels of expressed emotionality, rituals of dying in which prayers and beliefs enable the passage from one life form to another, and funeral rituals. For the home hospice worker, there is additional exposure to the home environment, which "makes the patient much more real." "Seeing the home and the things that the patient treasures or owns or doesn't own has often made it harder for me," commented one worker. She further stated, "Sometimes, the conditions in the home are very poor, sometimes unclean, and that is bothersome. And sometimes there are surprises when you find out something about the patient you could only know if you saw their home, such as the patient who was an amateur artist and had pictures he had drawn all over his home." In contrast, one inpatient social worker noted, "Seeing the patient on the unit takes away the intimacy of the home. It is very sterile in the hospital and the patient's sense of personhood is lost in the hospital. I have to try to make the hospital part more comfortable and comforting with each patient."

In commenting on being part of the interdisciplinary team, most social workers felt respected as a member of the team, with some reservations about communication between medical staff and social workers. Some home hospice workers expressed that teaming with nurses is essential because the nurses more readily have the ear of the doctor. In several service venues, the social workers, nurses, and doctors meet weekly or more often to discuss patients. Some social workers expressed that they felt they were the emotional arm of the multidisciplinary team and that they were often the ones to gather the team in the event of a patient's death.

When hospice social workers were asked to identify what conflicts or emotional concerns their work evoked, responses included:

"There is the need to understand that those who are irate and abusive of the staff are really angry at their illness, and try to not take it personally."

"Sometimes, it is hard for me to feel that I have done good work, as the patient always dies. No one really knows that work that has been done, and I occasionally feel the need for affirmation and cannot get it."

"If I meet a family and feel very comfortable, I say watch out to myself! Don't get too close, pay attention to the boundary demarcations, and keep professional boundaries so they and I can move on when the patient dies."

The social workers were asked to describe what drew them to their work and kept it meaningful. Several noted that they felt especially privileged to be allowed into the lives of their patients and their family, that they saw this as "an amazing moment." "My perspective on life and death is always changing," commented a home care social worker, and "The work has helped me to look at life and death differently, and I have met so many courageous people in the work. I feel that it is an incredible gift to be there for someone who is dying." Another commented on the level of strength she has witnessed in others and that she has "seen so many beautiful relationships with a generosity of spirit." On a more philosophical level, a social worker commented that he has begun to see death "not as a complete end but as part of a process, and that there are many things that can influence the process." "Our work will never be done," commented a social worker who had been involved in hospice work for 15 years, "And, I struggle to never put off what I want to do. Enjoy life; it can be taken away in a minute."

The interviews with the 15 hospice social workers helped clarify the range of activities experienced in hospice work. In many respects, the work is more patient and family centered than other medical social work situations, and although the outcome is never in doubt, the time spent with the patient and family may extend for many months, affording the social worker greater levels of interaction than in regular hospital-based work. The social workers were united in their belief that they provided a valuable service to their patients, families, and caregivers in an effort to help them attain a better quality of life in their dying.

Surely this work is not for everyone, and each of the social workers interviewed commented on periods when they had doubts about their work and their ability to continue in this area. But more often than not, the social workers liked what they did and felt convicted in their belief that their efforts were worthwhile. The benefits in the work cannot be measured by the fact that the patient did not survive; accepting death is one of the first tasks of the social worker, and once that has been accepted, the task of working toward safe passage is clearer.

Being part of an interdisciplinary team, having colleagues to share the burden of the work, and being able to rely on consistent supervision were mentioned as necessary aspects of the work situation that made a difference in how each felt about his or her participation in the hospice. All of the social workers saw themselves as part of a bigger effort focused on patient and caregiver care. As noted by MacDonald (1991) and applicable to those interviewed, "Identity for the hospice social worker rests not on a preconceived notion of his or her proper sphere of expertise, but on an ability to correctly perceive the hospice team's and the hospice movement's needs at any time and to respond appropriately" (p. 277).

One of the social workers interviewed was soon to leave the hospice where he worked to pursue a career in a totally unrelated field. He spoke about his struggle, because he so loved his work with the hospice yet felt that he had to try this alternative professional area. He commented on the level of strength people exhibit in their decline and that he felt, "Just to be present with these folks, and to offer comfort and compassion, makes this the best job. It is awesome, not shallow, and I will miss it."

Several mentioned that they had begun to wonder how they will die. For many, the work has stirred them to appreciate their own vulnerability and impermanence and has enhanced their appreciation of life.

6

ORGAN TRANSPLANT SOCIAL WORK

ABOUT ORGAN TRANSPLANTATION

Organ transplantation is a successful therapy for end-stage organ failure. Transplantable organs include the kidney, liver, heart, lung, pancreas, and intestine. Organs can be obtained from living donors, either family members or anonymous donors whose tissues and medical profile match the recipient's, or through donation programs. Organs obtained through donor programs are taken from deceased donors who made prior arrangements for their organs to be transplanted or whose family members arranged for the organ donation upon their death. During 2003, 25,468 organs were transplanted: 18,657 from deceased donors and 6,811 from living donors. Nationally, more than 73,000 people await an organ transplant; each day, approximately 16 will die without receiving one. More than 46,000 people await a kidney. Kidneys are the organ in greatest demand, followed by livers, hearts, and lungs (Organ Procurement and Transplantation Network [OPTN], 2004). The medical dynamics of organ transplantation are complex in that living organs are transferred from one human being (deceased or living) to another. In the case of a living donor, the recipient and the donor both go through experiences that require intensive medical and psychological attention.

As the technology of transplantation has become more sophisticated over the years, the success rate for those receiving transplants, measured in terms of length of life (survival) and quality of life, has grown. It is remarkable that the first kidney transplant was performed less than

50 years ago between identical twins in a hospital in Boston and now it is considered a highly successful and almost routine procedure for end-stage kidney disease. The first heart transplant was performed in 1967 by Dr. Christian Barnard in South Africa. Since that time, advances in understanding of the immune system and the development of cardiopulmonary bypass machinery have led to longer survival rates for those who otherwise would have succumbed to their diseases. Heart transplants accounted for 1,366 transplants in 2004 (OPTN, 2004).

It must be understood that the patient who is considering organ transplant faces two options: probable death due to their disease or the potential life-sustaining intervention of an organ transplant; the critical word here is potential, because it is not uncommon for the recipient's body to reject the donated organ. In most cases, the patient has had extensive medical treatment concerning the failing organ and has reached a stage in which traditional medical care has failed. One exception to this scenario is the patient who can be maintained on dialysis for an extended length of time while awaiting a kidney replacement. In every organ transplant situation, there are more recipients than donors, so criteria have had to be established to determine the suitability of a patient for a transplant. The politics of organ transplantation, while compelling, do not fall within the purview of this text.

Essential to understanding organ transplantation is the understanding that the transplanted organ will never be as effective as the original, undiseased organ and that life after transplantation is often disrupted by intense medical concerns, regimens, monitoring, emergencies, and uncertainty. Nonetheless, as a medical procedure, the success rate of transplantation, measured in survival rates, has risen over the years within each organ category.

Organ transplant will be described in this chapter as a generic experience for the patient, donor, and caregiver. Occasionally, I will reference a specific organ transplant, but the focus of the content will be transplantation in general.

THE PATIENT EXPERIENCE

The patient who is considering a transplant is experiencing a terminal illness for which medical intervention is no longer beneficial. When transplant is presented as a possibility, despite the extensive levels of risk, the patient may feel optimistic that he or she can regain aspects of pre-illness life. The process of transplantation breaks down into assessment, pretransplant, and posttransplant phases. Patients accepted into a transplant program must meet both the medical and emotional criteria for inclusion. The social work department performs a psychosocial assessment on the patient, and the medical members of the transplant team address the physical and medical needs. The goal of a social work assessment is to evaluate the patient's emotional status and support system with a view to predicting his or her ability to cope with the transplant program and its subsequent lifetime regimentation of medications and medical oversight. Also, it is important for the social worker to identify areas in which the patient may require assistance through the process (Bright, 1994).

Specifically, the patient is assessed for previous medical compliance, previous reactions to major stress, education and work history, coping behaviors, existence of mental illness, substance abuse, finances, interpersonal relationships, and the integrity of the family unit (Dhooper, 1994). The psychosocial assessment is considered critical due to the scarcity of organs and the need to find patients who will be able to maintain their transplanted organs and who will not sabotage — by neglect, drug use, or medical noncompliance — their medical regimen, thus defeating the transplantation procedure (Zilberfein, Hutson, Snyder, & Epstein, 2001). Personnel in many hospital programs will spend time interviewing potential donors in an effort to both assess and educate them regarding the anticipated procedure.

A patient who meets the medical and psychosocial criteria is placed on an organ transplant waiting list. During this pretransplant phase, the social worker remains available for support and can play a significant role in the life of the patient and family. The emotional intensity of the waiting period varies by the type of organ being transplanted: candidates for kidneys can be sustained for indefinite periods of time, whereas those waiting for a heart, lung, or liver may not be able to survive until the transplanted organ becomes available. In other words, the recipient may face death daily while time passes until the transplant.

In addition, the wait for the transplant may involve relocation near the hospital so that the patient is able to be at the hospital at a moment's notice when an organ becomes available. Some patients are expected to wear pagers to alert them that an organ has become available and to quickly arrange admission into the hospital to begin the transplantation procedure. The disruption to the patient and the family may be immense because they have to be near the hospital and away from family and friends; this may involve incurring the expense of maintaining two households, removing children from school, and so forth. The waiting time can be from a few days to weeks to months, depending on the organ and availability. Although the sickest are first in line for an organ, the sad reality is that all too often, patients die before an organ becomes available. Thus, in addition to the stress of waiting and having to put their lives on hold at a moment's notice, the patient and family must deal with the ambiguity of the outcome while the patient's condition continues to deteriorate, often requiring hospitalization and further life and family disruption (Bohnengel, 1983). "The social worker's activity in this stage can be directed toward first, helping these patients with relocation and assistance in adapting to their new environment; second, familiarizing them with the world of the hospital and transplantation related protocols; third, helping them to maintain their physical readiness for the transplant; and fourth, assisting them in retaining their hope and mental preparedness" (Dhooper, 1994, p. 76).

Once an organ has been secured, the patient is admitted to the hospital to await the scheduled transplant. The medical complexity of this time involves several physicians and staff from various disciplines who all work cooperatively to pull together the many pieces of the actual transplant surgery. While awaiting the transplant, patients and family members experience a wide range of emotions, from relief that the transplant is actually and finally happening, to fear of death and dying. Social work services can help address some of their concerns and present the transplant in a realistic light. Many patients and their families believe that all of their medical problems related to the transplant will cease after the transplant has taken place. Initially, patients and family members experience a sense of renewed hope because the long wait is over and new life is about to begin. However, the reality is that a transplant is not a cure but a treatment for the disease, and it comes with many life changes including side effects of lifelong transplant medications, the threat and fear of the possibility of organ rejection and the need for another organ, and the haunting memory of the presurgical and surgical experience (Zilberfein et al., 2001).

Irrespective of what organ is being transplanted, the recipient's surgery is long — typically from 5 to 12 hours — and the recovery trajectory is tense and physically demanding. After transplant, the patient is taken from the operating room to an intensive care unit. This is a critical time because the patient is medically unstable and the viability of the transplant is uncertain. The best outcome is that the newly transplanted organ will begin to function in a short amount of time (immediately or within hours of the transplant) and will be accepted by the patient's body. One of the major medical concerns during this time is whether the host's immune system will accept the donor organ or attack the foreign body that has been inserted into the host. Despite all efforts at matching donor and host, there are many instances of organ rejection.

As the organ begins to function and the patient begins to heal, he or she is moved off the intensive care unit onto a medical floor. During this period, the social worker is involved primarily with the family because the patient is heavily medicated for pain and is sleeping a lot (Bright, 1994).

Following the transplant, both the family and patient go through a time of euphoria, a honeymoon period marked by joy and relief. The threat of death before receiving the organ is gone, the symptoms of illness and accompanying feelings of helplessness have disappeared, and the patient feels the improvement that the transplanted organ has brought to his or her body. The patient has begun to function better and appears to be in better health (Dhooper, 1994). The initiation of lifelong immunosuppressive drugs that serve to keep the body from rejecting the new organ begins immediately following the transplant. These drugs can bring bouts of irritability, paranoia, and depression for the patient, along with other natural reactions to surgery.

Two outcomes are possible at this immediate posttransplant stage: either the patient responds positively to the immunosuppressant drugs and begins to heal or there is a rejection episode. In the event of rejection, the body fights the invasion of a foreign organ (the organ of the donor) and defeats it, rendering the organ inoperable. This is a serious setback and may even be fatal to the patient. It can mean that another transplant has to be considered; heroic medical intervention is initiated to keep the patient viable to accept another organ, should it become available. Needless to say, the patient and family are devastated at this turn of events.

As the patient begins to emerge from the intensive care phase of the transplant experience, support from family is central to his or her emotional well-being. As in many medical situations, family and friend support has a buffering effect on the experience of a critical illness. They help the patient feel cared for and cared about and, in some instances, literally help in the hospital because nursing staff is sometimes not adequate to meet the needs of the patient. Family members are also cushioned by social support; feeling that the burden of illness is carried not only by them but also by other concerned family members and friends.

In a study by Jones and Egan (2000), recipients of liver organs noted that not only were they supported emotionally by family, but also, in many cases, a family member was in the hospital with them all day and in some cases 24 hours a day, helping with some of the nursing responsibilities including feeding and changing dressings. Patients experience a variety of emotional responses in this early posttransplant recovery phase, with the opposing emotional poles of relief and fear, some of which is mitigated by emotional support from caregivers (Evangelista, Doering, & Dracup, 2003).

Feelings about the donated organ begin to emerge soon after the transplant. If the organ was from a deceased person, it is a challenge for the recipient not to equate the wish for an organ with the wish for someone to die. In an odd twist of thinking, but one that is understandable, some recipients in a recent study acknowledged that during the long wait for an organ, they wished for someone to die; then, when the death of a donor occurred, the recipient found it difficult not to think that he or she caused the donor's death — a kind of magical thinking. Recipients of a planned donation, from either a relative or another person who was compatible, expressed gratitude and appreciation directly, although in these cases the gratitude was not so simple to handle. Some recipients expressed guilt and anguish that they had hurt the donor in the process of receiving the transplanted organ; others tried to repay the donor with a financial gift or trip as a way of expressing their gratitude (Sanner, 2003).

Leaving the hospital, posttransplant, is another highly emotional time, as patients leave the protective safety of the hospital, fearing separation from the doctors, nurses, and other professionals. Family caregivers may be anxious about their ability to manage the patient's care at home, and other concerns begin to surface that may or may not have been considered when the transplant was discussed. Among these concerns are finances and the quality of life for recipient and family. One study found that neither the organ recipients nor their families were adequately informed about the high cost of posttransplantation medication. Most thought of the transplantation economics as including the surgery and post-inpatient care and were not anticipating the cost of subsequent immunosuppressants and the other life-sustaining medications needed by the patient. In addition, the necessity of intensive medical follow-up, especially in the first many months posttransplant, was surprising to most recipients and family caregivers (Jones & Egan, 2000).

Dhooper (1994) identified several areas of potential psychosocial problems in posttransplant adjustment for the patient: problems related to the organ, self-concept, illness, family and job, finance, and ability to cope. Organ-related problems include feeling like a different person, feeling unworthy of the donated organ, and feeling guilty at being alive at the cost of a donor's life. Altered body image due to changed appearance because of the side effects of the immunosuppressant medications (swelling, hair growth, weight gain), with attendant loss of self-esteem, is common. These feelings are compounded by the fear of organ rejection. Adhering to the medical regimen and acknowledging the chronicity of one's medical condition are the illness-related concerns. Family-related problems revolve around communication and the difficulty in asserting and redefining roles and status, and job-related concerns revolve around productivity, performance, and finding and maintaining a job. Finances are often strained by unaccounted and uninsured medical expenses with the escalating costs of medicine. Coping-related problems include reduced ability to handle stress, social isolation, and impaired social interaction. Of course, some recipients will handle many of these areas easily, whereas for other recipients it will be more difficult. Social workers can be helpful with some of these concerns through individual and family counseling sessions in which feelings are validated, aired, and shared among family members. Support groups for posttransplant recipients and their families are a valued venue for the discussion of these and other transplant-related concerns.

THE DONOR EXPERIENCE

Numerous factors influence the decision to become an organ donor, to "give the gift of life." Some people will donate an organ to an organ bank with no knowledge of the recipient; others will donate an organ to a specific person, a stranger, with whom they are medically compatible; some donate an organ to a compatible family recipient; and many others donate their organs upon their death, recipients unknown.

Living donors who give of their body to another when the recipient is unknown are giving of themselves in the most benevolent way imaginable, practicing a form of pure altruism. They are driven by no other motive than to give and sustain life. This form of organ donation is the least common. More frequent is the donor who gives to a specific person, and the most frequent form of live donation is among compatible family members. In general, "Most people who serve as donors appear to enjoy the psychosocial benefits of the donation act itself" (Fischer, 2003, p. 44).

On some occasions, family members exert pressure on someone in the family to donate an organ to save another. The pressure can be intense and heated and the family member may feel coerced into donating. In these situations, social work involvement with the family must help all members articulate their feelings and reach an amicable solution.

When a prospective donor has been medically cleared to donate an organ, social work staff is expected to perform a pretransplant psychosocial evaluation to help the person make an informed decision, to discern motives for donation, to gain an understanding of how the donor may respond after the transplantation and explain what the medical experience will entail. Specific areas of inquiry during the evaluation include an attempt to uncover any premorbid psychiatric illness, any relevant psychological or social pressures (this is especially important when the donation is for a family member), and the rationale and reasons for donating (Fischer, 2003).

Informed consent is an especially sensitive issue for the transplant team because donors place themselves at some degree of risk and must understand what awaits them during the transplant procedure. As such, the orientation to the transplant must be detailed and inclusive, explaining the medical and legal aspects of the transplant and establishing that the donor has not been coerced into making the transplant decision. The information must be presented in a way that the donor understands and the donor has to be able to demonstrate their understanding of the procedure to the satisfaction of the social worker. When this has been accomplished and the evaluation is completed, the donation can proceed.

Once compatibility has been established, the donor submits to a variety of tests and is hospitalized for several days before and after the procedure. The surgery usually spans several hours. Depending on the organ used, it may be several weeks before the donor feels as he or she did predonation. The donor also must receive medical care for months afterward to ensure there is maximal functioning without the transplanted organ.

THE TRANSPLANT UNIT SOCIAL WORKER

"In virtually all transplant programs, social workers have been available to help patients and families meet the challenges of organ transplantation. From the time of the initial referral, through assessment, waiting period, transplant admission, and post-transplant follow-up, it is the social worker who is responsible for patient and family psychosocial assessment, treatment, and rehabilitation" (Paris, Hutkin-Slade, Calhoun-Wilson, & Oehlert, 1999, p. 202). The social worker is an integral member of the transplant team, which includes medical and surgical physicians, nurses, physiotherapists, nutritionists, psychiatrists, and psychologists. Each team member contributes in significant and interlocking ways. Published studies have validated the benefits of clinical social work involvement, providing statistical support for such findings as reduced morbidity for recipients who were at high medical risk (Tazelaar, Prieto, Lake, & Emery, 1992); reduced family dysfunction and better overall adjustment for patients who attended a social worker-led transplant psychoeducational support groups (Suszycki, 1986); and fewer stress-related problems for patients who attended a social worker-led educational program to prepare them for the stressors anticipated during the transplant process (Gier, Levick, & Blanzia, 1988).

Jones and Egan (2000) detailed several areas of need identified by organ transplant recipients and their family members. For example, while awaiting the availability of an organ, patients needed information regarding costs during and after discharge. Before and after hospitalization, patients were concerned with what to expect as an inpatient and during the recuperation stages. Family members expressed concern over what the patient would be like after the transplant, whether the patient would be able to return to work, his or her ability to function, and what aftercare would be needed when the patient returned home.

The unique orientation of social work practice takes a holistic view of patients and considers not only their needs but the needs of the family as well. Within this perspective comes the mandate to be attentive to both patients and family members, addressing their emotional and concrete needs. No other discipline on the interdisciplinary team views the patient in this manner. In general, this perspective suggests that the major role for the social worker is to have a presence in the transplant unit to educate and assess, to advise on financial issues, and to help the patient and family make the bridge from hospital back to the community, facilitating whatever services might be needed for the patient to safely return home.

In terms of affective response to the transplant, Zilberfein et al. (2001) identified areas social workers typically encounter when counseling transplant patients and their families. Major topics were fear of death and dying, loss of independence both physically and functionally, anger, guilt about their survival depending on someone else's death, anxiety about obtaining an organ in a timely manner, and frustration about the lack of control in obtaining an organ.

These studies point to the complexity of the transplant experience and to the scope of social work intervention. Unlike for other medical procedures, those awaiting an organ live with unending uncertainty, even when they are experiencing the transplant procedure; so much hinges on the success of the transplant. The social worker must be attuned to these dynamics and be able to remain hopeful with the patient and family while injecting the possibility of organ failure. This stance is difficult for the patient and family but also for the social worker, who has probably developed a relationship with the key players over the period of pretransplant workup and hospitalization.

SOCIAL WORKER COMMENTS

I interviewed seven social workers who had primary responsibility on a transplant unit. Two of the social workers spent more than half their time being responsible for interviewing potential donors, both for specific patients and for unknown recipients, while also being responsible for patients and family members on the unit.

For the social workers, all of the patient and family concerns that were identified in the literature were common counseling and support areas. The greatest frustration social work staff identified on behalf of their patients was the long, often interminable, wait for organs to become available. Patients who are hospitalized on the transplant unit are waiting for an organ and are too ill to be able to be maintained at home. As such, they can be in the hospital for weeks and in some cases, many months, until an organ becomes available. Because of the longer hospital stays, the social workers get to know the patients quite well and identify with their frustration and anguish. Watching patients become sicker as they waited for an organ was very hard for each social worker to handle. The most difficult moments described by the social workers were when a long-term patient died while waiting for an organ; this loss was keenly felt by each social worker and by the other team members as well.

In some instances, the hospital stay is shorter; a patient comes in, is transplanted within days, stays through recuperation, and is discharged. The shorter stay patients demanded much less from the social workers both in terms of service and emotional needs. Yet, even for the shorter term patients, the workers identified common areas of challenge: struggling not to judge their patients, dealing with difficult situations in which family members and patients behave in such a way as to endanger the newly transplanted organ, and witnessing the emotional toll for the patient and the family when an organ is rejected.

In terms of patient behavior and passing judgment, the social workers spoke about the patients who need a liver, for example, who have created the organ need by their drinking or drug abuse habits. Or the kidney patients who have not been conscientious about dialysis and have abused their bodies to such an extent that dialysis is no longer an option. Heart patients were sometimes the most frustrating to the social workers because obesity, smoking, and diet — all areas that a person can potentially control — were so abused or neglected that the heart was destroyed, creating the need for a transplant. Liver patients must be sober for 1 year before they can be considered for a transplant (overindulgence in alcohol is known to destroy an individual's liver due to cirrhosis). Several social workers spoke with frustration about liver transplant patients who had maintained their sobriety to obtain a liver and, as the wait became intolerable, returned to drinking, causing them to be taken off the transplant list. In short, the social workers felt the struggle not to "blame the victim" to be a difficult aspect of their work.

Social work staff described several difficult family situations. Often a dysfunctional family will enable behaviors that are not considered health affirming for a transplant patient. One social worker was quick to state, "These behaviors are quite provocative in light of the scarcity of organs. If there were more than enough organs around to address the need, well, so be it. But, there is such a scarcity that I want the organ to go to someone who will take care of his or herself and cherish the life that has been given to them through this procedure." She added, "It burns me when I know that the family or the patient will mess up all this good work that the doctors have done." Another area of frustration felt by the social workers on behalf of both family and patient was the high cost and quantity of drugs needed after the transplant. As one noted, "The drugs can cost between $10,000–$15,000 for the first year. The costs go down after the first year to maybe $5–$7,000 and will stay at that rate for the rest of the patient's life. This is a staggering amount of money and no matter how many times we tell family members about this, they seem shocked when they have to face that reality."

But, clearly, the hardest area of the work identified by each social worker was when a transplant failed and the person had all their hopes shattered. "This so difficult," said one social worker, "I had a 42-year-old patient who was on the list for a liver for 6 months, in and out of the hospital, and when it finally became available and he was transplanted, he developed a series of infections and finally the liver was rejected. He was a broken man and my heart went out to him and his family." In these cases, the social worker has to "be there for the patient and family, allowing them to ventilate their frustrations and anger while feeling a sense of impotence over the whole situation."

All social workers interviewed spoke of their units working as a team, feeling a valued member of the team and a central player. All but one social worker noted that they felt they were privileged to work with such dedicated and professional staff members — doctors and nurses — who were so talented and good at what they do. The dissenting social work voice came from a long-time worker, ready to retire, who, although appreciative of the talent of the medical team, had been struggling for some time with the changes she had seen over the many years of her professional career working in transplants. She was in a hospital that had experienced severe cutbacks in terms of staffing and she felt that these changes were harmful to patients and their well-being.

Her feelings about her "team" were more reflective of her feelings about the hospital and the administration and the impact of the recent cutbacks.

The joy of the work was described by all as occurring when a transplant succeeds, which was more often than not: "You see the patient become well, often in a matter of days, when they receive a new kidney or liver or heart. From an invalid, they turn into an almost well person who has energy and strength that was all but gone before the transplant. This makes it all worthwhile!"

7

PEDIATRIC ONCOLOGY SOCIAL WORK

ABOUT CHILDHOOD CANCERS

An estimated 9,200 new cases of cancer in children ages 0 to 14 were expected to occur in the United States in 2004. In comparison to the statistics for adults, childhood cancers are rare. The types of cancers children develop are generally different from those that develop in adults. An estimated 1,210 deaths are expected to occur in this age range in 2004, about one third due to leukemia. Leukemia is a cancer in which large numbers of abnormal white blood cells are produced in the bone marrow. These abnormal cells crowd the bone marrow and bloodstream, interfering with the production of other types of blood cells, creating anemia and bleeding problems for the child. There are several types of childhood leukemia; as a group they account for 25% of all childhood cancers and affect 2,200 young people each year. Other forms of childhood cancers include brain and spinal cord cancers, neuroblastoma (a cancer of the nervous system), Wilms' tumor (a kidney cancer), Hodgkin's lymphoma (cancer in the lymph nodes), and various forms of sarcoma. Despite its rarity, cancer is the chief cause of death by disease in children ages 1 to 14. Mortality rates from childhood cancer have declined by about 49% since 1975 (American Cancer Society [ACS], 2004). Since then, combination chemotherapies, bone marrow transplantation, and new supportive and surgical techniques, some in combination with standardized treatment approaches, have led to the survival of many children who would have been considered incurable in earlier times (Patenaude & Last, 2001).

This shift in detection and treatment has increased the likelihood that a child treated for cancer today will survive. Depending on the site of the cancer, 5-year survival rates range from 68% for those with neuroblastoma to 94% for those with Hodgkin's lymphoma. The current overall survival rate for childhood cancer is 75%, with improved outcomes attributable to aggressive multimodal treatments (ACS, 2004; Kazak et al., 2004). Childhood cancer is now considered either a single-episode illness or a chronic, but mainly treatable, disease.

The diagnosis of childhood cancer is stressful and anxiety producing for the patient and the entire family system. The tensions around initial diagnosis, treatment, and an uncertain future place inordinate stress on family relationships. Because most patients now enjoy long periods of remission or health after diagnosis and treatments, it has become easier to identify psychosocial issues common to this illness experience. For many, the psychosocial challenge of childhood cancer lies not only in the disease itself, but also in understanding how those affected cope with their ordeal (Derevensky, Tsanos, & Handman, 1998).

In similar ways to adult cancer diagnosis, childhood cancers are determined through biopsy of a tissue sample to confirm the presence of a malignancy. When the cancer is diagnosed, it is in the best interests of the child and family to be referred to a pediatric cancer specialist who is familiar with treatments specific to childhood cancer. Staging of the cancer — whether a tumor is localized to its site of origin or whether it has spread to nearby tissues or to organs that are more distant — has to be determined and becomes the basis for a treatment plan. Central to the treatment approach is the understanding that pediatric malignancies often grow rapidly, generally spread to various body parts, and often respond to aggressive treatment. Surgery, chemotherapy, and radiation are the most common approaches to treatment (Pizzo, 1993).

THE CHILD WITH CANCER

When a child is diagnosed with cancer, both patient and family enter the complex, often frightening world of modern medicine. Although there is surely legitimate hope for a cure, childhood cancer therapy creates an illness trajectory that alternates acute phases with intermittent periods of relative good health and normalcy. The trajectory is unpredictable and can include relapse, sustained remission, long-term acute phases, or death from the illness or treatment. "The improvement in outcome for most, but not all, children with cancer has thus created a powerful paradox of increased optimism accompanied with enduring uncertainty" (Stewart, 2003, p. 394).

As described by Stewart (2003), "Childhood cancer presents children with an inherently uncertain context that they must navigate in order to manage their illness" (p. 404). Most children, when or if they think about the future, cannot conceptualize life beyond the immediate. Even in the post-911 era, children have the ability to be able to stay in the moment and eternalize events. Cancer changes that and thrusts the child into issues of life and death, with his or her existence ruled by doctors, treatments, and uncertainty. A child's inherent trust in his or her parents as protectors is shattered. The view of the world as a safe place is upended dramatically with the cancer diagnosis. Despite these emotional assaults, most children on the oncology unit, assuming they have some strength and are physically able, will be upbeat, will interact with staff and other children, and will remain perhaps more optimistic than their medical situation warrants.

At each level of the illness, certain factors serve to exacerbate or mitigate some of the psychosocial stressors. But, "A reasonable summary (of existing literature) argues that some survivors of childhood cancer have managed to grow in positive ways as a result of their cancer experience, most probably are relatively normal in psychosocial terms and on most psychosocial measures ..." (Zebrack & Chesler, 2002, p. 133). Not all are unscathed, and a small minority of children experience depression, social adjustment problems, and uncontrollable anxiety.

Initial Diagnosis

The initial phase of cancer, the diagnosis phase, is often described as the most stressful time, with uncertainty permeating every aspect of the experience. The parents have a sick child whose illness has yet to be identified, but they realize their child is seriously ill. The child is probably frightened and feeling ill, missing school and life's daily routine, and struggling to make sense of what is happening to him or her.

The developmental stage of the child and his or her response to diagnosis are strongly correlated. The very young child is not necessarily able to understand and integrate the reality of the illness. The separation from mother and father and all that is familiar may make the initial diagnosis period particularly difficult. For a toddler, who is beginning to exert independence, confinement in a hospital or care facility for a diagnostic workup, even if the child is feeling ill, is not accepted well. Children of this age will experience separation acutely and it is to be expected that the child will exhibit emotional withdrawal and loss of interest in the environment with diminished responsiveness. The 3- to 4-year-old, although somewhat more relaxed in terms of dependent attachment to the parent, will also exhibit signs of confusion and disorientation. The older child, who is able to understand the complexity of having a diagnosis of cancer, will struggle with some of the same existential questions as adults: Why me? How much will it hurt? Will I die? Including the older child in discussions of the diagnosis and treatment plan is very important; the more the child knows, the better armed he or she will be to handle the rigors of treatment. This belief in inclusion is reflected in the fact that in the United States children over the age of seven are empowered and expected to sign forms for many treatment protocols (Patenaude & Last, 2001). The adolescent, in this initial stage of diagnosis, begins the descent into a separate world from their peers: a world of health concerns, pain, and sickness. Well adolescents are not grappling with a developing awareness of their own mortality and facing the possibility of their death. Instead, they are beginning the time in their lives when they are less dependent on their parents and more on their peers, are developing a fuller awareness of their bodies and themselves as physical beings, and are beginning to see and interact in the world as aspiring adults. Emotionally, most adolescents suffer more than younger children because the turbulence of adolescence is experienced through a veil of illness and treatments (Ross, 1993).

Treatment

Treatment usually requires a period of hospitalization; for school-age children, this means separation from home, friends, peers, and school. Hair loss from chemotherapy, physical disfigurement from surgical procedures, and burning from radiation treatments all have the potential to make children feel stigmatized, ashamed, self-conscious, and doubtful about their acceptability to their peers. With repeated hospitalizations, it becomes very difficult to access peer support. For adolescents in the treatment phase, the symptoms and treatment can significantly disrupt their normal psychosocial development. Treatment-related side effects such as nausea and vomiting, mouth sores, muscle pain, and fatigue can result in varying amounts of time missed from school. In addition, intense treatment regimens and the risk of infection due to low white cell counts can mean isolation from peers and social life. The illness increases adolescents' dependency on family members at a time when most young people their age are beginning to distance themselves from these ties. What adolescent wants to spend time with his or her parents? Most adolescents want to be with peers, doing peer-sanctioned things, belonging to a group, and absorbing the cultural norms of their friends. Adolescents with a cancer diagnosis become isolated from peers for an extended amount of time, and treatments can result in disfiguring scars, weight gain, hair loss, and even amputation, all of which can be damaging to an adolescent's fragile self-esteem (Chesler & Barbarin, 1987). At a time when planning for the future is the order of business, adolescent patients are dealing with uncertainty about how long their illness will last and what its ultimate outcome will be (Derevensky et al., 1998; Koocher, 1986). Adolescents with cancer are threatened by the loss of their autonomy, freedom, and socialization (Fearnow-Kenney & Kliewer, 2000).

Younger children often tolerate the physical treatments better than older children, but children of all ages suffer from the intense emotional and physical strain that treatment imposes. A child who has successfully been treated for cancer has probably suffered some disruption in a critical stage of physical or emotional development. Although this stage of illness is considered very challenging, the literature supports the fact that many youngsters have a sense of pride and confidence in themselves because they have successfully mastered the ongoing stress of their illness (Ross, 1993).

Posttreatment

When treatment ends, children typically go through an adjustment period during which fears and anxieties may emerge from the perceived lack of protection that treatment once provided. Even children who are in remission and are returning to precancer health status continue to be vigilant about lumps and other symptoms that may be the signs of a recurrence and a return of their illness.

In summary, the diagnosis, treatment, and posttreatment stages all pose significant emotional and physical challenges to the child and family system. In a comprehensive review of the literature, Van Dongen-Melman and Saunders-Woudstra (1986) found that adjustment difficulties in children and adolescents with cancer are typically mild and transient. In a more recent analysis, Stewart (2003) noted that children in her study described "… a process of adapting to and accommodating to the day-to-day uncertainties of cancer, thereby regaining a sense of normalcy and routine that supports their view of themselves as ordinary children with an ordinary life" (p. 405). Contrary to Stewart's observation, it should be noted that children who have survived cancer are not the same as children who have not had a serious, life-threatening illness. In general, childhood cancer survivors are more serious, perhaps more adult than their years, and seem to feel the weight of their illness for many years after treatment. Even children who are in full remission are subject to periodic checkups with their oncologist, reminding them of the cancer experience.

THE FAMILY EXPERIENCE

The parents of a child with cancer suffer great distress over the course of the illness and beyond. Parents must cope with this distress along with their other responsibilities while serving as their child's primary source of physical and psychosocial support (Suzuki & Kato, 2003). Because the family is the primary social support system for the child, how they manage and approach the child's illness can influence aspects of the illness trajectory. Numerous studies have documented the impact of parents' coping behaviors on the ill child's adjustment to the illness. Good coping by parents and family members, family support, parents' strong marital relationship, parental cooperation and optimism, lack of concurrent stress, and open communication within the family have been associated with good coping among childhood cancer survivors (Kupst & Schulman, 1988; Sanger, Copeland, & Davidson, 1991). Conversely, poor parental coping has been associated with poor outcomes in young patients, provoking feelings of anxiety, hopelessness, and externalizing behaviors of aggression in the ill child (Blotcky, Raczynski, Gurwitch, & Smith, 1985; Frank, Blount, & Brown, 1997; Sloper, Larcombe, & Charlton, 1994).

Some studies have isolated gender differences in parental coping. Chesler and Barbarin (1987), for example, found that fathers most commonly coped by working through their feelings alone, using avoidance strategies and emotionally withdrawing, whereas mothers were more likely to cope through emotional release, using a more confrontational style and talking through their emotions. Shapiro and Shumaker (1988) described different communication styles of mothers and fathers and reported that mothers preferred more open and frequent communication to maintain their emotional well-being. Goldbeck (2001) studied parents during the first 3 months of treatment, noting that mothers were more likely to stay with their child in the hospital, whereas fathers tended to stay home or return to work after a short time. Some of these findings reflect economic necessity, but when there was a choice about staying at the hospital or going to work, the fathers opted to go to their jobs more readily than the mothers. These findings suggest that mothers were more integral to the day-to-day activity of their child's illness. Although mothers seemed more involved in supporting their sick child, parents reported no measurable difference in their quality of life. In other words, both parents were deeply upset by their child's illness.

Additional factors in understanding the experience of the parents include the medical status of the child, social and economic conditions, and the parents' perception of the child's coping. Barakat et al. reported that the child's age, age at diagnosis, and time since diagnosis were not related to measures of parental anguish or the development of posttraumatic symptoms in parents (Barakat, Kazak, Meadows, Casey, & Stuber, 1997). Parents with lower socioeconomic status showed greater overall distress in their lives (Kupst & Schulman, 1988; Van Dongen-Melman et al., 1995). The perception of how the child is coping was correlated to parental coping in three studies. Kupst et al. (1995) reported that the child's adjustment and the parents' adjustment were related, and Barakat et al. reported that the parents' perception of the surviving child's quality of life was significantly and positively related to their own. Zebrack and colleagues showed that the anguish and worries of mothers was significantly related to their perceptions of their child's worries and the meanings they attached to their own and their child's cancer experience (Zebrack & Chesler, 2002; Zebrack, Chesler, Orbuch, & Parry, 2002).

The siblings of the cancer patient are often overlooked in discussions of the family experience. "The sibling of a child with cancer is in an exquisite double bind. He or she must attempt to reconcile the opposing strong feelings associated with the combination of sibling love and profound resentment. . . . A sibling can recognize how parents' hopes and dreams, once focused on all the children, now seem to reside in the fate of one particular child. A sibling's own need and desire for parental love and attention is moderated by feelings of guilt and shame" (Ross, 1993, p. 207). That siblings suffer along with their ailing brother or sister cannot be denied. In addition to what has been described, siblings may wonder whether they too will get sick: If so, will their parents be able to care for them at the same time they are caring for their sibling? Will the family's economic situation be seriously affected? Will we all be okay?

As this review demonstrates, all members of the family are affected by the diagnosis and treatment of a child with cancer. Surely, some families cope better than others, and many factors and variables influence that difference. What all families share is upset, anguish, and fear when the doctor declares their child has cancer.

THE PEDIATRIC ONCOLOGY SOCIAL WORKER

The social worker in the pediatric oncology unit of a hospital traditionally is involved in two forms of service: concrete and support services. Concrete service includes referrals to community agencies, assistance with transportation, discharge plans, and financial aid. Supportive services include counseling with patients and family members to deal with diagnosis, treatment, and possible death while leading the family to an understanding of the scope and depth of changes they are experiencing and will probably experience in their adjustment to the illness of their child (Lang & Mitrowski, 1981). Managed care (discussed in another chapter) has affected the delivery of some of these services while shortening the typical hospital stay for an ill child. Nevertheless, the role of the social worker in several different areas is central to the hospital experience for the patient and family.

As part of the multidisciplinary team, the social worker performs numerous roles including assessment, crisis intervention, supportive counseling, and overall case management. To clarify these roles, Shields et al. (1995) used a family needs survey to study the caregivers of children with cancer; they identified seven areas of need. First is a strong need to receive and share information related to their child's diagnosis and treatment, especially for those newly diagnosed. The hospital social worker can be a valuable resource to parents, especially during the initial phase of treatment. The offering of information may be based on the social worker's assessment of the parents' ability to absorb and process information at any given time. Family and social support, needed by most family members to help them cope with their child's cancer, was identified as the second need; the social worker may be instrumental in helping the family access social supports both from within their social circle and beyond. In going beyond the family for support, the social worker can facilitate meetings with other parents, direct the family member to a self-help support group, and hold group meetings on the unit with family members.

Financial guidance was identified as the third area of need, with costs of medical care one of the greatest stressors parents face. Most families felt inordinate stress as they struggled to pay for medical care and buy special equipment and medicines while carrying their usual financial obligations. As case manager, the social worker can assist the family by providing them with information about available federal and state-supported income maintenance and medical programs, helping them fill out necessary paperwork and forms, and referring them to appropriate community agencies. Responses to the survey further identified that parents need assistance in explaining to others and their own children what is happening in their lives. Social workers can counsel parents on how to communicate with others while stressing the need for open communication about the illness. Another identified area of need for parents was childcare support and respite care. Social workers can help facilitate this need by accessing community resources and linking the family to those available to help. Professional support for counseling falls within the scope of social work services in the hospital, and the family can be referred to community social workers who specialize in cancer support services. The final area of need was being able to access community support — a dentist who works with children with cancer or a different doctor, for example — which social workers can address through connections developed over time and with familiarity of community referrals.

In some of their work with families, social workers come to know families in crisis. Crisis intervention techniques such as active listening, validating responses, and encouraging expressions of anger, fear, and other emotional responses are relieving for the patient and family members. Supportive counseling is aimed at maintaining functional behaviors in all family members. The work of the social worker is to help with the varied adaptations that need to be made by the child and the family, to help the family anticipate problems, and to keep the family system as intact as possible as it is being stressed during the illness (Stovall, 1993).

In direct contact with the child cancer patient, the social worker must be attuned to the developmental stage of the child and be sensitive to behavior norms that are being challenged by the cancer and hospitalization. For the young child, being away from parents and feeling ill creates feelings of anxiety and fear that the social worker can address by being as attentive as possible and just by being a presence for the child when the parents are away from the hospital. Older children may be more distractible, but they still need the attention of the social worker and may need to be encouraged to discuss their fears and reactions. Adolescent cancer patients are struggling with school, peer, and independence issues that the social worker can help manage through counseling. In addition to in-hospital work, the social worker can help families access oncology camps; special programs that cater to children with cancer and their families, such as the Ronald McDonald Houses; and school intervention programs for the sick child (Cincotta, 1993).

An area not well researched in the social work literature is how patients and families are to be cared for in the event of a relapse. This is a particularly devastating time for all. The patient and family's hope that the child will be well has been shattered, and they realize that treatments, hospitalization, and major life disruptions will begin again. The anger provoked by this setback can go in many directions, and the stance of the social worker is to be accepting of this level of emotion and attempt to encourage the child and family members to discuss the feelings associated with the relapse.

SOCIAL WORKER COMMENTS

"The most profound professional experiences take place here," said one of the social workers interviewed. "This is the center of human drama, and I am a part of that experience for the child and parent." All of the nine pediatric oncology social workers interviewed described the intensity of their unit and the work that they do. Caseloads varied from 24 to 60 cases.

One described her job using a cliff metaphor: "When a child is very sick, he or she and their family can easily go off the cliff, either emotionally or physically, falling one way or the other. I see my job as holding them on this side of the cliff." Another worker said, "What I tell parents is, "You are normal people in an abnormal situation, and we have to work to make the best of this situation."

In describing the role and function of the social worker, they agreed that much of their work is done with the parents. This is consistent with the systemic view of social work that the patient is part of a family system and all parts of the system influence each other. For the social worker, the patient includes the sick individual and the family members or caretakers. One worker described the experience of the parents as "having the control taken out of their life, and that the illness takes over the control of all that subsequently happens. As such, I try to give each parent some degree of control, even if it is minimal, so that they feel connected to the process of the illness." One social worker described his job as serving as the bridge between the hospital and the patient and family, functioning as an educator, service provider, and advocate. As the bridge, he made it a point to try to be where the patient and family are emotionally, to help them understand the medical aspects of what is happening and then to be able to see beyond the medical issues to the bigger picture of what lies beyond the illness. This social worker makes a special effort to educate parents using language that they can understand, to help them deal with the emotional and social aspects of the illness experience: "I educate to reduce the anxiety for both the kids and their parents." In direct work with the children, he attempts to get to know the child with the aim of getting the child to focus away from the medical situation and instead on an activity. The hospital has films, activity rooms, game areas, and volunteers, who attempt to keep the child who is able, active and involved with others. This helps the child and family appreciate that the patient is still a child and has the needs of all children to play and interact, despite the illness. These venues of activity also give the family a place to relax and have "normal" interaction with their child and temporarily, perhaps, forget their problems.

In accord with the literature, most of the social workers identified the initial period of diagnosis as the most trying, requiring conscientious intervention with family members: "Our job at that juncture is to educate about resources, help the family mobilize, and connect them to others who have gone through the experience of cancer with their own children, to help ease this initial overwhelming burden. After all, parents expect to have a healthy child and this is the worst blow that anyone could receive."

One social worker eloquently described her interactions with patients and family members, stating that for her it was a matter of "bearing witness. I sit and listen to what the child or the parent is saying, having developed respect for the process of acceptance of what this diagnosis means. In time, most are able to adapt and handle much of what is hurled at them, but in the beginning it is so hard." "I listen a lot and try to empower at every opportunity. I see the family as a whole and make my assessments and interventions with a systems perspective, trying to hold up those parts of the system that are the weakest," said one worker. As eloquently articulated by the social workers, being able to be with the family at this most trying time is essential because their need to talk and examine their responses and feelings ultimately translates into their ability to manage the impact of diagnosis and care for their child.

Each worker, in one form or another, said that death is a constant on the unit and that periodically it becomes overwhelming, especially if they have known the child and family for a long time. When a death occurs, the role of the social worker is to console the parents and do whatever concrete tasks — make phone calls, arrange with a funeral home, etc. — need to be done. Typical comments about death on their unit were, "Even when expected, the child's death is shocking and parents seem to freeze. So, I try to be as available to help with concrete tasks as much as possible." "The skills in handling death are so complex, I try to prepare the parents and educate them toward end-of-life choices that they can make." Although not cited specifically in their comments, the social workers mentioned that despite all the preparation for death coming from the medical staff and social workers, the moment of dying is overwhelming for most parents and even comes as a surprise. In response to this, one worker stated, "I want to be able to address the emotion of the moment, so I stick close by when death is pending."

Difficult cases were defined not necessarily by severity of illness or age of the child but more in terms of whether the child had needed social support and whether the family was able to manage the care needed for the child. "When the parents lack the social supports or they themselves have lots of problems such as chaotic lives, abuse problems, emotional problems, that make it impossible for them to adequately care for their child, that makes for a difficult case," explained one of the workers. "I have trouble when the patient is low on the priority list of the family," explained another.

Another area of difficulty for several of the social workers was navigating between the managed care requirements of shortened hospital stays and addressing the needs of the child and the family. This struggle was illustrated in this way: "When the child is really too sick to go home, or the family is not able to care for the child and we don't have time to arrange the needed resources for the safe care of the child, the frustration and pressure are way too intense to be healthy."

The work is not without its stresses and strains. For some, the anguish of seeing sick children has "spilled over to myself and I find myself worrying about my nieces and nephews [this social worker has no children] and then myself." Boundary issues assail some of the workers as they struggle not to allow the parents' anguish to become their own anguish. A version of the boundary struggle is being able to "not let the daily insults of upset parents or staff get to me and not to allow the beliefs of others about me remain."

The most satisfying aspect of the work was in knowing that they had contributed to the well-being of a sick child. "I thrive on being able to do for the patient, being able to round out the edges of a very difficult time and situation," said one social worker. The ability "to create a lot out of a difficult situation and learn more about the human condition," motivated one social worker. "The patient is a living person and seeing the effect we have on them and what happens in their life is so gratifying." Something interesting identified by each social worker as a positive aspect of the work was their role on the interdisciplinary team; they felt their role was critical on the unit and on the team.

One social worker explained that he gives children a postcard when they are discharged and asks them to mail it in a few weeks to tell him how they are doing. "I love getting mail," he said "especially when the kid sounds upbeat and seems to be getting on with life."

8

ONCOLOGY SOCIAL WORK WITH ADULTS

WHAT IS CANCER?

Cancer is a group of diseases characterized by uncontrolled growth and spread of abnormal cells. Cancer occurs when a cell in the body mutates to an abnormal state and begins to multiply uncontrollably. It is not one disease but many; because there are numerous types of cells, there are many types of cancer. If the spread of the mutated cells is not halted or controlled, it can result in death. Typically, the cancerous cells begin to grow on an organ of the body and, if not treated or if the cancerous growth (tumor) is not removed, a metastasis can occur. Metastasis means cancer cells from the original site have broken away and traveled through the body in the bloodstream or the lymphatic system and the cancer cells have spread to other organs where new tumors can grow.

Almost every family will have at least one member in each generation who will become ill with cancer. The American Cancer Society (ACS) estimated that, in 2004, more than 1,368,000 new cancer cases would be diagnosed in the United States. Since 1990, more than 18 million new cancer cases have been diagnosed; 563,700 Americans are expected to die of cancer, more than 1,500 people each day. In the United States, cancer accounts for one in four deaths. The National Institutes of Health estimate that overall costs for cancer in the year 2003 totaled $189.5 billion (ACS, 2004).

Survival rates are somewhat encouraging, having increased over the years; the 5-year survival rate for all cancers combined is 63%. This number represents people who are living 5 years after their diagnosis. Five years has been used as a standard because, statistically, if the cancer is going to recur or if a metastasis is going to happen, it will have happened during that time. The likelihood of a recurrence of cancer after 5 years is statistically and significantly reduced. However, these rates vary greatly by cancer type and stage at diagnosis (ACS, 2004).

Cancer is an equal opportunity disease: anyone can develop cancer. However, the rate of occurrence increases with age and most cases affect adults beginning in middle age. About 75% of all cancers are diagnosed in individuals age 55 and older. In the United States, men have less than a 1 in 2 lifetime risk of developing cancer (half of all men will have cancer at some time in their lives); for women, the risk is a little more than 1 in 3 (one in three women will have cancer in her life). It is estimated that 5 to 10% of cancers are hereditary. For example, a woman's chance of developing breast cancer is higher if her mother or sister has had the disease (Rosenthal, 1993). The remainder of the cancers are not hereditary but result from damage to genes (mutations) that occurs throughout the lifetime. These changes may be due to internal factors such as hormones or external factors such as tobacco, chemicals, and sunlight (ACS, 2004).

The question of prevention haunts cancer researchers and those affected by its diagnosis. Research has demonstrated that all cancers caused by cigarette smoking and heavy use of alcohol could be prevented completely. The American Cancer Society estimated that, in 2004, more than 180,000 cancer deaths were attributed to smoking and tobacco use. In addition, lifestyle factors are known to increase the likelihood of a cancer diagnosis. About one third of the 563,700 cancer deaths expected to occur in 2004 were related to nutrition, physical inactivity, being overweight or obese, and other lifestyle factors, and thus could have been prevented. Many of the more than 1 million skin cancers predicted for 2004 could have been prevented by diligent avoidance of sun exposure. The best offense in an effort to reduce the intensity of a cancer diagnosis is through regular screening examinations with a health care professional; cancers that can be detected — breast, colon, rectum, cervix, prostate, oral cavity, and skin — account for half of all new cases of cancer. Not all cancers are readily detectable before they have reached critical, life-threatening levels. Of those that are detectable, the 5-year survival rate is 84%. If all of these cancers were diagnosed at a localized stage through regular screenings, the 5-year survival rate would increase to 95% (ACS, 2004).

When cancer is suspected, because of symptoms, history, or physical exam, a diagnosis can be confirmed only on the basis of a tissue biopsy and pathologic study of the tissue removed. The pathologist grades the cancer according to the tumor's virulence or rapidity of growth; grade is a major determinant of prognosis (Rosenthal, 1993). Staging is the process of describing the extent or spread of the disease from the original site of the cancer. It dictates the choice of treatment and follow-up disease management. The cancer's stage depends on the size of the primary tumor (a collection of cancer cells that have formed into a mass), its location in the body, and whether cancerous cells from the original tumor have spread to other areas of the body. The pathologist assigns a stage of I, II, III, or IV, with I being the least advanced and earliest stage. Prognosis worsens as the staging numbers increase.

TREATMENT OPTIONS

Three basic treatments for cancer exist: surgery, radiation, and chemotherapy. Most people with cancer will have some type of surgery, because it offers the greatest chance for a cure for localized cancers. The surgical procedure is designed to remove the cancerous tumor and surrounding tissue to prevent cellular spread of the original site. Advances in surgical procedures allow for less invasive surgeries, with the goal of preserving as much normal function of the afflicted area as possible. In some cases of breast cancer, for example, although a small part of the breast is removed — the part where the tumor resided — the entire breast is preserved. Many surgeries of this type are done on an outpatient basis, whereas the more extensive surgeries require several days in the hospital.

Radiation treatment uses a stream of high-energy particles, or waves, to destroy or damage cancer cells. This treatment approach is used in more than half of all cancer cases. Many patients become cancer free after surgery followed by radiation treatments. All cells in the body grow and divide, but cancer cells do so at a rapid pace. Radiation treatment targets cancer cells to deliver high voltage to the cells, breaking the DNA within the cell to prevent growth and further dividing. In the process of radiating a precise area, the radiation waves can cause local irritation, burning, and discomfort. Radiation treatments are given either in the hospital or at special radiation centers, where trained professionals calculate the dosage and frequency of treatment. Radiation may also be used to prevent growth of cancer cells in other areas of the body beyond the primary site of the cancer (ACS, 2004). Radiation treatments are usually done daily to the affected area for a period of weeks.

Chemotherapy, the other common form of postsurgical treatment, is the administering of certain chemicals or drugs, usually intravenously, to the blood stream of a cancer patient. It can also be administered through injection or in pill form. A cancerous tumor is a collection of cells that has grown at a very rapid rate. The chemicals in the chemotherapy are designed to attack fast-growing cells and destroy the cancerous mass. The chemotherapy may be given weekly or monthly depending on the type of cancer and what length of time research has shown to be ideal for destroying the offending cells. The drugs used in chemotherapy are very strong and are not able to differentiate between the fast-growing cancer cells and other fast-growing cells in the body. These other cells — hair cells, cells in the mouth, certain blood cells, cells that line the esophagus and intestines — are also destroyed, often causing side effects that are unpleasant for the patient. Many patients lose their hair, develop sores in their mouth and skin, develop a form of anemia with resulting exhaustion, and experience nausea, vomiting, and stomach upset. When the chemotherapy stops, the symptoms disappear, but this form of treatment for weeks or months debilitates many patients after treatment until blood counts rise and energy returns.

Immunotherapy is treatment that uses certain parts of the immune system to fight disease; it is often used with other treatments to effect management and cure of cancer. This orientation to treatment is geared toward stimulation of the patient's immune system by vaccination of tumor cells. Specific cells, called T-lymphocytes, are inserted through the blood system and directed toward the tumor. This approach has been shown to be effective with small cancers and with some metastases and is still being developed as a viable treatment strategy. Monoclonal antibody therapy uses antibodies produced in a lab to stimulate the immune system of the cancer patient. This treatment technique is relatively new and is being evaluated through extensive clinical trials (ACS, 2004). Immunotherapy holds promise for treating cancers.

THE CANCER EXPERIENCE FOR THE PATIENT

Many people's first experience with cancer begins with the discovery of a lump or other symptom that is associated with cancer. This could be a breast lump, a sore that has changed appearance, a persistent pain, blood in the stool or urine, or a sore throat or cough that does not go away. From this moment of discovery, the uncertainty of cancer begins. "But this moment, before the doctor has even been called or a single test been done, often transforms a person's life from general well-being and confidence to one of enormous anxiety and uncertainty about the future. This pervasive sense of uncertainty probably characterizes the journey of cancer more than anything else" (Holland & Lewis, 2000, p. 40). Medical attention is sought, tests performed, perhaps a biopsy of tissue is taken and analyzed, and the moment of consultation and confirmation occurs. From then on, life changes irrevocably.

"Of all life events, a cancer diagnosis is one of the most startling and disturbing. With this unpleasant surprise, life suddenly changes. Although the person with a new diagnosis may have been feeling perfectly healthy, in an instant, the future becomes uncertain" (Cordoba, Fobair, & Callan, 1993, p. 43). Every existential fear the person has is realized when the diagnosis is received. No matter how positively this information is delivered, no matter how persuasive are the statistics, newly identified cancer patients face uncertainty and challenge unknown to them until that moment. "The landscapes of most human lives are permanently altered by a cancer diagnosis. Even when some positive changes or insights result, returning to 'the way things were' is simply not possible" (Koocher & Pollin, 2001, p. 363). Even though significant improvements to survival rates have occurred due to advances in detection and treatments, cancer remains a potentially life-threatening disease; as such, it represents a potentially catastrophic stressor to those diagnosed (Kilbourn & Durning, 2003, p. 108). Who among us does not equate cancer with death or debilitating illness? Understandably, the cancer diagnosis awakens feelings of anxiety and fear, as well as vulnerability and awareness of personal mortality. Immediate reactions to the diagnosis may include disbelief, denial, anger, depression, anxiety, and confusion. This level of distress can be crippling, with questions such as "Will I die?" and "How long might I live?" (Andrykowski, Carpenter, & Munn, 2003).

Most people, upon diagnosis, experience a period of denial and disbelief, similar to a crisis response in which the individual is initially paralyzed by a shocking event. Similar to a crisis response, within a short time many will begin to mobilize their inner and outer resources, seek medical direction, and gather information related to their diagnosis. Ensuing surgery and treatment is initiated and the difficult adjustment to the diagnosis and what comes after become embedded in the lives of the patient and those close to him or her. Recovery from surgery to remove a tumor may be protracted, perhaps involving a period of hospitalization, or it may be relatively short if the surgery was not extensive or debilitating. Often there is pain associated with the surgery and the follow-up treatments.

Patients whose cancer is far advanced may not have the option of surgery, and treatment choices may be limited. These patients face an uncertain future and have to embrace the notion that their cancer is fatal. Palliative measures to keep them pain free and comfortable, along with the initiation of hospice intervention, is sometimes the most one can offer to an advanced cancer patient.

PSYCHOSOCIAL CONSIDERATIONS

A cancer diagnosis is a traumatic event for most individuals and their loved ones. Patients may question the accuracy of the diagnosis and attempt to distance themselves from its reality. Difficulty sleeping, eating, and concentrating and mood swings are all characteristic of the early phase. Upon diagnosis, the primary coping task confronting patients is to attempt to maintain cognitive and emotional equilibrium; they need to be able to maintain effective decision making abilities regarding treatment preferences (Andrykowski et al., 2003). In the initial stage, the most frequent source of stress cited by patients and spouses was the uncertainty associated with not knowing what to expect. Of the 54 couples interviewed in the research, 51 were concerned about their ignorance of medical procedures, hospital routines, the course of the disease, and the side effects of treatment (Vess, Moreland, Schwebel, & Kraut, 1988). Over time in the cancer experience, reactions and responses will differ, but the initial period for most is marked by confusion, stress, and anxiety.

Although many people adapt well to a diagnosis of cancer, it is estimated that approximately one third of all cancer patients experience some psychological distress during the course of their illness (Zabora, 1998). Although statistical documentation is variable, studies have substantiated that patients with cancer diagnoses score significantly higher than the general population, but significantly lower than psychiatric populations, on measures of depression (Kilbourn & Durning, 2003).

A variety of variables correlate with adjustment to cancer. Demographic variables include age (younger patients seem to have a more difficult time psychologically with their diagnosis and treatment [Kilbourn & Durning, 2003]), race (for all cancers, African Americans have a higher mortality rate than Caucasians [ACS, 2004]), gender (generally men seem to have more difficulties than women do in social adjustment and psychological distress [Peleg-Oren, Sherer, & Soskolne, 2003]), income (more affluent patients who have better access to medical care outlive those who are not affluent [ACS, 2004]), level of education (better education correlates to better awareness and more self-care responses [Andrykowski et al., 2003], and marital status (married people adjust better to their disease [Kornblith et al., 1998; Schnoll, Knowles, & Harlow, 2002; Taylor, 1995]).

Emotional correlates to adjustment include the buffering effect of higher levels of social support, optimism, and degrees of communication with health care providers. The strongest predictor of positive adjustment is social support. Social support has been documented as having a major role in reducing or buffering negative psychological responses such as hopelessness, despair, and depression in cancer patients. Having someone to whom patients can confide their fears and concerns, a loving and supportive spouse or friend, appears to enhance their emotional state while facilitating the ability to cope more effectively with their illness (Blanchard, Albrecht, Ruckdeschel, Grant, & Hemmick, 1995). Hopelessness has a particularly corrosive impact on the cancer patient's emotional state. Patients who perceive cancer as a death threat and view their life as meaningless have more symptoms of depression, with hopelessness as an outcome of those feelings. Patients who have less social support have more symptoms of hopelessness (Gil & Gilbar, 2001).

At different stages of the cancer experience, different stressors affect the emotional and psychological well-being of the patient. Once the course of treatment has been established, the patient may have to cope with discomfort from surgery and side effects from chemotherapy or radiation. There can be pain, nausea, and fatigue. In addition, patients may need to cope with temporary or permanent cosmetic changes such as hair loss or the loss of a limb or breast resulting from surgery. The patient may fear abandonment, may be unable to perform sexually, or may be afraid of risking further pain with certain physical exertion. In all instances, the primary coping task for the patient is to be able to minimize the experience and impact of these side effects in order to continue with as many routine daily activities and social roles as possible. In doing so, the patient is more likely to maintain the morale and motivation necessary to complete his or her treatment (Andrykowski et al., 2003).

During the treatment phase, a major concern for some patients is their physical decline and the threat to psychological and financial well-being. Because many patients are unable to work during their treatment, they miss the sense of self-esteem and pride they used to get from their work. This casts many patients in only the sick role. The very real concern, faced by many, of financial insecurity and significant loss of family income forces some debilitated cancer patients back to work before they are able. In addition, physical decline, which prevents patients from fulfilling their former duties in the home, provokes frustration and anxiety (Vess et al., 1988).

The period immediately after chemotherapy or radiation treatment is completed can be seen as a time of celebration or of heightened anxiety. Despite the side effects associated with treatments, many patients derive comfort from knowing that they are actively combating their disease. However, completion of treatment can trigger anxiety about recurrence, can provoke a shift in the patient's network of social supports, and may heighten concern due to longer periods between medical visits. One must begin to make the shift away from the patient role and move into formerly held roles. This is not easy, because the threat of recurrence haunts most cancer patients (Andrykowski et al., 2003). When recurrence occurs, many of the original emotional and psychological reactions reoccur, sometimes with greater intensity, as the hope of "beating the disease" begins to fade.

THE CAREGIVER EXPERIENCE

Cancer affects not only the patient but the family or caregivers as well. As in most illness experiences described in this volume, the view of the illness transcends the needs of the patient and extends to the entire family and its functioning. "It is now recognized that the patient's experience of being diagnosed with and treated for cancer can be as distressing, if not more distressing in some cases, for the partner(s) than for the patient" (Carlson, Bultz, Speca, & St. Pierre, 2000a, p. 40). In fact, a link exists between patients' and partners' levels of distress: when one partner is distressed, the other tends to be similarly distressed (Northouse, Dorris, & Charon-Moore, 1995). This link between patient and caregiver can be a source of extreme comfort but also an arena of stress and strain.

Caregiving is often a balancing act between the psychological and the logistical. Besides the task of giving emotional support, the caregiver may be involved in appointment scheduling, paying medical bills, handling insurance, keeping track of medication, and taking care of the physical needs of the patient (Holland & Lewis, 2000). In addition to assuming greater responsibilities, the caregiver carries the mantle of worry about the future, has to adjust to the physical limitations the illness provokes, has to cope with the patient's mood changes, and lives with the uncertainty of the patient's health status (Ey, Compas, Epping-Jordan, & Worsham, 1998).

Conclusions from research by Carlson et al. (2000) on partners of cancer patients show that husbands experience distress both before and after their wives are diagnosed with cancer and during the treatment phase of the illness. The issue of loss of control contributes to the distress felt by partners as well as patients, especially in the case of husbands, who become distressed in situations characterized by a high degree of uncertainty and helplessness and a low sense of perceived control. Over time, most husbands seem to adjust to changes caused by their wives' cancer and return to normal psychological functioning. When husbands are patients, it appears that wives are more distressed after the diagnosis than are the patients themselves. The wives tend to accept the burden of caregiving with less assistance than their husbands in a similar situation. The women continue to perform household chores and care for the children but are often distressed by feelings of loneliness and helplessness. Like the husbands, most wives seem to resume previous coping levels over time. Same-sex couples struggle in similar ways, with role changes that are imposed by the illness and juxtaposition of responsibilities.

Sales, Schultz, and Biegel (1992) found that the spouse's distress was greater when the patient had a poorer prognosis, the patient was in a terminal stage of illness, and the illness was prolonged. Despite these stressors, most family members managed to cope without experiencing severe pathology. Sales et al. also noted that younger partners were more at risk for adjustment problems because they often felt frustrated and angry, whereas older partners were often more burdened by caretaking demands and had a greater tendency to feeling overwhelmed. Wives generally had more adjustment problems earlier in the illness. The better the quality of the marriage before the cancer diagnosis, the less strain partners experienced during the diagnostic and treatment phases of the illness. Couples with preschool-aged children experienced the greatest role demands, those with school-aged children experienced the most conflict, and those with adult children exhibited the least disruption.

ONCOLOGY SOCIAL WORK

Considering that today less than half of those diagnosed with cancer will die of the disease, this leaves enormous room for psychosocial interventions to improve the psychological or functional status of those coping with the disease (Cwikel & Behar, 1999a). Psychological sequelae to a cancer diagnosis are understandable. Thoughts of death and dying loom following diagnosis; although sometimes not appropriate to the diagnosis, it is understandable nonetheless. Study after study has documented the impact of the diagnosis and treatment demands for the cancer patient and caregivers. In numerous studies, depression and anxiety have been found to be particularly prevalent in cancer patients. "To achieve mastery of the cancer experience, a significant number of patients and families will benefit from counseling interventions and a comprehensive evaluation of their psychosocial needs" (Herschel & Vaitones, 2004, p. 6).

Psychosocial support has long been demonstrated to be a crucial factor in moderating the effects of difficult life stressors. Social workers are uniquely qualified to offer such interventions with the systems perspective, clinical expertise, and academic preparation. Psychotherapeutic intervention offers a safe context in which to manage the intrusion of painful and frightening thoughts and fears of death, which can overwhelm patients who have little or no opportunity to fully express themselves elsewhere. Patients who have a time and place to deal with them can better manage these normal, yet terrifying feelings. This is an area in which the oncology social worker can significantly affect the life of the cancer patient (Spiegel & Diamond, 2001). In the hospital, the oncology social worker will attempt to help the patient and family adjust to the illness. Upon discharge, most hospitals identify referral outlets for patients and families, directing them to social workers in their community who are able to counsel oncology patients and family members. Many of these social workers have had additional training in working with people with a serious illness. In some communities, outpatient mental health agencies have social workers on staff who deal specifically with these referrals.

Blum (1993) suggests basic principles of oncology social work interventions:

- Social work interventions must be based on an understanding of the patient's specific cancer diagnosis and treatment plan, as well as the patient's emotional, financial, and social situation.
- Social workers must make themselves available; some patients are reluctant to seek out services, so accessibility facilitates connection.
- Social work services are designed to help patients and the families feel more in control of a situation and less helpless. Interventions should focus on helping people cope with the medical, emotional, and social problems they encounter at different points in the cancer experience.
- The diverse population of cancer patients — varied by race, age, socioeconomic status, education, and developmental stage — has needs that vary over time. The social worker must understand these variables and be sensitive to them. (p. 107)

COUNSELING

The overall goal of individual counseling is to help the patient adjust to changes associated with the diagnosis and make plans for the future (Kilbourn & Durning, 2003). The person with cancer commonly experiences diminished feelings of self-worth, increased dependence on others for activities of daily living, and fear of pain and death. The foundation of counseling is to ask meaningful questions that elicit feelings and concerns while attempting to promote adaptive functioning by helping the patient focus on specific concerns and set achievable goals (Herschel & Vaitones, 2004). Frequently, the individual counseling will take place in the patient's hospital room or in a clinic. In the hospital setting, the social worker must realize that time is short and that traditional insight-oriented psychotherapy is not a realistic option. Counseling the patient — dealing with the reality of the situation and helping the patient assess and plan — are realistic goals of the hospital-based social worker. Individual counseling can also be used to help the patient who, based on his or her health crisis, is now ready to make some changes in his or her life, to reevaluate goals and values and to find a new direction. The social worker may provide family counseling to help family members cope with feelings similar to what the patient is experiencing — feelings of confusion, fear, and helplessness. Financial concerns may directly affect family viability; caring for the patient may impose serious hardships on the functioning of the family. Social work support of the family may include education, facilitation of resources, promotion of enhanced communication, and general support of their struggles.

Group interventions can also be useful for allowing the patient or caregiver to get emotional support and share information with those who have had or are having a similar experience. Group members have the opportunity to practice new skills with other patients and witness how others handle the multiple stressors — emotional, psychological, financial — associated with cancer treatment and cancer survivorship (Kilbourn & Durning, 2003).

The timing of interventions, either group or individual, may be a factor in their effectiveness. In an analysis of research on interventions for this population, Cwikel and Behar (1999a) found that intervention is most common and achieves the most effective results during the treatment phase. This seems reasonable in light of the level of denial and chaos that characterizes the initial period of diagnosis and treatment. When the denial of the initial period crumbles, most people begin to lose hope and question what will happen to them. Noting that both individual and group interventions were equally effective in their review of research studies, the authors summarized that the value of working with a social worker potentially increases the patient's hope, feelings of self-efficacy, and expectation for improvement while minimizing alienation, loneliness, and stigma. Although difficult to assess, it must be assumed that when patients have a more positive psychological profile, it affects their ability to tolerate their treatments, some of which are very uncomfortable and debilitating, and to rally toward wellness.

SOCIAL WORKER COMMENTS

Of the 10 social workers interviewed, there seemed to be unanimous agreement that the work was very challenging but that it afforded them a high level of satisfaction. In hospital settings, the mandate of managed care has attenuated hospital stays, making long-term relationships with patients very rare. The brevity of these relationships was a source of frustration for those interviewed. On some of the oncology units, patients return for additional treatments or with critical incidents that connect the social worker to them for a longer period of time. Patients who are hospitalized may be at an early stage of diagnosis, possibly having undergone surgery; they may be undergoing treatment; or they are in the terminal phase of life. At each stage, the social workers defined their role and function and the challenges they face.

For the newly diagnosed, the social workers saw their task as offering emotional support and facilitating discussion between the patient, the family, and the doctors. Several social workers felt that their approach to the newly diagnosed was to apply crisis intervention techniques for both the patient and family. Education of family members was a strong component of their intervention strategy, based on the belief that the more the patient or family knows, the better prepared they will be for what occurs. It is essentially an empowerment approach, consistent with social work values.

Working with the family was described as being as important as patient-related work. Often the family members are in denial and have to be educated to the needs of the patient, or the family is devastated and needs social work support to be able to mobilize their resources to care for the patient. Social work intervention with the doctors on behalf of the patient, either for more hospital time or for needed education for the patient or family, was part of the social work role.

For those further along in their disease, those who are experiencing a recurrence, or those who are terminal, the social workers described their task as one of helping the patient and family live with the disease, enhance relationships, and realistically explore options. For the terminal patient, the role was to help the patient and family tie up loose ends and to "be there for the family and patient in whatever ways they need me."

The social work skills mentioned as useful in their work included assessment and crisis intervention. Each patient and family must be assessed for social supports, level of education about the disease, and ability to manage the demands imposed by the cancer. Because part of the job of the social worker is discharge planning, he or she must get the sense from the family that the patient's needs — physical and emotional — will be met when the patient returns home. Part of the assessment includes determining what additional services must be put in place for the patient to return home to a safe environment. Active listening, especially for those patients who are struggling during their treatment, is a crucial skill. The social workers also mentioned the necessary skill of trying to "listen with the third ear" (i.e., the ability to hear what the patient is saying on one level and understand that he or she might mean something different). Serving as an advocate for the patient to access resources, especially for problem cases that involve Medicaid or insurance entitlements, or for patients who have no money, consumed a lot of the social workers' time, often keeping them from spending time with patients and families.

All the social workers felt that their unit operated with a team approach, with the doctors, nurses, dieticians, and physical therapists pulling together on behalf of the patient. Except for one social worker, the feeling was that each of them had a voice in decision making and was a respected member of the team. Several of the workers described an interesting aspect of their role: taking care of the team members when a patient dies. The nurses look to the social workers to help the family, but they also look to them to help with their own reactions to a patient's death. Although every death is different, several of those interviewed felt that each one was a traumatic event on their unit. During one week, one of the social workers reported that she had had two deaths on her unit and that all the staff was "shaken and upset for quite some time."

As expected, the most difficult cases involved younger patients and those who were terminally ill. For a woman in her mid-30s with lung cancer, two young children, and no significant support system, the social worker struggled to get medically trained aides to come to the home for the patient and arranged hospice care for her at no cost. Although this was a satisfying piece of her work, the social worker was challenged by the fact that the woman was very close to her own age and it awakened her own fear. One social worker who had had a family member die from cancer noted the potential for overidentification with the patient's struggle. She felt that, especially with the younger patients, she could never do enough and that there were times when she felt "sucked dry" by the demands of the work.

Equally sad yet satisfying was the situation with a 40-year-old woman with breast cancer that had metastasized. The patient was terminal, and she did not want her teenaged daughters to see her in the hospital. She asked the social worker to talk to her children, which she did. But the social worker urged the mother to speak directly to her daughters, and eventually the mother agreed to see them. The social worker was acting out of a belief that although it might be difficult for both the mother and daughters in the moment, in the long run, it would be important for the daughters' well-being to have had some time with their mother before her death. There were several visits before she died. On the day of her death, her 13-year-old daughter came to see her and was with her when she died. For the social worker, it was a very sad moment, but she had the satisfaction of knowing that she had made a significant impact on the situation.

The satisfaction in the work comes from being able to facilitate a good discharge plan: the patient is sent home with needed services and to a safe environment. The immediate gratification this offers sustained many of the workers. The frustrations occur when needed services cannot be accessed, insurance companies create obstacles to patient care, and the hospital exerts intense pressure to discharge.

The conflicts and emotional concerns mentioned by the interviewees involved the separation of their job and their own lives. Many have ongoing feelings of frustration because of wanting to fix many aspects of the cancer patients' lives in a short amount of time in a system that "values discharge over good care."

When asked if the social workers had fears for themselves after seeing so much illness, the majority responded that they have a different view of life since beginning their work with oncology patients. "I treasure every day. So many things can happen, cancer being one of them, that I do not take my health for granted. I began exercising and stopped smoking after 2 months on the unit."

Even with the intensity and gravity of the diagnosis, this group of social workers felt that they were in positions to make a significant impact in the lives of their patients and the caregivers. They seemed to feel a strong pull to their work and agreed that, although this service was not for everyone — they were witness to a lot of suffering — they found it satisfying and gratifying.

9

THE HIV/AIDS SOCIAL WORKER

ABOUT HIV/AIDS

AIDS (acquired immunodeficiency syndrome) was first reported in the United States in 1981. The first cases were documented in California and New York and presented as an unusual array of infections that responded poorly to therapy and ended in death. Physicians were puzzled by this situation because none of the patients suffered from any condition known to predispose them to infections. They rightly concluded that the patients had developed an illness never before described in the medical literature. They named the condition AIDS: acquired immunodeficiency syndrome, a name that encompassed many aspects of the presenting illness, specifically that each patient had had a severely compromised immune system with the resulting inability to fight infections and that the illness was acquired, not inherited or the result of other recognized conditions. What was also unusual was that the majority of those who were suffering with this illness were gay men. Those who were studying this medical situation assumed it had something to do with gay social behavior (Curran, 1983). By the mid-1980s, researchers had isolated the virus that causes AIDS and termed it HIV (human immunodeficiency virus). In the intervening years, thousands of people had been diagnosed with AIDS and it had caused countless deaths. Since isolating the virus, researchers have devised numerous treatment regimens, but the numbers of new cases and deaths has continued to rise, as has the picture of AIDS as a gay disease.

In 2003, the cumulative number of diagnoses of AIDS in the United States was 929,985 and the estimated cumulative number of deaths since the epidemic began was 524,050 (Centers for Disease Control [CDC], 2003). Globally, as a worldwide epidemic, 40 million women, men, and children are currently infected with HIV/AIDS; throughout all continents 5 million new HIV infections were reported in 2003, with a total death count of more than 3 million (UNAIDS/WHO, 2003). Although AIDS is a worldwide epidemic, the observations in this chapter relate only to the situation in the United States.

People who contract HIV are susceptible to AIDS; people with AIDS almost always get life-threatening diseases called opportunistic infections, which are caused by microbes and viruses that do not usually make healthy people sick. In the early years of the epidemic, with medical knowledge limited, those who contracted HIV were certain to develop AIDS and were destined to die of it. As knowledge of the illness grew, some treatments were successful in slowing down the progression of HIV, but, to date, no cure exists.

HIV infection begins with minimal flu-like symptoms, including a fever, headache, tiredness, and swollen glands, and within a short time (about a week) symptoms subside. Many people do not know they have been infected, suspecting some other viral infection. More severe or persistent symptoms of illness may not occur for a decade or more after the virus enters the body. During this asymptomatic period, the virus is multiplying, infecting, and killing cells of the immune system. The cells most frequently affected by the virus are the CD4+ T cells (T4 cells), which are the body's major infection fighters. As the immune system deteriorates, a variety of complications and illnesses ensue. This may be the person's initial recognition that something is seriously wrong and that he or she may have been infected with HIV. The individual may also notice a lack of energy, weight loss, fevers and sweats, frequent yeast infections, shingles, skin rashes, and short-term memory loss. Medical intervention at this point would be to treat the infection and do blood analysis to determine whether the person is HIV positive. Various tests are done, including viral load. The viral load test measures the amount of HIV in a sample of blood and is thus a good predictor of AIDS. People with a high viral load usually develop AIDS more rapidly than those with a low viral load.

The diagnosis of AIDS, the most advanced stage of HIV infection, occurs when a person's blood shows less than 200 T4 cells (healthy people have counts of 1,000 or more T4 cells) per cubic millimeter of blood. In addition, the person will have one or more opportunistic infections, which would not affect healthy people but can be fatal to someone with HIV/AIDS. Symptoms of opportunistic infections in people with AIDS include coughing, shortness of breath, seizures, lack of coordination, painful swallowing, disorientation, severe and persistent diarrhea, fever, vision loss, weight loss, extreme fatigue, severe headaches, coma, and certain cancers (Kaposi's sarcoma, lymphomas, and cervical cancer). In addition, pneumocystis carinii pneumonia (PCP) is recognized as a common illness in people with HIV, occurring in more than 60% of cases, and is often the first AIDS-defining illness (Holtom, 1992). Many people are so debilitated by the symptoms of AIDS that they are incapable of holding jobs or doing simple household chores, whereas others have periods of illness followed by periods during which they function normally (Matthews, 2003). It is the idiosyncratic nature of the illness, its unique manifestation in each patient, that makes HIV/AIDS difficult to predict and treat.

Currently, there is neither a vaccine to prevent HIV infection nor a cure. Treatment of HIV includes medications that strengthen the immune system and fight both HIV infection and its associated infections and cancers. The first drug to treat AIDS was AZT (azidothymidine, generically known as zidovudine), approved by the U.S. Food and Drug Administration in 1987. Initially heralded as a wonder drug to defeat HIV, its effectiveness waned over time as the virus mutated to overcome the drug. Currently there are two major groups of drugs used to fight the virus (Matthews, 2003). One group is designed to prevent the early stage of the virus from making copies of itself; these drugs slow the spread of the virus in the body and delay the onset of opportunistic infections. A second class of drugs, protease inhibitors, interrupts replication of the virus at a later stage in the life cycle. Within each group of drugs, individual drugs have significant side effects. With the introduction of these two groups of drugs and a recent treatment innovation for AIDS called HAART (highly active antiretroviral therapy) introduced in 1997, the health of many people with AIDS has been improved. With treatment advances, people with HIV can and do live longer and more productive lives. However, data suggest that strict adherence to the treatment regimens of HAART and the combination therapies must be maintained for the medications to work fully. Long-term side effects of HAART have created other medical conditions, including neurological and coronary difficulties (Thompson, 2003).

Combination therapies seem to be the most effective at lowering viral loads and decreasing HIV-resistant mutations, but they are expensive, ranging from $12,000 to $18,000 per year (Gant, 1998), in some cases covered by insurance and in others not. If a patient qualifies for Medicaid (i.e., patient is disabled, at a certain income level, and unable to work), the costs for medication and medical treatment are covered by the government. Although HAART and the other medications cannot cure HIV/AIDS, HIV-positive patients are living longer and maintaining healthier and more productive lives than ever before, creating a situation in which AIDS can be seen as a chronic illness rather than the death sentence it had originally been considered (Fesko, 2001).

Having unprotected sex with an infected partner is the most common cause of HIV. The virus can enter the body through the lining of the vagina, vulva, penis, rectum, or mouth. It can also be contracted through infected blood, either through transfusions or by contact with someone who is contaminated by the virus through sexual contact, kissing, or the exchange of bodily fluid. HIV frequently is spread between injection drug users when they share needles or syringes carrying very small quantities of contaminated blood. One drug particularly associated with HIV transmission is crystal methamphetamine (crystal meth), a recreational drug often used by younger homosexual men, especially in urban areas. The drug facilitates, enhances, and prolongs sexual encounters but its use can lead to lapses in judgment with regard to safe sex, increasing the risk of HIV transmission (Urbina & Jones, 2004).

In an unfortunate twist of medical fate, women who are HIV positive can transmit HIV to their babies during pregnancy or birth and also through breast milk. Approximately one quarter to one third of all untreated pregnant women infected with HIV will pass on the infection to their babies (Matthews, 2003).

In the earliest stages of the AIDS epidemic in the United States, homosexual and bisexual men accounted for more than 90% of all cases, with cases of intravenous drug users and heterosexuals a distinctly unusual minority. Over the years, this identification has shifted, but it was particularly stigmatizing and disenfranchising for those who were first diagnosed with the virus. Since the early years of the epidemic, the virus has spread across demographic groups, gaining access to new populations through individuals who overlapped groups. During the 1980s, more and more women became infected with HIV. No longer a "gay plague," HIV/AIDS began to claim women and heterosexual men in its mounting statistics. In addition to intense fear about the effects of the disease, people infected with HIV/AIDS experienced intense stigma from family, friends, and society at large in repeated scenarios of violence and discrimination (Bacon, 1987; Christ & Wiener, 1987).

Since 1992, injection drug use has become a frequent mode of transmission, and between 1986 and 1993, heterosexual transmission increased 1,200% (Gant, 1998). Because of the lifestyles associated with

HIV/AIDS — sexual promiscuity, homosexuality, and subsequently intravenous drug use — those who were first diagnosed suffered at the mercy of both political and religious forces that condemned their life choices and ostracized them for their behaviors and illness. Many of the initial social taboos that first were associated with the disease have shifted, but HIV/AIDS remains a powerful social issue, manifesting in areas of health care, employment, and family and personal stigma. The following quote from Pryor, Reeder, and Landau (1999) reflects the views of many from the early years of the epidemic:

> In the early 1980's we witnessed the beginning of one of the most complicated and bewildering social problems ever faced by contemporary society: the epidemic of infection with human immunodeficiency virus which caused Acquired Immunodeficiency Syndrome (AIDS). For both the social/behavioral sciences, the AIDS epidemic has spawned a brood of perplexing questions. ... Truly amazing are the power and scope of AIDS stigma. At the hands of their fellow humans, people with HIV infection have received negative treatment in employment, health care, housing, insurance coverage, public accommodations, educations, and immigration policies. (pp. 1193–1194)

How differently this history could have been written if President Reagan and those in government and other positions of power before him had publicly recognized the disease, before more than 25,000 people had died from HIV.

HIV/AIDS: THE PATIENT EXPERIENCE

When a person is infected with HIV, he or she may be unaware that transmission of the virus has occurred. As such, the flu-like symptoms and malaise that may follow transmission may well be neglected and thought to be "a touch of the flu" or "a virus" with no further concern or anguish. People who are newly infected usually have few or no symptoms, whereas those further along (i.e., months or years later) may have profound immune deficiency, leaving the body open to opportunistic infections and the diagnosis of AIDS. Such infections are defining of AIDS. Typical sites of opportunistic infection include the lungs, skin, gastrointestinal tract, lymph nodes, brain, and eyes. For any of these illnesses, the average person might expect to be hospitalized and treated with antibiotics or other medications specific to the illness. People who have compromised immune systems, however, may not have the biological and physiological reserve to adequately fight the infections.

In its most virulent stages, HIV-related opportunistic infections consume the body, causing pneumonia, serious skin disorders, inability to eat or metabolize food, and other serious conditions. In the early stages of the epidemic, photographs of Rock Hudson, ravaged by AIDS, looking gaunt and depleted by AIDS-related illness, invited the shocking and inevitable comparison to the picture of health he once was and brought public attention to the destructive power of this disease. Pictures of children and adults in present-day Africa, emaciated because of AIDS, serve as a similar reminder.

Since the advent of new treatment options, which began in the mid-1990s, an interesting psychological shift has occurred in the HIV/AIDS world: from AIDS as a death sentence to living with AIDS with improved physical functioning and longer or long-lasting immune capability. Known as the Lazarus phenomenon, many people diagnosed with AIDS have made the shift from living out their anticipated shortened lives due to the virus to now beginning to live their lives, albeit cautiously, as long-term survivors. Now that patients have regained a future, many practical and financial problems have developed for the many who spent their savings, sold their life insurance, resigned from the world of work, and foreclosed relationships, all because they assumed death was imminent and they did not dare to hope that they may have a future. For so many HIV-positive patients, this new lease on life has allowed for resumption of healthy relationships and family bonding and created opportunities to reinvest in living. But, as Sowell (1997) points out, "... even with a more stable disease status, a large number of those individuals remain chronically ill and face the uncertainty of not knowing when they may experience a drug failure or deterioration of their condition" (p. 43). Rose (1998) calls it the "roller coaster of hope," noting that uncertainty is a fact of life for those with HIV. Because so many have died from AIDS, it is hard to reconstitute life and relax into one's own wellness.

WOMEN AND HIV/AIDS

Overall, women represent an increasing proportion of new AIDS cases, with African American women representing a greater number of AIDS cases than White women (Kaplan, Tomaszewski, & Gorin, 2004). In the United States, women account for 19% of all people with AIDS and 27% of HIV-positive individuals. AIDS is the fourth leading cause of death among women aged 24 to 44. Three quarters of the female adults with

AIDS are either black or Hispanic (CDC, 2003). Although initially women did not appear to be prone to HIV/AIDS, over the years of the epidemic, more and more women have been diagnosed with HIV. This has been attributed to women having been victims of sexual assault, having had sexual partners who were infected, using intravenous drugs, or having unprotected sex with drug users. The high percentage of minority women with the virus is striking. This can be understood in the context of cultural norms that prescribe unprotected sexual contact and the higher use of intravenous drugs in the minority community.

Men and women have similar experiences with HIV, but women are prone to a host of different opportunistic infections including vaginal candidiasis, genital infections, and pelvic inflammatory disease. The incidence of some malignancies is lower for women, specifically Kaposi's sarcoma. One of the most common and disturbing side effects associated with combination therapies is visible changes in body composition and appearance. These changes result from a redistribution of body fat (the cause is not known or understood); fat moves from the face, arms, rear end, and legs and subsequently accumulates around the gut, at the base of the neck, or in the breasts. These changes commonly accompany abnormal lab tests indicating elevated cholesterol, triglycerides, glucose tolerance, and other changes. The medical term for these changes is lipodystrophy. Women are more prone to lipodystrophy than men and seem to have more dramatic changes in body configuration. Because physical appearance is often of greater concern to women, this manifestation of their disease can cause additional stress and anguish (Matthews, 2003).

Emotionally, women experience the profound impact of the illness on themselves with equal emphasis and concern for their children. Childcare concerns and caretaking roles are severely strained by the illness; couple this with the fear of more severe illness and death and the rate of depression in women with HIV/AIDS is quite high, approaching 65 to 70% (Matthews, 2003). Another area of major concern is the social stigma associated with HIV and its impact on both the woman and her children. Loss was a constant theme in one study of HIV-positive women: loss of their future, of potential love relationships, of family and friends, and of a future with children and grandchildren. Indeed, one of the most challenging tasks for the women in this study was telling their children of their HIV status (Goggin et al., 2001). Transmission issues loom large for many women, because they may have inadvertently infected their children with HIV either through breastfeeding or while pregnant. This can be a torturous situation for the woman involved.

THE FAMILY/CAREGIVER EXPERIENCE

Although many people with AIDS are living longer and fuller lives, many still suffer the disabling effects of the virus, with the increasing need for long-term care and support. Frequently, people with AIDS turn to their family of origin for that support, although gay men are more likely to seek and receive support from friends and partners than from their family of origin (Kadushin, 1999). The family's response may vary from acceptance to bitter anger and rejection depending on various circumstances of family history, how the family member became infected, socioeconomic issues, and ages of family members. Finances are a major concern because of the extreme costs of medical care for people with AIDS. Family members faced with the reintegration of a drug user into the family may experience tension and anger over events from the past. An AIDS diagnosis may necessitate the disclosure of homosexuality to unknowing family members. All of these issues suggest that people with AIDS who return home for care may experience difficulties related to family dynamics in addition to their struggle with the effects of the virus and their debilitated condition (Cates, Graham, Boeglin, & Tielker, 1990).

In discussing the needs of the caregivers or family members, one must be sensitive to a broadened definition of family. Family for a person with HIV/AIDS may include the partner or friends, who may be the primary support system for the individual.

> Friends, partners, and family members substantially influence the quality of life experienced by persons with AIDS. Caregivers are involved in virtually every aspect of the illness, from pre-diagnosis care to making postmortem plans. They influence medical decision making and discharge dispositions, run the household, provide nursing care or arrange for its provision, negotiate financial and legal matters, counsel the dying. (Land, 1992, pp. 199–200)

Understanding the unique "family" make-up can be an important aspect of care. It behooves the social worker involved in working with an HIV family to be aware of the various combinations and permutations the patient's life has assumed. Sometimes the family of origin and the partner can engage in a battle for control of the patient's medical care. Consider the family of origin of a gay man; upon learning of their son's hospitalization, the parents arrive at the hospital and want to take charge of and be involved in his medical care. The patient defines his family of choice as his partner. Thus the patient is caught in a battle for control over who has the right to be involved in decision making about his care. A dilemma of this sort suggests that regardless of gender, sexual orientation, or means of transmission, all family members (no matter how family is defined) are heavily impacted by the illness and the stigma that still accompanies HIV (Babcock, 1998b).

Once AIDS has been diagnosed and the opportunistic infections become more frequent, the needs of the AIDS patient increase as the illness becomes more and more debilitating. As the patient becomes sicker, autonomy decreases and dependency needs increase. Depending on the severity of the opportunistic infections, caregiving can be managed at home with a modicum of ongoing care. Eventually, people with AIDS are unable to care for themselves, requiring care beyond the capacity of most home situations. This level of illness provokes immeasurable stress for caregivers, and as a result of this tension, physical work, and emotional turmoil, they too may become depleted and require supportive services (Land, 1992).

THE SOCIAL WORKER AND HIV/AIDS

When a person with AIDS is admitted to the hospital, it is usually under acute circumstances: the person is too ill to be cared for at home and needs intensive medical intervention. The hospital social worker is often the first nonmedical staff person to see the patient. If this is a first hospitalization, it can be a very confusing and frightening time for the patient, especially if this is the first illness that confirms the AIDS diagnosis.

Hospitalization for any illness exacerbates a patient's sense of powerlessness and lack of control; for the first-time AIDS patient these feelings are common along with their reaction to the shattering of their life that this illness represents. When a person enters a hospital, they have to accept or struggle to accept that they are handing over their body and well-being to the care of the medical staff. Even when fully informed, patients struggle with being able to understand and grapple with the realization that their bodies have gone haywire, that the illusion that they can control a disease process is a myth, and that they are essentially powerless to control what is happening to them.

Social workers often must help patients exercise as much control over their diagnostic workup and treatment as they can manage (Furstenberg & Olson, 1984). This is done by encouraging and supporting patients' efforts to communicate with physicians and other health care staff. The social worker also can help facilitate discussions of sensitive matters between patients and physicians; patients may be reticent to bring up issues or concerns out of fear that their care will be compromised. Social workers can ease such fears by bridging the gap between patients and medical staff and by providing information to both patients and families to help reacquire a much-needed sense of control over medical decisions (Sternberg, 1992).

As hospitalizations lengthen or become more frequent, the patient may need to access a broader range of social work services, such as financial assistance, legal services, housing, home health care, long-term care, hospice, childcare, transportation, and supportive counseling. The role of the social worker in each of these areas may differ, but often the social worker is needed to make the initial contact on behalf of the patient and facilitate access to services. It is essential, especially in working with this population, for the social worker to be knowledgeable about community services, to know the established help programs, and to be creative in finding solutions to patient problems.

Babcock (1998a) outlines what social workers need to know about basic concrete services to be effective with the HIV/AIDS patient:

What resources are available in the community for providing AIDS-sensitive support?

Where is the nearest AIDS service organization and what resources can it provide to someone in the community?

What can the state Department of Health offer? Local home care? Financial assistance?

Does the patient's insurance have HIV case management services?

For the patient, each hospitalization provokes a predictable crisis: a time of fear, vulnerability, having to face his or her own mortality, having to answer numerous questions about transmission and behavior, and fear that current treatment is not working. What social workers need to remember when working with the patient at this time is that basic social work values apply: respect the worth of each individual while working with a mindset of nonjudgmental acceptance. "Our best help is often that of listening to the patient (and caregivers) and then clarifying for the team what is the patient's/family's experience of the particular phase of the illness" (Babcock, 1998a, p. 92).

In many hospitals, the social worker's primary goal is discharge planning. Because of the imposed time constraints, discharge planning is often viewed as planned short-term intervention. As such, the social worker, upon admission and assessment, begins to develop a care plan to address the specific needs of the patient. The care plan must include answers to the following: What level of care does the patient need and what options exist to provide that care? Is the patient's judgment impaired? Can the patient make his or her own decisions? Does the patient need drug rehabilitation assistance? (Babcock, 1992). Armed with answers to these and other questions, the social worker is better able to construct a safe and well-researched discharge care plan.

The social worker in the HIV/AIDS unit may have to overcome internal emotional barriers in order to be fully effective. The most effective social workers are able to fully accept the patient, regardless of history and behavior and are able to look for the patient's strengths. The social worker offers respect for the patient's ability to draw upon these reserves, is prepared to advocate for the patient and his or her needs, is able to move beyond the stereotypes and see the patient as a person, and can tolerate the level of fear and self-recrimination often voiced by the patient.

Working with the families of AIDS patients may be as important as working directly with the patient. What makes this aspect of the work crucial is that in most cases, the support of the family is integral to the illness trajectory for the patient. Most HIV patients ultimately need a lot of personal care to manage their lives. Sometimes social worker intervention is needed to mobilize the family to be able to care for the patient. Under the most reasonable of circumstances, family conflicts are normal, but in the case of HIV/AIDS, an illness that is so emotionally laden, conflicts and stress often run high. Families need encouragement and support to express hurt, anger, and fear; the social worker needs to help families identify their conflicting emotions and help them make sense of their reality and begin to establish some control over their situation (Sternberg, 1992).

In summary, the social worker's role within the hospital setting focuses on the psychosocial aspects of AIDS and involves making attempts to minimize the negative impact of AIDS on the patient and family. This can be facilitated by linking the patient with available community resources while maintaining a supportive role that respects the uniqueness of each individual and looks beyond the cause of the illness toward best-care outcomes.

SOCIAL WORKER COMMENTS

Fourteen inpatient HIV/AIDS social workers agreed to be interviewed. Those who had been doing the work for several years were better able to comment on the impact of the newer drug regimens and how they have changed the AIDS experience. Several of these social workers spoke of the fact that patients are living longer and, although they are in and out of the hospital with some frequency, are better able to survive the acute situations. In addition, the social workers now have longer term relationships with many patients and caregivers, seeing them through several hospitalizations.

Caseloads were very high in these units, but this may be misleading because of the continuum of care orientation. This means the patient is followed from inpatient to outpatient. If a patient is followed through the hospital, he or she can be treated as long as possible as an outpatient and is admitted to the inpatient service while still being tracked by the same social worker. Therefore, when an inpatient social worker speaks of a caseload of 200, most of these patients are outpatients and only fall under the social worker's direct care when admitted for an acute episode. Nevertheless, inpatient units were always full, with a typical inpatient caseload of 15 to 30 patients.

When patients are admitted for the first time, the social workers are expected to do an initial assessment and convey their findings to the unit team. Each of the social workers, from five different hospitals, spoke of the strength of the unit and the necessity of its cohesion. All social workers felt valued as team members and felt that the patients benefited from the strength of the team. "If someone works with AIDS, they want to be there and they are very devoted," commented one social worker. Burnout does happen, however, and the most common causes, as reported by the social workers, are "... too many cases, too much death, or too many patients who undermine our efforts." The undermining takes several forms: noncompliance with medications, medical treatments, or appointments, resumption of drug use, and general lack of caring for the self. The theme of frustration over treatment compliance was noted by all interviewed. "I become frustrated when patients will not cooperate or collaborate with the team. What they don't realize is if they have a degree of self-control, they can be well." An additional frustration for these social workers was nonavailability of resources, with the most pressing need identified as housing.

Social work tasks, uniformly identified by those interviewed, were initial assessments, some time to do supportive counseling with both patients and caregivers, lots of education, creation of care plans, and a lot of direct discussion about sexual practices, drug use, and high-risk behavior. The general feeling was that the work had to focus on here-and-now issues to help the patient avoid more serious medical situations; motivational interviewing, highlighting strengths, was often used. In direct work with the patients, being nonjudgmental was seen as essential. "Patients pick up on judgmental attitudes and are very sensitive to them. They sometimes feel that they could have prevented their infection with the virus and they need social workers to understand their dilemma and be sympathetic."

A frequent situation that emerged for the social workers, especially with patients admitted for their first opportunistic infection (signaling full-blown AIDS), was the question of disclosure. It is often difficult for patients to accept that they have converted from HIV to AIDS and then to feel the burden of whether and how to disclose to family, children, partners, and others. It is not unusual for social workers to be asked to help in these situations and often they are present when the disclosure is made. Most of the workers reported this is a difficult part of practice.

Death was a constant on the units. The less experienced social workers were more affected by the losses. What seemed common was the reaction of one social worker, who said, "I feel each loss and often will be there when the death occurs. I do my best to help the patient. For me, though, there is no time to process the loss and to react to it, as the needs of the other patients must be managed." "As the years have passed," commented a social worker who has been engaged in the work since the beginning of the epidemic, "I am less and less affected. I am here to do whatever I can do at the moment, but when the time is up, it is up. I do struggle with those patients I have known a long time, but others will come in and die, and I accept the death easily."

In defining their role and function, one social worker stated, "I do a little bit of everything: HIV education, medication adherence counseling, crisis intervention, concrete services. I get involved with many things." To this list, some of the workers added supportive counseling around coping with the illness. As one worker noted, "I try to give patients hope, especially the newly diagnosed. I have to tell the patients that they can be well for a very long time but that they will have to take many medications and they have to adhere to certain medical regimens very strictly. The problem is that many of the patients say they will adhere to their treatment plans, but life intrudes and they sabotage themselves."

In working with partners and family members, the social workers made themselves available as often as time permitted to educate and keep them informed about the patient's condition. But sometimes, the family was uncooperative and blamed the patient. In these circumstances, one social worker said, "We have to intervene to protect the patient, who is usually feeling self-blame even without the family. I will often tell the family that they have to move on and begin dealing with what is, and not what could have been. I know that these are just words, but there is not much else to do. I will encourage dialogue and releasing of emotions, but the reality is that the patient's life has changed with the diagnosis and everyone has to start dealing with it."

In general, the workers interviewed felt a kinship toward their patients and their struggles. Perhaps more so than on any other medical unit, a level of dedication to the patient was needed for the workers to sustain some of the frustrations encountered daily. These frustrations included not only patient behaviors, but also the recalcitrance of the medical system, with limited resources and options for caring for the patients, and sometimes frustrating behaviors from family members.

Despite their frustrations — with the patients, the system, and society (and its tendency to blame the victim) — the social workers gained satisfaction in being able to intervene and do something positive for the patients. "In working with these patients, I feel that I am touching a part of my own humanity as I help another." "When I touch another life, I know that the work is meaningful. This disease has killed so many, and if I can help to fight that and keep the spirits up of one who has it, I go home at night and feel that my work and my life are meaningful."

10

SOCIAL WORK IN THE REHABILITATION UNIT

ABOUT HOSPITAL REHABILITATION

Patients who have been treated for a given medical condition and need additional rehabilitation before they can be transferred home or to a long-term care facility utilize the rehabilitation unit in a hospital. The goal of a rehabilitation unit is to restore patients to their former capacity of functioning. Patients placed on the unit may have a variety of illnesses, but the three main types are stroke, spinal cord injury, and traumatic brain injury. A brief overview of these three illnesses and the psychosocial impact on both patient and family follow. Although these are three distinct disabling illnesses, a good deal of overlap exists among the conditions and the impact of the medical conditions on the patient and family.

STROKE

According to the American Heart Association (2004), every 45 seconds someone in the United States has a stroke. A stroke is a sudden impairment of brain function. On average, someone dies from stroke every 3 minutes, with stroke accounting for 1 of every 15 deaths in the United States in 2001. A stroke creates potential for damage within the brain. The two main categories of stroke — hemorrhage and ischemia — are diametrically opposite conditions. Too much blood within the closed cranial area characterizes hemorrhage whereas ischemia is characterized by too little blood to supply an adequate amount of oxygen and nutrients to a part of the brain.

Each year about 700,000 people in the United States experience a new or recurrent stroke, with men's stroke incidence rates 1.25 times greater than women's. African Americans have an overall stroke incidence that is 70% greater than Caucasians. This higher incidence is caused by the prevalence of high blood pressure in African Americans hypothesized to occur because of diet. Rates of stroke increase with age, history of heart disease or diabetes, cocaine use, and bleeding disorders (Caplan, 2000).

Heavy smokers and people with high blood pressure have an increased risk of stroke, whereas those who are physically active have a decreased risk; this is true across all racial, gender, and age lines. The aftermath of stroke may be life altering and is the leading cause of serious, long-term disability in the United States. In 1999, more than one million American adults reported difficulty with functional limitations, activities of daily living, and other impairments resulting from stroke. In 2004, the estimated direct and indirect cost of stroke was $53.6 billion, with the largest component of acute care costs going toward hospital room care, medical management, and diagnostic costs (American Heart Association, 2004).

The course of the stroke can be relatively fleeting in that the effects of the damage to the brain may be short lived and the patient recovers sometimes within hours or days. A more serious clinical picture occurs with permanent damage to the brain resulting in paralysis of limbs, speech impairment, facial paralysis, and damage to other parts of the brain involved in thought and muscle control. Muscle strength, range of motion, and gross mobility are frequently affected. In the more serious cases, a stroke often results in a loss of functional independence. Stroke can alter the individual's capacity for role functioning and "can render untenable a self-concept grounded in a sense of autonomy and mastery" (Palmer & Glass, 2003, p. 256). Most stroke survivors are eventually able to resume their lives in their communities, but for those who have had a crippling stroke, a difficult and demanding rehabilitative challenge awaits.

Patient adjustment to stroke cannot be understood in isolation because "… changes occur not only in the physical and cognitive capacities of the stroke survivor but also in the broader pattern of social relations in the family. Thus, stroke brings about a psychosocial transition that requires the reconstruction of patterns of family functioning to accommodate both the temporary and permanent changes that are caused by the stroke" (Palmer & Glass, 2003, p. 258). Between

40 and 60% of people who have had a stroke have residual deficits that require assistance with activities of daily living. For example, paralysis of one side of the body can make walking and movement difficult; they might have difficulty speaking or swallowing; they might struggle to manage self-care activities. These, often permanent, deficits resulting from the stroke mean that patients and caregivers are linked in the recovery and transition period.

For the severely impacted stroke survivor, major physical and emotional transitions occur, especially if residual and permanent physical limitation exist. From functional to limited, from adept to reliant, and from independent to dependent — these mark the changes for the patient. Caregivers face numerous shifts and challenges as caregiving responsibilities and burdens emerge. Facing significant changes in social, economic, personal, sexual, and emotional realms of their life, many caregivers are prone to depression. Because family members provide 80% of home care for stroke patients, it is not surprising that, over time, caregivers tend to develop a declining quality of life, including depressive behavior and deteriorating general health and life satisfaction (Grant, Elliot, Newman-Giber, & Bartolucci, 2001).

The struggle for both patient and caregiver revolves around the need to create a balance between providing care and assistance while encouraging the stroke victim to regain independence. Stroke survivors may require some degree of help with self-care while being encouraged by family members to become more self-sufficient, as they learn a whole new way to navigate and negotiate their lives. They often need support to establish a pattern of accommodation to the consequences of the stroke (Palmer & Glass, 2003, p. 257). Purk and Richardson (1994) investigated the interrelationship of care receivers (husbands) and caregivers (wives), finding that the morale of care-receiving patients had a positive effect on caregiver morale and vice versa.

SPINAL CORD INJURY

The onset of spinal cord injury (SCI) is a major stressful event, often the result of a traumatic accident. Approximately 247,000 people in the United States live with spinal cord injuries, with 7,800 new injuries occurring each year. SCI primarily affects young adult males. Since 2000, the average age at injury has been 33.4 years; 82% of injuries are sustained by males. Motor vehicle crashes account for 44% of reported SCI cases; acts of violence (primarily gunshot wounds), 24%; falls, 22%; and recreational sporting activities account for the rest. Fifty-three percent of SCI patients are single when injured. Life expectancies for persons with SCI continue to increase but are still somewhat below life expectancies for those with no SCI.

Since 1988, 45% of all SCIs have resulted in complete paralysis, 55% incomplete. Complete paralysis means total loss of sensation and function below the injury level; incomplete injuries result in partial loss. Less than 1% of people who sustain spinal cord injuries fully recover, although all can improve from the initial diagnosis. The most common descriptors of SCI are quadriplegia (limited or no use of arms and legs) and paraplegia (use of arms but little or no use of legs). People with SCI may experience permanent paralysis and altered bowel, bladder, and sexual functioning. They may also deal with both physical distress (e.g., pressure ulcers, urinary tract infections, and chronic pain) and psychological distress (e.g., physical and attitudinal barriers in society) for the rest of their lives (Weaver, Guihan, Pape, Legro, & Collins, 2001).

Overall, 85% of SCI patients who survive the first 24 hours are still alive 10 years later. Mortality rates are significantly higher during the first year after injury than during subsequent years, particularly for severely injured persons. Respiratory ailment is the leading cause of death (National Spinal Cord Injury Association, 2004).

The emotional impact of spinal cord injury is significant and affects how patients see themselves and their situation. Subjective well-being (SWB) is an individual's evaluative reaction to his or her life. The concept can be separated into affective or cognitive aspects. The affective aspect reflects positive emotions such as joy and pleasure and negative emotions such as anxiety and sadness. The cognitive aspect reflects general life satisfaction (Fuhrer, 1996). The SWB concept has been applied to the field of spinal cord injury. Current theories about adjustment to SCI and SWB note that after the initial trauma of SCI, some individuals exhibit depressive symptoms that warrant a diagnosis of clinical depression whereas others are able to adjust to their disability in a relatively short time. The difference in SWB among people with SCI appears to be related to demographic and psychosocial factors (Livneh & Antonak, 1997). People who have acquired a SCI at a younger age, have a higher level of education and income, are married, and have a job, tend to have higher levels of SWB than those who acquired the disability at an older age, had less education and income, were divorced or separated, and did not have a job (Boschen, 1996; Chase, Cornille, & English, 2000; Crewe & Krause, 1991; Krause & Dawis, 1992).

In terms of the impact of psychosocial factors on SWB, perceived social support and self-efficacy beliefs (person's judgment about his or her ability to perform certain tasks and activities) were closely related to SWB. In research by Hampton (2004), results of interviews with 127 individuals with SCI demonstrated that gender was not a factor in SWB and that people with SCI have different levels of SWB. These differences related to the level of the client's general self-efficacy beliefs, perceived social support, perceived health, and age at injury.

In dynamics similar to those in families in which a member has had a stroke, the family members of a spinal cord survivor face a number of adjustments and challenges. As noted by Meade and her colleagues, "[Family members] are disrupted not only by the stress of injury, but also by the necessity of taking on new and unfamiliar responsibilities" (Meade, Taylor, Kreutzer, Marwitz, & Vera, 2004, p. 151). In several research studies, one of the most frequently mentioned needs of family members was information regarding the patient's condition and prognosis, assurance regarding quality of care, and emotional support (Hart, 1981; Stanton, 1984). Stanton (1984) added to this list: demonstrated concern for the patient by the rehabilitation unit, honest and informed communication about patient treatment, care, and progress, reassurance from staff, need for a consistent contact person, need for someone to talk to, and the ability to visit the patient whenever desired. In the short run, during hospitalization and rehabilitation, the family needs to be advised on numerous dimensions, including the prospect for recovery and the options for care that exist outside of the hospital or rehab unit. Many resources in the community must be mobilized to help the patient and family adjust to a new and altered lifestyle and pace of life and to potential economic concerns.

TRAUMATIC BRAIN INJURY

Traumatic brain injury (TBI) is an injury to the brain caused by impact (e.g., a fall or car accident), internal damage (e.g., a gunshot or surgical intervention), or loss of oxygen. Traumatic brain injury results from a trauma imposed from without. Although some aspects of TBI are similar to a stroke, a stroke is an internal event that disrupts the brain in specific ways. Traumatic brain injury can be focal (confined to one area of the brain) or diffuse (involving more than one area of the brain). Symptoms of a TBI may include seizures, headache, nausea, confusion, and other emotional and behavioral problems. TBIs contribute to a substantial number of deaths and cases of permanent disability annually. Each year in the United States an estimated 1.4 million people sustain a TBI. Of those, 230,000 are hospitalized and survive, which is 20 times the number of hospitalizations for spinal cord injury. Approximately 50,000 people die from TBI and 80,000 to 90,000 people experience the onset of long-term disability associated with TBI. Not all TBIs are serious; approximately 75% are concussions or other forms of mild injury.

At least 5.3 million Americans (2% of the U.S. population) currently live with disabilities resulting from TBI (Centers for Disease Control [CDC], 2004b). African Americans and other people of color have higher TBI incidence than Caucasians, and TBI rates are lower for people with some college experience compared with those with only a high school education. TBI increases as socioeconomic status decreases (Cunningham et al., 1999). These statistics reflect the lower incidence of violence among people with more education and higher socioeconomic status or advantage.

Depending on the severity and amount of injury, TBI can cause problems with cognition (concentration, memory, judgment, mood), movement (strength, coordination, balance), sensation (touch, vision), and emotions (instability, impulsivity). TBI can also cause seizure disorders such as epilepsy. TBI affects males at twice the rate of females, with those ages 15 to 24 at highest risk. In the more debilitating TBIs, those that are life altering and carry severe consequences for the survivor, the cost of care averages $1,000 per day for rehabilitation, with the lifetime cost for one person surviving a severe TBI totaling as much as $4.5 million (CDC, 2004b).

For the patient, the experience of a mild TBI (a concussion, blow to the head, etc.) can be brief, requiring only rest and monitoring to be certain that the extent of injury is contained and that no symptoms of trauma occur. Immediate treatment for more serious injuries include surgery to control bleeding in and around the brain, monitoring and controlling intracranial pressure, ensuring adequate blood flow to the brain, and treating the body for other injuries and infection.

TBI severity is classified as mild, moderate, or severe. The diagnosis is based on depth and length of coma after the injury, duration of post-traumatic amnesia, neuroimaging, electrophysiological studies, and measures of brain stem function. As severity levels increase, the range and extent of possible long-term physical, cognitive, and psychosocial impairments increase (Degeneffe, 2001).

Medical staff routinely use the Glasgow Coma Scale to rate the extent of injury and chances of recovery. The scale involves testing for three patient responses: eye opening, verbal responses, and motor responses (National Institute of Neurological Disorders and Stroke, 2004). Upon admission to a hospital, patients need immediate assessment to stabilize them and determine a course of treatment, whether it is surgery or medications designed to shrink the swelling in the brain to avoid serious damage. Patients who are severely injured may go through a period of time in which they are unable to speak, think, or communicate meaningfully. As the injury to the brain starts to resolve, some of the initial damage may be reversed. If the symptoms prevail, the course of treatment and rehabilitation begins; treatment may be short term or lifelong. Patient adjustment to the long-term impact is similar to that with stroke or spinal cord injury, with the propensity toward depression, diminished self-esteem, and anxiety based on increased dependency and care needs as an altered lifestyle evolves.

For the patient, severe traumatic brain injury interrupts personal development and life plans and interferes with career goals, relationships, and identity. Post-injury life is often characterized by problems of daily survival while dealing with body parts that no longer respond, having difficulty in making oneself understood, and learning how to manage with an unreliable brain, sometimes with wildly ranging emotions. Cognitive and behavioral impairments are the greatest compromisers of patient quality of life, because the personality changes that occur in the majority of cases do not necessarily improve over time (Rowlands, 2001).

The family struggles along with the patient, because so much of what happens for the patient reverberates with and affects the family. Because most TBI survivors live with their families, family members becomes acutely aware of the skills that have been lost and the activities patients can no longer perform by themselves. "Families of people with TBI face numerous challenges and stresses in providing care. They face living with and providing care for a person that in many ways is different from who he or she was before the injury. The injured family member may demonstrate a variety of physical and behavioral care needs that make family caregiving especially stressful and burdensome" (Degeneffe, 2001, p. 260).

In addition, family caregivers frequently face levels of stress and burden that do not lessen over time and in some instances increase over time. For the family, especially the parents, the initial offerings of social and tangible support begin to decrease as the long-term, lifelong nature of the resulting disability manifests. Caring for the patient may limit opportunities for the caregiver to develop new relationships and affect the social and economic fabric of the family (Rowlands, 2001). Domestic partners of people with TBI in committed, intimate relationships face the potential of living with someone who has changed dramatically since the injury. Spouse caregivers and partners face an adjustment to their relationship with the TBI patient in which they have to make decisions on behalf of their injured spouse or partner and, in the event there are children, adjust to a single-parent status, because the injured spouse or partner may be unable to perform traditional roles. Siblings of those with TBI may feel neglected in deference to the care of the injured person. In summary, the whole family system and the relationships and roles within the family are dramatically altered in the event of a severe TBI, especially if extended care is needed (Degeneffe, 2001).

One of the strategies that has been identified as helpful to families of hospitalized TBI patients is having as much information as possible about the patient's current and future situation. Family members appreciate professional guidance and medical care information, with honest answers to questions and information on physical problems. Because TBIs are sudden and tend to result from accidents, family members generally are totally unprepared for this episode and are uninformed about what to expect and how to proceed (Kreutzer, Serio, & Berquist, 1994).

PSYCHOSOCIAL ADAPTATION TO DISABILITY

There are many ways to understand the psychosocial adaptation to disability. Underlying each approach is the recognition that the disabling condition causes mild to profound changes in affected individuals and the people who care for and live with them. In each of the illnesses described previously — stroke, spinal cord injury, and traumatic brain injury — and others, the impact on both patients and families can be permanently life altering and profound. Problems of psychosocial adjustment manifest in areas of depression, stress, self-esteem, and social connectedness (Nosek & Hughes, 2003).

Livneh and Antonak (1997) theorized that psychosocial adaptation to disability flows in a series of reactions, unfolding in eight stages: shock, anxiety, denial, depression, internalized anger, externalized hostility, acknowledgment, and finally acceptance or adjustment. These stages are reminiscent of the stages outlined by Elisabeth Kübler-Ross (1969), who described a terminally ill patient's stage preparation for death; in a way, the disabling impact of permanent disability resonates as a death of hope, plans, and expectations about life. The eight stages are grouped into three clusters: (a) earlier reactions (shock, anxiety, denial); (b) intermediate reactions (depression, anger, hostility); and (c) later reactions (acknowledgment and acceptance). In Livneh and Antonak's view, each of these stages and clusters is further affected by the sociodemographic characteristics of the individual, the personality attributes, and the physical and social environment.

Some reject the stage theories in favor of an analysis of variables that affect the patient and family and enhance or defeat the psychosocial recovery process. Others look primarily at the functionality of the individual as the greatest predictor of psychosocial adjustment, with those who have greater functionality thought to be less depression prone and better able to handle the adjustment process. Coping style is another variable that has been proffered as primary in the psychosocial adjustment process (Livneh & Wilson, 2003). Research by Eide and Roysamb (2002) with 1,391 people with disabilities showed that the level of difficulty with performing and participating in daily life activities led to or contributed to increased psychosocial problems, which influenced the outcome and pace of the rehabilitation process. Each theory of adaptation has merit. From a social work perspective, an understanding of the family's impact during the recovery and rehabilitation stage is central to any conceptual framework.

THE REHABILITATION UNIT SOCIAL WORKER

The social worker is in a pivotal position on the rehabilitation unit, providing much-needed services for the patient and family. Initially, the family and patient needs involve counseling to help them adjust to the reality of the injury and its subsequent effects on the family system. Long-term care services focus on supporting families for the move of the injured person from the hospital back into the home or to a rehabilitation facility (Hosack & Rocchio, 1995).

The role of the social worker in an inpatient rehabilitation setting has been described as the "four A's": (a) *anticipate* the patient's needs, through an assessment of the patient's psychosocial functioning and through a biopsychosocial orientation to care that includes the patient and family; (b) *answer* patient and family questions and provide education through supportive counseling, information, and referral to community resources; (c) *advocate* by identifying gaps in service and promoting the patient and family's ability to become their own advocates; and (d) *alleviate* patient and family fears by providing counseling to help the family cope with the illness or disability (Flaherty, 2004). This role definition applies to the three illnesses described in this chapter and to any other patient needing care in a rehab unit (Flaherty, 2004).

An overriding orientation to the social worker's practice employs a collaborative or generalist as well as a family systems approach. The collaborative approach to working with those who are disabled and in need of long-term rehabilitation is founded on the fact that people with disabilities are people first and disabled second. They are neither their diagnoses nor their conditions. In many instances, the services a disabled person may need from a social worker may not be disability related, including emotional support, career counseling, addiction counseling, financial advice, and so forth. From the generalist perspective, practice principles are grounded in support for self-determination and empowerment and guided by the need to assist the individual toward greater participation in their own recovery (Gilson, Bricout, & Baskind, 1998). From the orientation provided by a family systems perspective, the patient in not only the one who has sustained an injury; the 'patient' is the injured survivor and the family. The family is the focal point of intervention and every intervention validates the family's central role in the care of the patient. The social worker is expected to form a therapeutic alliance with the family that can facilitate their ability to better communicate with medical professionals, anticipate and solve psychosocial problems, and develop a sense of confidence in caregiving (Palmer & Glass, 2003).

Another aspect of the social work role is to encourage and facilitate opportunities for social support for the family and patient. By accessing community resources or offering groups in the hospital setting, the social worker helps provide needed social and peer support so vital to the rehabilitation experience.

A crucially important role for the social worker is that of educator. Family members highly value information from professionals relating to the patient's care, physical problems, and cognitive difficulties; the information needs to be delivered in honest, understandable terms (Meade et al., 2004). Often, the social worker is the most accessible member of the health care team and is able to "translate" the medical jargon into more usable and familiar language for the patient and family.

In dealing with the patient, the social worker should make an effort to identify areas in which the patient lacks confidence and help develop interventions to increase confidence in the rehabilitation process. This enhancement can be facilitated by helping clients retrieve past successful coping experiences that have been overlooked or unidentified, thus building successful coping strategies, providing positive reinforcement, using role models, and providing appropriate counseling to reduce negative feelings (Hampton, 2004).

SOCIAL WORKER COMMENTS

Ten social workers contributed their thoughts and reactions about their work on the rehab unit in their hospital. Units varied from hospital to hospital with caseloads that ranged from 21 to 36 patients. On each unit, patients received physical therapy for 3 to 4 hours per day and occupational therapy as warranted. Unlike units in which shorter stays are the norm, the rehab floor has patients for weeks at a time and sometimes up to 2 months, awaiting stabilization to return home or for transfer to a long-term rehabilitation facility.

The major social work responsibility articulated by the social workers was discharge planning. Unlike shorter term hospitalizations, resources for patients with disabilities must be in place and caregivers must be educated about the care needs of the disabled person; the social worker has to be assured that the patient is returning to a safe home in which his or her needs can be adequately met. Because the social worker has the time to get to know the patient, counseling opportunities present themselves, often around issues of adjustment. The most frequent lament of the patient, as described by several of the social workers, is depression over not being able to function as before. One social worker explained that, during down time, she will "just sit with a patient and wait for something to come up." "One patient," she explained, "stated that part of his body had died (due to a stroke at age 29) and was gone and he didn't know how he would be able to deal with his very uncertain future." The needs of the patient are directly fused with the family, and most social workers felt that an understanding of family dynamics was essential to helping the patient. The general observation was that if a family was dysfunctional before the accident or illness, then they would be just as dysfunctional afterward. The displacement of anger by the family onto the social workers was mentioned by several, who noted that the family's anger at the patient and hospital system were pronounced and often got in the way of being able to work smoothly with the family. One of the challenges for the social workers was to be able to absorb this displaced emotion and not respond to it other than to recognize it as a necessary part of the reactions of the family.

Assessment by the social worker is ongoing in the rehab unit. Initially, it is used to understand the patient: who were they before the illness, what were their activities, and what will change because of this illness or disability? As time goes on and the rate of improvement is becoming known, the social worker assesses the capacity of the family to care for the injured patient and the scope of disability to determine what services will be needed to assist and care for the patient when he or she leaves the hospital. At each stage, the social worker strives "to strengthen whatever coping mechanisms there are and to do as much supportive work as possible."

Treatment issues, as defined by the social workers, differed according to the age of the patient. "The younger patients, under 35, are eager to get back to their lives and to begin working toward rehabilitation goals. The older folks have a harder time." Several workers noted that they have internal struggles regarding those who have had disabling accidents or conditions that could have been prevented. "It is maddening to look at an 18-year-old male who will be forever unable to walk because he didn't want to wear a helmet when on his motorcycle. Or to see the total crippling effects of a stroke, especially in someone who has never taken care of himself."

An aspect of the work that has not been explored in the literature involves forensics for the rehab unit social worker. On occasion, when a patient is admitted to the rehab unit, the social worker will suspect abuse or other violence has occurred. An example of this, according to one worker, involved a female rehab patient who had been living in a shelter. Her abusive boyfriend had pushed her down a flight of stairs, causing traumatic brain injury and several fractured bones. The social worker contacted protective services on behalf of the patient, police were involved, and the boyfriend was arrested. The social worker must be attuned to the possibility of forensic situations because falls or other injuries may be caused by domestic violence or other forms of violent behavior.

The two most difficult aspects of the work, as identified by those interviewed, involved young people who had sustained serious and crippling injuries and thus had their lives ruined and working with unhelpful, unresponsive families who often worked against the well-being of the patient. Some of the difficulties on the unit are shared; both of the hospitals where social workers were interviewed work with a team approach.

The conflicts and emotional responses of the workers who were interviewed ranged from "being more conscious of how suddenly a life can change" to "being very sensitive to the limitations of others" and "an appreciation of how randomly things happen." A practice concern that was raised by one worker involved how much information a patient or family member should be told. The worker struggled with whether a patient should be told the seriousness of his or her injury and the grim prognosis for full recovery and whether having this knowledge depresses the patient and makes the rehabilitation process more complex.

One worker said that she thrives "on the stress of the unit. The work is so intense and the potential to see people change makes it exhilarating!" Even a negative was turned into a positive, as one worker said,

"I love fighting with the insurance companies who routinely turn down our requests for services. It gets my blood going and I feel so good when I finally succeed."

One worker felt, "I will never be the same person again, after having worked on this floor (rehab unit). I feel that I am doing exactly what I am supposed to be doing. I believe that I am here to open doors for my patients and help them through the door into the next chapter of their life — a life that is now marked by a changed physical reality. It is scary and exciting at the same time."

11

THE SOCIAL WORKER IN THE BURN UNIT

ABOUT BURNS

Each year in the United States, 1.1 million burn injuries require medical attention; approximately 50,000 of these require hospitalization, with 20,000 patients having major burns involving at least 25% of their total body surface. In addition, someone dies in a fire every 2 hours, and someone is injured due to a burn every 23 minutes (Karter, 2001); up to 10,000 people in the United States die every year of burn-related infections (Centers for Disease Control [CDC], 2004a). Burn injuries rank fifth among major causes of death among persons 15 to 55 years old (CDC, 1999).

Most burn victims are taken to hospitals for specialized treatment. About half of the total number of burn victims go to one of 125 specialized burn treatment centers across the United States and the rest go to the nation's 5,000 other hospitals. Each burn center averages 200 admissions per year, other hospitals less than 5 (American Burn Association [ABA], 2002). Most burn centers employ a multidisciplinary approach to patient care that includes physicians and nurses who have special training in burn care as well as social workers and psychologists. Palliative care specialists are frequently dispatched to help manage the pain of the more severe burn cases.

Burns are described in terms of degree and size. Burn injuries range from minor sunburns to major thermal injuries. First-degree burns involve the top layer of skin and are not particularly serious. A first-degree burn would be sunburn. This type of burn is red and hot, but there is no blistering or swelling. Second-degree burns involve the first two layers of skin. The skin is light red and blistery, somewhat swollen, and moist and oozing. The pain is severe and often these burns will require medical attention. Third-degree burns involve all layers of skin. The burn destroys the nerves and the blood vessels of the skin. Initially there is little pain; the burn penetrates the entire thickness of the skin and permanently destroys tissue. These burns require immediate and specialized care and surgical repair. Fourth-degree burns go through all layers of skin and down into the muscle and bone. Although they look like third-degree burns, they are more serious and do great harm to the body structure. Oddly, because the nerves are burned, there is little pain with this degree of burn.

The size of a burn injury is scaled according to the amount of body surface that has been burned — termed the total body surface area (TBSA). The average size of a burn injury admitted to a burn center is about 14% TBSA; burns of 10% TBSA or less account for 54% of burn center admissions because they are usually serious and demand medical attention. About 6% of people admitted to burn centers do not survive; most of them have also suffered severe smoke inhalation injury (ABA, 2002). Advances in medical management of burns have dramatically decreased mortality rates from burn injuries. Critical care medicine, advances in infection control techniques, and the development of new and more powerful antibiotics have helped decrease the number of deaths due to infection. These and other strides have made burn injuries as large as 80% TBSA survivable and have allowed children with burns as large as 50% a good chance for survival (Danks, 2003).

Data from the American Burn Association (2002), accumulated over a 28-year period in which 49 hospitals in Canada and the United States participated, documented more than 73,000 burn cases. Of these, 70% were male and the average patient was 30 years old. Infants accounted for 13% of cases and patients 60 years and older were 11%. In addition, the data showed that the three most common causes of burns were thermal (flame or fire), scalding, and contact. It is generally thought that about one third of all burn victims suffer physical or psychiatric disorders or alcohol or drug addiction prior to their injury (Williams & Griffiths, 1991). The problems faced by people with psychiatric disorders or addiction problems may lead them to be careless when handling matches, cigarettes, and so forth. Their judgment may be impaired by psychiatric disordered thinking or drugs or alcohol, putting them at greater risk in the presence of a fire.

THE PATIENT EXPERIENCE

What happens when a person is burned varies according to the depth of the burn, which depends on the degree of heat to which the person was exposed and the length of the exposure. The depth refers to how much damage has been done to tissue, muscle, and bone beneath the superficial layers of skin. The deeper the burn, the more serious and even lethal it is. Adult burn survivors not only face a painful and extensive physical recovery process but also are challenged to cope with losses in personal relationships, lifestyles, occupation, and personal identity. These losses can be compounded by social stigma if they have a disfiguring injury. The stigma and disfigurement can provoke self-esteem issues for burn survivors (Carter & Petro, 1998).

In Erving Goffman's remarkable book, *Stigma: Notes on the Management of Spoiled Identity* (1963), he comments on stigma as the public's attitude toward a person who possesses an attribute that falls short of society's expectations. The person with the attribute is reduced and is tainted. One category specifically mentioned as a target of stigma is people who have a physical deformity; the deformity referred to as an abomination of the body. The stigma felt by a burn victim emerges out of this conceptualization. Pallua, Kunsebeck, and Noah (2003) found an increase in depression among patients with burns to areas of the body that are normally exposed compared with patients whose burns are not easily visible. Patients with clearly apparent burn scars appear less frequently in public (Taal & Faber, 1998). Bernstein (1988) sums up the experience of the burn survivor, calling it "the social disorder that comes with disfigurement" (p. 5).

Survivors of severe burns face overwhelming issues of adjustment and multiple stressors during the recovery period. These issues may confront them for the rest of their lives. Treatment is often prolonged and painful, involving years of rehospitalization, skin grafting, and plastic and reconstructive surgery. Beyond the lengthy hospital stays, extended periods of treatment, and the surgeries, the dominant initial physical manifestation of a serious burn injury is pain. "The burn injury represents a severe trauma involving damage to body integrity, personal appearance, functioning, and psychological well-being" (Thornton & Battistel, 2001, p. 93).

A poignant result of third- and fourth-degree facial burns is the disfigurement that occurs when facial muscles have been damaged. When a burn damages nerves and muscle, it alters the communication system of the face by immobilizing facial expressions. In essence, due to the burn damage, the face has lost its signaling and response capacity; the face is no longer able to register emotion. This is a powerful and devastating outcome of burn injury (Bernstein, 1988).

On an emotional and more symbolic level, Gilboa (2001) describes the unique characteristics of the burn-injured person. She notes that on a more primitive level of thinking, "the skin has a concrete role in holding the different parts of the body together, uniting them into one unique whole. Without it, the body would be divided into parts and fall apart. Without the skin (or if the skin is seriously mutilated) one would break and there would be no healing. … The sense of invasion or leakage in the part (the skin) that holds, protects, unites, and distinguishes the individual as a unique human being is liable to create a whole set of feelings of disintegration and existential fear" (pp. 335–336). This interesting observation helps explain the depth of the despair and rage burn survivors experience.

Almost all who experience a serious burn deal with a sense of confusion, anxiety, depression, helplessness, anger, guilt, low self-esteem, low self-confidence, and other negative feelings that ultimately may lead to withdrawal and social isolation. These feelings may be accompanied by a deep sense of loss, a response not unlike mourning, and in some cases, the loss of the will to live (Bernstein, 1982; Tempereau, Grossman & Brones, 1989).

PHASES OF RECOVERY

Summers (1991) describes three phases of burn care recovery: resuscitative, acute, and rehabilitative. Each phase has both medical and psychosocial aspects. The resuscitative phase lasts from the time of injury until approximately 2 days hence. Medically, the goal is to prevent burn shock and preserve vital organ functioning; all activities are directed toward survival. The patient is usually emotionally in shock because most burns are unexpected events and most people have little or no experience with burns and the trajectory of the burn experience. Initially, the patient is oriented and alert, before major pain medication alters thinking and responses. Soon, anger, fear, and anxiety permeate the responses of the patient and family. In many cases the patient will begin to have nightmares and flashbacks. Within the first few days, as the patient becomes physiologically stable, deeper levels of anxiety may be perceived as the reality of the burn injury starts to set in. Support and ventilation by the patient and family are to be encouraged.

The acute care phase, phase 2, lasts until the burn wounds are closed. Medically, the goal is to prevent infection, maintain fluid balance, and control pain. During this phase, the patient may exhibit signs of emotional regression, with less control of emotions, flashbacks, anger, and anxiety being the most common. Pain is almost always a constant in this phase and the medications administered may alter the patient's responses. The patient may continue to exhibit depression, anxiety, and other psychological difficulties, including sleep disturbance, nightmares, flashbacks, and confusion (Rossi, Vila, Zago, & Ferreira, 2005).

In phase 2, patients should be supported in whatever efforts at independence and decision making they have initiated. Due to the burn, they might become tentative about moving in certain ways for fear of pain or injury to the burned area. They might not initiate certain activities (e.g., self-care, feeding), preferring to have someone care for them. This ultimately results in diminished degrees of independence; patients should be encouraged to do as many things as possible for themselves that will not result in pain. In terms of decision making, it may be difficult for patients to think beyond their most immediate needs for pain relief and care, but often decisions must be made about jobs, relating to other people, financial situations, for example, and patients, as often as possible, should be empowered to make decisions on their own behalf, thus retaining as much selfhood as possible during this very difficult time.

Phase 3 is the rehabilitative period, a time of recuperation and transition from hospital to home. Physically, this phase can last years as reconstructive and cosmetic surgeries attempt to correct residual defects. Psychologically, patients attempt to regain specific personal goals related to achieving as much preburn function as possible. Although self-confidence may begin to increase, depression is likely to surface as they realize the extent of their loss of functioning. Patients commonly express fears about reintegrating into their lives, wondering how they will be accepted by others and whether they will be able to assume some of their preburn responsibilities and activities.

PAIN MANAGEMENT

Beyond the lengthy hospital stays, extended periods of treatment, and the surgeries, the dominant physical manifestation of a serious burn injury is pain. Pain management is a central aspect of care for the seriously burned patient who is hospitalized. Burn pain is acute pain that may or may not be intermittent, because nerve endings are exposed and damaged by burning of the skin that encases them. In addition, as part of the management of the burn, debriding or the removal of the burned skin is part of daily hospital care. This procedure is done either at the bedside or in special tank rooms where the patient is bathed as well. This is especially painful and most patients require pain relief medication before and during this daily and sometimes twice daily procedure. Equally painful are changes of dressings and physiotherapy. There is a psychological aspect to pain control: survival and fear of disfigurement cause depression, and with depression there is less energy to tolerate pain (Noyes & Andreasen, 1971). The sense of severe stress, accompanied by anxiety and anger at the world, also leads to emotional exhaustion and reduced capacity to handle any discomfort.

THE FAMILY EXPERIENCE

In ways that parallel the experience of the burn patient, the family goes through many changes as a result of the injury. Upon hearing of the burn, the family is shocked because they did not expect it to occur, and the fear of the unknown and the uncertainty of the patient's condition is deeply unsettling. At the least, family members perceive the event as a threat to the family unit and are anxious about the survival of the patient. As knowledge as gained, as the family interfaces with the medical staff, as the extent of what has happened becomes known, the family begins to make the necessary initial adjustments to the situation.

Depending on the degree of burn, the patient may soon leave the hospital, but the more severely burned patient may well remain in the hospital for weeks. In this case, in the second phase of recovery, while the burns begin to close and are being treated, families are beginning to adjust to a new routine while facing uncertainties concerning the future role of the burn patient in the family and concurrent economic concerns.

During the rehabilitation period, the family becomes the source of much needed support as the patient begins the difficult task of reentering the world as a burn survivor. As departure from the hospital nears, the family, along with the patient, experiences a mixture of happiness and fear about what is to come next. Depending on the patient's ability to be self-sufficient, to be able to resume some aspects of self-care, this period for the family can be difficult but manageable. However, if the patient is seriously debilitated, is seriously depressed and disfigured, or is facing many operations and hospitalizations, the family may suffer with the patient over the long period of recuperation.

"The most consistently recognized contributing factor in determining quality of psychosocial adjustment seems to be the family support system" (Blakeney, Herndon, Desai, Beard, & Wales-Seale, 1988, p. 661). Family support can greatly influence the recovery of burn patients and must be considered a part of the treatment plan. It is through this network that the concerns and fears of acceptance, the burden of guilt, and the addressing of needs can be best managed. Burn patients are assailed with numerous psychological difficulties created by the burn. Social support that "envelops" the injured person —in both a concrete and metaphorical sense — enables coping. This can be forthcoming from family as well as friends. Research supports the view that patients given such support have been found to possess a higher body image, experience their body as more valuable, and display higher levels of self-esteem and lower depression relative to their counterparts who do not enjoy such levels of support (Orr, Reznikoff, & Smith, 1989). Burn units should encourage the presence of friends and family at the adult patient's bedside.

Social support is important not only during the acute phase, when stress and physical need is at its greatest, but throughout the rehabilitation and reentry period. Social support becomes an essential component of the healing when the patient has to encounter society, and when the signs of the injury are noticeable and may evoke reactions of revulsion (Gilboa, 2001).

Rossi et al. (2005) note that the changes stemming from the burn injury may be seen by the family in a negative way, i.e., the patient may be blamed for the burn, could have caused the burn inadvertently, may have provoked havoc in the family and financial ruin. If the family holds a negative view of the burn experience or the patient, they may have difficulty being as supportive as they need to be to help the patient. In some cases, sadly, the reaction of the family may not be helpful to the patient. This observation about family support suggests that the family needs as much support and counsel as the patient. For this reason, many burn units initiate individual and group services for family members to buttress them during the extended recovery period.

THE BURN UNIT SOCIAL WORKER

"Social workers and other helping professionals can play a key role in helping the burn survivor navigate the enormous adjustments and transitions that they have been catapulted into" (Williams, Davey, & Klock-Powell, 2003, p. 73). Social workers provide numerous services on a burn unit, from case management to discharge planning, as well as various counseling functions. From the systems perspective of social work, the burn victim is only one area of concern; the systems perspective acknowledges that the family and caregivers should be considered equally in the counseling and supportive activities offered by the social worker. In addition, the social worker needs to be knowledgeable about community resources and be able to collaborate and coordinate helping activities with the multidisciplinary team.

Typically, the social worker interventions include assessment of the patient to gain an understanding of the patient's prior physical and psychological health and coping skills, assessment of the availability of the family and other social networks, and evaluation of the economic situation. The information obtained during the assessment is fed back to the other members of the multidisciplinary team to ensure that all have a working understanding of the patient's situation. This assessment will underpin social work intervention during hospitalization and will be helpful in formulating a comprehensive discharge plan (Thornton & Battistel, 2001). Concrete concerns about insurance and benefit entitlements are also the domain of the social worker. Equally important are the necessary health care proxy and instructions for resuscitation and so forth, which must be obtained from the family to cover the possibility that a critical care moment could occur. These documents give direction to the medical team, and it behooves the social worker to make certain these documents have been filled out and filed.

In addressing the psychological needs of the patient and family, the primary role of the social worker is to help the individual ventilate their struggles, anger, frustrations, fears, and guilt. This form of supportive counseling is offered to the patient and the family on a fairly intensive level, with daily interaction as the norm. Families need support to cope with the multitude of changes wrought by the burn episode and to manage the altered appearance, functionality, and emotional state of the burn victim. The burn patient has to be helped to adjust to an appearance-conscious world that is not accepting of the visage of people with serious burns and to be shepherded through grieving the many losses associated with serious burn injuries (Miller, 2000). In preparing for discharge from the safe environment of the hospital, many patients will go through a crisis of confidence and revert to more emotional ways of relating, with angry outbursts more often seen at the beginning of the hospitalization, including regression and feelings of being incapable of managing event the simplest of tasks. In research involving 68 patients with burn injuries, the majority reported that the period in the hospital was difficult; but more than half reported that they experienced psychological difficulties on discharge from the hospital and in the months that followed (Wisely & Tarrier, 2001).

With particular awareness of the phases of recovery described by Summers (1991), the social worker is attentive to both patient and family members as they emerge from the shock wrought by the burn to the more concrete physical needs of the patient. In some cases, in which the burn destroyed a home, for example, the social worker must assist the family in finding shelter, thus advocating with various systems in the community. While in the hospital, the patient may have more contact with the social worker than with any other member of the professional team. And, the contact is of a nonphysical nature. In other words, both doctors and nurses interact with the patient over issues of medical care, whether it is literally doing some procedure in caring for the burn or discussing the medical situation with the patient. It is the social worker to whom patients will most likely turn to discuss what has happened to them.

Kleve and Robinson (1999), who studied 71 adults with burn injuries, reported that burn-injured people often do not want to overburden family members and found that they needed more specialized help to improve coping and to ventilate their fears and concerns. This research suggests two directions: that social workers provide more direct help to family members to give direction to their interaction with the patient, and that family sessions (which include the patient and family, working with the social worker) address the concerns of all parties to help ease emotional burdens. Of note in this research was the finding that levels of support, in particular during hospitalization, did not meet patient needs. In fact, many patients indicated that they felt the need for significantly more psychological help than was available. This felt need was expressed to exist at discharge and beyond, especially when the patient was struggling with issues over disfigurement.

Williams et al. (2003) eloquently describe the role of the social worker: "The skilled helper (social worker) is needed to listen without pity and tolerate hearing stories of indescribable loss as they provide needed support during a long grief process. By sharing their stories, burn survivors can simultaneously make sense of the enormity of their experience while allowing others to witness the reality of their ordeal" (p. 74).

Forensic Burns

Another social worker role is involvement in cases in which the cause of a burn is suspicious and might be the result of intentional injury. This is especially true when children have been burned. Each burn must be evaluated and the burn pattern assessed to determine whether intentional burning or child abuse has occurred. An example of a suspicious burn would be scald burns on a child's feet. This type of burn creates a classic "stocking feet" pattern, and although it could be that the child incurred this type of burn on his or her own, abuse must be explored or decided upon. The physicians and nurses are also involved in this area and often will alert the social worker of their suspicions. The social worker is often detailed to investigate the possibility of this type of burn situation and take the necessary actions to protect the child and prosecute the offending agent (Danks, 2003).

SOCIAL WORKER COMMENTS

Eight burn unit social workers were interviewed. Each worked in a designated burn unit center within a major medical center. Of the eight, seven spoke enthusiastically about their work and found it "compelling," "dynamic," and "very gratifying." The other social worker acknowledged that she had been on her unit for many years and that the changes brought by managed care had so altered her sense of the work that she was finding few rewards or satisfactions in the articulation of her job.

The social workers defined their role and function differentially based on whether the patient was going to be on the burn unit for a short time (i.e., had a less severe burn requiring less than 1 week's stay) or longer. For the short-term patients and families, the social workers performed a psychosocial assessment of the patient and family, leading to a fairly rapid discharge plan. Within the discharge planning role, the social worker made certain that appropriate care for the patient was available, arranging for home care when needed. Sometimes this was more difficult than expected, because some of the patients, as described in the preceding sections, either had active drug or alcohol abuse histories or pre-existing psychological problems. In some cases, patients were homeless. Each situation required that the social worker spend a substantial amount of time negotiating various systems to ensure safe discharge for the patient. In these instances, most of the social workers felt degrees of frustration because they did not have the time to provide the supportive counseling the patient needed to adjust well to the situation. Each of the social workers spoke of the pressures within their respective hospitals to discharge quickly, responding to managed care imperatives imposed on the hospital structure.

For the burn victims who are longer term, the social worker role was described in broader terms, including more work with the patients and caregivers. For the patients, the social workers often employed a crisis intervention approach, which allows patients to ventilate their emotions and express the rage, guilt, and frustration of their situation before dealing with the longer term consequences of their burn. Education of both patient and family or caregivers was also described within the role and function of the social worker. Few people have experience with burns, so the social worker's focus of education is to describe the trajectory and complexity of the medical experience, to normalize the experience as part of standard burn care, and to explain that there will be long stretches between periods of gain. Education regarding the emotional and psychological experience of burns is equally important, and the social worker needs to address this area as early as possible to prepare family members for the "emotional roller coaster" often seen in burn patients.

For all concerned, although the burn is an injury, it has to be seen both as an illness and as a chronic disease necessitating lifestyle changes and adjustments, especially if there is scarring and disfigurement. Burn patients may not be able to resume normal activity levels, may feel so physically changed that they do not want to engage with (i.e., be seen by) people, and may have periods of depression and withdrawal. As such, changes in the patients' levels of confidence and self-esteem, their ability to work and interact, their sense of their future, and their family and other relationships may have to be redefined. Some patients are in the hospital for many weeks, thus affording the social worker time to develop a counseling relationship that can address these concerns. The dominant psychological fear described by the social workers I interviewed was how society would react to the disfigured patient. Several of the social workers spoke of the difficulty in being able to be fully reassuring to patients that their concerns were not realistic. In some cases, referrals were made to a staff psychiatrist for medication for anxiety and depression relief to help patients manage their concerns.

Death is a constant reality on the acute burn unit, and what seems to cushion the social workers' reactions to this aspect of the job is the sense of cohesion and closeness of the staff. Each social worker spoke of the successful team approach in the burn center and how all staff members seem to take care of each other when needed. In one unit, the social worker described how the entire team — doctors, nurse manager, and social worker — meets with a family when death approaches. One social worker expressed concern about the level of awareness of the other patients on the burn unit. Most of the burn units are rather small, with an average of 15 to 20 beds. When a patient dies, other patients may not know because many are in private rooms, isolated from other patients. However, family members and caregivers surely are aware of a death, and this sends a shock wave through the unit that the social worker may need to address.

In all the burn centers, children are accommodated either on the unit or in a separate part of the unit. Two of the social workers stated that dealing with the pain and anguish of the children was the hardest part of their job. On the other hand, they stated that burns on children always look worse than they are and that the children rebound so much faster than the adults, which helps enormously. The forensic aspect of children being burned was also discussed, with a particular case described. It involved a 6-year-old boy with cerebral palsy who was brought to the burn unit with second- and third-degree burns. The parent stated that the child was burned while in the bathtub with his sister. The parent had put water in the tub but the sister decided to add more and the boy was burned. Was this a case of neglect? The parent appeared to be very conscientious but was overwhelmed with responsibility. The team met and decided to call in the case as a child abuse situation. This resulted in an investigation that ended with the parent keeping the child but also with the addition of more help in the house.

One social worker described a more satisfying case involving a 24-year-old homeless man who was found on the street with fourth-degree burns (bone involvement) over his face and hands. He had been thrown out of his house 6 weeks earlier because of his drug abuse. During the several months he was in the hospital, the social worker talked with him a lot about his life, his drug use, the circumstances that led to his burn, and what the future held for him. In time, the social worker was able to involve the patient's mother in his situation. He enrolled in an inpatient drug rehab program upon discharge from the hospital and has kept in touch with the social worker, reporting that he is still drug free.

In another case, a 20-year-old man lost his arms and legs in a house fire and what remained of his body was terribly disfigured. He was in the hospital for 8 months, requiring critical care and crisis intervention medically and emotionally. He had multiple surgeries and by the time he was ready for discharge, he had been fitted with prosthetic devices that allowed him to navigate on his own. The substantial multidisciplinary care for this case involved the burn unit and physical therapy staff. He had an electric wheelchair and by the time he was ready to leave the hospital, a natural and gradual reentry process was successful. He was able to return to college and graduate near the top of his class. It is this type of bravery, strength, and recovery that sustains burn unit social workers.

In describing what satisfactions the burn unit social workers derive from their work, each mentioned that once they were able to get past the physical changes caused by burns, they were able to see the person under the burn. "Things that shocked me a year ago," stated one social worker, "don't bother me now and I am able to relate to the person." Reaching for that person and bringing them back to the surface, seeing change happening slowly yet consistently, and being part of a dedicated staff were sources of satisfaction for each worker.

12

SOCIAL WORK IN THE EMERGENCY ROOM

ABOUT THE EMERGENCY ROOM

Most hospital emergency rooms (ERs) across the United States offer social work services. Although no exact definition exists of the range of services offered, Bristow and Herrick (2002) explain that social workers provide psychosocial assessments, bereavement counseling and initial grief support, substance abuse assessment and referral, discharge planning, referrals for community services, emotional support, and education and advocacy for patients. Because many people use the ER as their first contact with medical care, the range of problems faced by the emergency department, especially in urban settings, necessitates the continuous presence of social work staff in the ER. In addition, government policies and regulations have mandated specific social work services for those dealing with the effects of drug abuse, family violence, and psychiatric illnesses, and many who are poor, homeless, without insurance, or lack access to other sources of medical treatment (Ponto & Berg, 1992). Many of these problems fall within the traditional description of social work service provision and naturally fall to the social worker to address in the ER setting.

"The hospital emergency room offers social workers an opportunity to work in what is often the front line of health care — the patient's first contact with the hospital" (Healy, 1981, p. 36). In addition, the ER social worker is expected to interface with families and deal with their concerns and issues related to the patient. The ER social worker carries responsibility for both the patient and the family, providing support, education, and referral services.

ER social workers describe their work as exciting and challenging, fast paced, and extremely difficult. The variety — the many different diagnoses, life situations, and presenting problems — and range of service provision is part of what makes the work exciting (Soskis, 1985). Brown (1996) eloquently describes the urgency of life in the emergency room: "The emergency department is a crucible of emotions. The anguish, fear, need, and gore are wearing. Survival in this place requires a deep kindness nestled in a very dark sense of humor, and a strong faith tempered with cynicism" (p. 5). However, as van Wormer and Boes (1997) point out, "Of all medical care units in which social workers might choose to practice, the ER in an inner-city public hospital is one of the most stressful. The struggle against burnout is constant" (p. 92).

As anyone who has visited an ER in an urban hospital knows, the pace and intensity are remarkable. In my efforts to interview social workers for this chapter, I had to spend time in the emergency room. One ER was so packed that it was almost impossible to walk through the area, with patient waiting times of more than 4 hours. In another ER, the social workers shared an office that had been a closet, with boxes and files piled up so that there was virtually no open floor space. These working conditions, exaggerated by the life-and-death quality of the situations that often present in an ER, account for the burnout referred to by van Wormer and Boes (1997).

THE SOCIAL WORKER IN THE ER

In the ER setting, crises, deaths, and severe client problems must be assessed and addressed as quickly and efficiently as possible. The social worker–client relationship in this setting is fleeting and emotionally laden (van Wormer & Boes, 1997). The pressure for immediate action is intense and the social worker is on call and alert for whatever problems arise (Dziegielewski & Duncklee, 2004). Working as part of a multidisciplinary effort, the social worker is in constant negotiation with the medical team and is responsible for case management activities such as referrals and resource finding and for patient and family counseling, including grief counseling and management of emotional stress (Ponto & Berg, 1992), all delivered over a period of minutes or hours, not longer than the patient is in the ER. Unlike social work that is practiced on a specific hospital unit, where patients with like illnesses are cared for, in the ER, patients with a variety of issues need to be treated immediately and sent home or be sent to a floor in the hospital. Time is always of the essence, especially in a busy ER, with a steady stream of cases and situations that present to medical and social work staff. It is not unusual for the social worker to juggle several different cases and situations simultaneously.

Typically, the patient problems fall into diverse life-threatening situations, such as accidents, sudden illness, death, substance abuse, and the results of violent acts (e.g., rape or other sexual assault), which cast the social worker in different roles. In cases of accidents and sudden illness, the social worker is the main conduit of vital information to the family as the medical staff tends to the patient. In most situations, the doctors will have some contact with worried family members, but it is to the social work staff that the family members will turn with questions regarding the implications of a diagnosis or treatment plan.

If the patient is being admitted into the hospital, the social worker educates the family regarding hospital protocol and so forth. If the patient is being discharged, often the social worker helps to formulate plans for future care involving complex decisions and procurement of needed community-based medical resources (McLeod, Bywaters, & Cooke, 2003). The social worker must be sure the information conveyed to the family is given in such a way that they are fully able to understand it. Less medical jargon and more direct factual expression of the situation is warranted as family members and friends struggle to incorporate the reality of what has happened to the patient. Not essential, but frequently sought, are social workers who are bilingual, especially in a city hospital ER.

Beyond being the conduit of information, the social worker must deal with the emotionality of both patients and family members in the ER. It behooves the social worker to try to create a caring and nonpressured haven for the family in the midst of a chaotic environmental situation so that the family can adjust better to the unfolding situation with the patient (Dziegielewski & Duncklee, 2004). It can be assumed that people who are in the ER are there because they need immediate care, either because something sudden has happened to them medically or they have been in an accident. As such, the patient and family members have not had time to prepare for the situation; emotions run high, especially if the patient is critically or seriously ill. Social workers find that they must manage some of this emotion to keep family members focused. Many emergency departments have small rooms adjacent to the ER in which anguished family members can wait and use the telephone to contact others.

In cases of death in the ER, the role of the social worker is to respond to and care for the patient's relatives and friends in the emergency room. As the critically ill or injured patient is rushed into the ER, the medical team takes over the medical care and needed lifesaving measures, leaving family and friends to wait for news or information regarding the condition of the patient. In the event of death, either after or before arrival in the ER, the situation for family and friends reaches high levels of stress because they have had little time to prepare themselves emotionally for the loss they have sustained. All concerned are best served if the social worker is realistic regarding the severity of the patient's condition; immediate intervention and the initial acceptance of the family's grief are the social worker's goals (Holland & Rogich, 1980).

Wells (1993) offers specific guidelines for the social worker who must convey the news of serious illness or death to a family waiting in the ER. The first rule is to place the patient's family in a private area while sharing as much information about the patient as possible. The family must be made aware of the patient's medical situation, with the intention of reducing the element of surprise should the patient die. Keeping the family informed of the seriousness of the situation helps them better handle the news of a death. Wordiness and excessive use of medical terminology usually serves to confuse and escalate anxiety rather than assuage it. Codes (internal communication within the hospital that signal immediate emergency activity on behalf of a patient, usually involving dramatic lifesaving procedures) need to be explained and the family must make a decision as to the limits they want the medical team to pursue on behalf of the patient. In the event of death, the family must be told of the hospital protocol regarding funeral arrangements and care of the body. Under all circumstances, the social worker is to be seen and is to use him- or herself as a comforting figure.

As appropriate, the social worker can encourage discussion regarding the deceased while giving as much attention as possible to helping the family begin their grief process. The most difficult time for most family members, second to hearing of the death of the patient, is when they view the body. The inescapable physical reality of the death must be faced; family members should be advised that there may be tubes and other equipment still in place that will alter the visual status of the body. The social worker may accompany a family member to view the body or stay with the other family members (Wells, 1993). Holland and Rogich (1980) sum up the role of the social worker when there is a death in the ER: The social worker is the stabilizer and manager in the crisis of death. How do families relate to the social worker at these moments? Sometimes, the social worker can become the target of the anger a family members feels toward the medical establishment for "letting the patient die." Other times, the social worker is seen as a force to keep emotion in check until it can be dealt with in a different venue. One of the frustrations cited by social workers interviewed for this chapter is the short contact they have with patients and families, especially when there is a death and the option for follow-up does not exist.

Two other roles for the social worker are in the area of substance abuse, when patients are brought to the ER either intoxicated or having overdosed on drugs, and in cases of sexual assault or domestic violence. The social worker's task in cases of substance abuse is to gather as much information as possible, conduct a thorough assessment, and refer the patient to available services for substance abuse. In cases of sexual assault, the patient must endure a rigorous physical exam while struggling with the emotional impact of the assault. The social worker is required to complete an assessment, document the experience with needed paperwork and information, and comfort the patient. A thorough risk assessment should consider severity and frequency of abuse, past and current patient injuries, and criminal justice interventions that have occurred. In some cases, the hospital protocol requires the social worker to provide documentation and pictures of the injured area on the body of the assault victim. Referrals are always necessary after this type of injury and this task, naturally, falls to the social worker on staff. The overriding task for the social worker is to make sure the patient is discharged to a safe place.

In cases of substance abuse, the patient must be assessed and referred for treatment. In both of these circumstances — substance abuse and suspected sexual assault — the social worker must assess and access family supports to ensure follow-through of the referral. In some instances, the social worker is expected to go beyond the hospital setting to follow-up with court-mandated appearances. In cases of suspected child abuse, social workers are required by law to report any suspicions they have to local child abuse agencies for follow-up.

Homeless people represent a growing segment of ER patients; these are people who have no insurance, no entitlements, and no ability to pay for medical care. These patients, more frequently seen in urban hospital settings, present a host of medical and social problems to the ER staff. The social worker must find resources to assist the homeless who are not hospitalized, who are being put back out on the street, while attempting to ensure their safety and well-being. The mindset of administrators in many inner-city hospitals is to "Treat 'em and street 'em," which suggests that in the interests of efficiency and cost-effectiveness, homeless people are the least desirable patients and should be expediently handled and evacuated from the ER (van Wormer & Boes, 1997).

As suggested by this review of the literature, the role of the social worker in the ER is to provide for the psychosocial needs of the patients and their families in a time of crisis. Working in tandem with the medical staff, the social worker performs a vital service that, because it is in an emergency situation, cannot be monitored or performed by the medical staff. In addition, with social work's systems orientation and grounding in counseling methods and crisis intervention, the social worker is best suited to render services of this type.

SOCIAL WORKER COMMENTS

Six emergency room social workers were interviewed, three in urban settings and three in suburban hospitals. The overriding sentiment of all those interviewed was that what drew them to the work was the fast pace of the ER. One worker, who had been in the ER more than 5 years, said the ER was so much better than the traditional social work setting of the hospital because the energy, challenge, and diversity of situations and age groups were constantly stimulating.

For the most part, the social workers defined their role and function, as described in the literature, as a source of comfort and education for the family. Each affirmed that in the ER, the family is the patient; it's not just the person being ministered to by the medical team. "We are the middle person," explained an 18-year ER social work veteran, "when it comes to psychosocial needs. We advocate for the patient. The doctors like to fix things, but we have to take care of the details for both the patient and family." It was pointed out that the social worker often spends more time with the patient and family than any of the medical team's members and that the social workers are better able to explain things to family members than the nurses or physicians. It was suggested that each discipline — medicine, nursing, and social work — has its own area of expertise but that a well-functioning ER will have some areas of blended roles and overlap while still respecting the unique contributions of each professional.

Particularly challenging cases include those that use the ER as their medical home. They highlight the deficiencies in the medical system to the social workers and the frustrating lack of resources for those less fortunate. Cases of child abuse and sexual assault provide serious levels of challenge. In one case, reported by an inner-city social worker, a young child was brought into the ER with burns on her legs and genitals; 80% of her body was burned. The burns carried the telltale markings of a child who was burned through neglect or intent. The social worker was called in to evaluate the situation and gather the information needed to determine whether to call protective services on behalf of the child or to call the police. The social worker spoke with the mother, who claimed she had done no wrong and that she was always attentive to the child.

Although the mother denied any wrongdoing, her story did not add up and in time the mother admitted that she had neglected the child, indirectly causing the burn. Child protective services were called, but the child died of her injuries and the mother was jailed. "We do the work that no one in the ER wants to do. The doctors don't have the time for this type of investigation and the nurses are running around as well. So, it falls to us," exclaimed the worker. While lamenting this aspect of his job, the social worker also acknowledged that being the investigator is sometimes the most interesting aspect of his work.

An example of a very satisfying case involved a repeater (a patient who comes to the ER frequently, sometimes using it as a place to get a meal and a clean bed for a night) in a suburban setting. The patient was a homeless woman in her mid-50s. She had an extensive alcoholism history and came to the ER on a regular basis. With each visit to the ER, she was put into a cubicle, fed, and allowed to sleep off her intoxication. Even though the woman was never admitted to the hospital to a unit, the social worker gained more information about her and had come to know her in a way. By spending some time listening to the patient's concerns and fear, the social worker convinced her to try to stop drinking and to seek admission into a homeless shelter.

As described in the literature, death is a constant in the ER and social workers deal with distraught family members on a daily basis. In working with the family, social workers make an effort to involve them to say farewell to the deceased. The workers find themselves making phone calls to arrange funerals, calling family members, and consoling those who are in the ER. It is difficult and sometimes frustrating to the social workers, who feel that they are there only at the beginning of the grief response and cannot be there for a longer period to help the family. Often referrals are made to grief counselors.

In all the ERs, the social workers were frequently called in to minister to staff when a death occurred. It is an interesting use of their skill in helping people talk about what they feel and have experienced as a first step in being able to deal with their experience. The social workers are seen as functioning beyond the medical situations with the ability to help the medical staff deal with their losses. When death occurs, the nurses, and sometimes the physicians, will seek on-the-spot counseling and additional support from the social work staff. It was not unusual for staff to gather after a particularly difficult day or shift in the ER when there had been numerous very serious or fatal situations, with the social workers helping staff and themselves "to vent" about the various events.

The work is not without its level of frustration. The medical staff often ignores repeaters, which, in turn, can be a source of irritation to the social workers. These are the homeless and the substance abusers for whom the social workers will advocate, but frequently they "hit a brick wall" because there are not enough resources to address the needs of the patients. Many people use the ER "as a way station, and we don't have enough resources to manage all their needs. The doctors and nurses don't seem to understand this and keep at us to right these people while we don't have the resources or services to do that," explained one of the workers.

Internal to one of the ERs, a social worker identified the struggle to get along with the different disciplines in the ER, each with a different stake in the patient. "We are all trying to help but sometimes we are at cross-purposes with each other and we get in the way of the helping. The ER is a medical place and I have to respect that as the first priority, with the psychosocial needs put aside and then reevaluated as the emergency unfolds." This social worker was responding to the emergency aspect of medical care that has to be administered to in the setting. If a patient is in the throes of a heart attack, his or her psychosocial needs are not an issue; if a patient has a broken bone, it has to be set and a cast applied, and then the psychosocial issues can be addressed. It falls to the social workers on the units to extend the psychosocial care needed. While in the ER, the social worker moves the patient and family along, as they begin their entry into the medical establishment.

Is the ER a workplace for everyone? Most of the social workers were clear that if one needs more time to plan and execute interventions or a calm atmosphere in which to work, then the ER is not the place. For those who like quick turnover, rapid-fire assessment, and the challenge of finding rapid solutions, the ER is the perfect place.

13

RURAL HOSPITAL SOCIAL WORK

RURAL SOCIAL WORK

Social workers function in diverse venues and with diverse roles. It is inaccurate to assume that social workers function the same way in every venue, because differing circumstances and resources dictate how social workers articulates their role. This definitional difference can be seen when comparing the urban and rural hospital social worker. In this chapter we look at the rural hospital social worker, noting the differences and similarities between these workers and their urban counterparts. The assumptions regarding rural communities are that the area is not dominated by large metropolitan cities, the lifestyle is more relaxed, there is more open land, and, as such, less density of population and activity.

Nonmetropolitan areas of the United States have all of the problems of large metropolitan areas including the challenge of offering quality medical care to residents. Access to health care is a national problem, felt especially by those not covered by health insurance or other third-party programs. This problem, however, seems to be even more acute in rural areas. Rural settings do not have as many physicians, nurses, pharmacies, or hospital beds per capita as there are in metropolitan communities. Often, medical professionals prefer to work in urban areas, where they are more likely to have larger caseloads and the ability to pursue specialized practice, and where they are likely to have better services and schools for their families (Ginsberg, 1993).

In rural areas, social work practice has to be specifically adapted to the small community. What that means in terms of the hospital social worker is that the smaller community will have fewer resources than the large city; the social worker will have to provide a more comprehensive package of services than the metropolitan social worker and will probably have to make do with less for the people served. This view, however, applies to formal community supports and does not consider the many local, personalized, noninstitutional supports that may become available to residents when they are ill. Small communities operate on a highly personalized basis, relying on informal supports such as the church, family, and peer group. For the rural social worker, knowledge of the community and the ability to be a member or participant in the life of the community are essential to being able to provide quality and caring service to patients and clients.

Other variables that define and delineate social work practice in a rural community are the impact of geography, the characteristics of the population, and the service providers. Geography affects practice because of the distances people have to negotiate to access service, because people live more isolated lives in rural areas, and because rural persons have a greater tendency toward certain social problems than urban dwellers. There tends to be a higher frequency of depression in rural areas, in part because of the distance between individuals and community life. One could speculate that the diversion of city living, missing in the rural community, could serve as a distraction from the problems of everyday life that provoke depression.

In terms of the characteristics of the people, rural dwellers are seen as more conservative in their values. Social workers have to be attuned and responsive to more traditional lifestyles. The rural community relies more on informal helping networks and decision makers than does the urban community. As such, rural social workers must have a generalist orientation to be able to address the multitude and variety of tasks presented to them by the constituents. Another way of viewing this is to say that social workers in a rural setting must engage in activities that subsume a wider range of roles than is the case for the urban worker and have to be aware of and make us of informal networks in their work (York, Denton, & Moran, 1989).

HEALTH CARE IN RURAL AREAS

In general, the health of urban dwellers is better than that of rural residents. Within the rural population, the health status of low-income residents is not as good as that of residents with higher incomes. Similarly, poor rural residents are in worse health than poor urban dwellers. This can be explained by limitations due to economic reasons as well as by geographic barriers and the shortage of medical providers in rural areas. The geographic barriers to receiving health care are significant: often the population base is not large enough to support medical facilities and practitioners, and travel to medical care can be overwhelming with limited or no public transportation available. The scarcity of medical providers and the vulnerability of rural hospitals — with the growing number of rural hospitals forced to close or consolidate their services — presents a major barrier to receiving health care. In the absence of primary care providers, the rural dweller will use the hospital for medical care. As rural hospitals continue to close, the level of health care in the rural community will, consequently, deteriorate even further (Summers, 1993).

Financial barriers to medical care in rural areas include high poverty rates, lack of health insurance for a substantial proportion of the population, low insurance reimbursement rates for certain rural groups, and a high percentage of small local businesses that do not offer medical coverage to their employees. The policies of federal entitlements in the form of Medicare and Medicaid also contribute to the rural picture; reimbursement rates vary from state to state, but generally eligibility rates tend to be more restrictive in rural areas than in urban-dominated states (Summers, 1993).

The general picture presented here suggests that a disparity exists between rural and urban areas in terms of how and to what extent services can be delivered to people who are ill. The impact of this disparity defines how medical social workers in rural areas approach their work and how they deploy resources, a significantly different picture from how the urban medical social worker functions.

THE RURAL MEDICAL SOCIAL WORKER

In ways similar to their urban counterparts, rural medical social workers are involved with assessment, helping the patient and family adjust to the medical experience while in the hospital, resource procurement, and creating a safe and reasoned discharge plan (Egan & Kadushin, 1995). Although their tasks may be similar to those in an urban setting, how they accomplish their work does differ.

One reason for this difference resides in the financial resources of the patients or families, the hospital, and the community. As stated previously in this chapter, residents of rural communities are generally poorer than in urban areas, more residents lack health insurance or other medical coverage, and rural employers tend not to provide health care coverage (Ginsberg, 1993). Under these conditions, the assessment function of the social worker must take into account the limited financial resources of the family, the possibility that medication and treatment compliance might be compromised due to financial constraints, and the tendency for rural residents to use and utilize health services less than urban dwellers (Summers, 1993). It implies a high level of patient follow-up on the part of the social workers, not a routine part of the urban worker's role definition.

Rural hospitals represent half of all community hospitals in the United States but have been hit more severely than urban hospitals in terms of reimbursement policies. A community hospital is defined as a nonfederal, short-term, general facility. The American Hospital Association estimates that there are 4,895 community hospitals in the United States (AHA, 2005). There is a constant economic struggle in rural areas for hospitals to remain financially solvent; a high percentage of hospital closings have been reported each decade since the 1980s. A primary reason rural hospitals have experienced financial difficulties relates to changes in Medicare reimbursement rates initiated by the federal government in 1983.

Faced with sharply escalating Medicare costs, the federal government switched from a fee-for-service model to a prospective payment system (PPS). Under this system, hospitals receive a fixed amount for treating patients diagnosed with a given illness, regardless of the patients' length of stay or type of care received. This shift in reimbursement levels was difficult enough for urban hospitals, but it had even more serious implications for rural hospitals that rely more heavily on Medicare admissions. The lower levels of reimbursement left rural hospitals financially vulnerable. To compound the problem, the rural rates of federal reimbursement are lower than urban rates. Finally, rural hospitals are small and experience low occupancy rates, exacerbating the financial tenuousness of these institutions (Coward & Dwyer, 1993; Mick & Morlock, 1990). The implications of these financial differences suggest that the staffing and levels of care and aftercare for ailing rural residents may be affected by the financial position of the hospital. The social worker must be more cost-conscious when offering services, because types of services may be limited and services may have to be rationed selectively. In addition, on a practice level, because many rural social workers are not employed full-time workers, continuity of service often suffers (Egan & Kadushin, 1995).

The rural social worker uses the community in a more integrated way than the urban worker. As described previously, the community serves a vital function in the care of the rural dweller and is seen as a source of support in times of difficulty. It is therefore incumbent on the social worker to be fully versed in the resources of the diverse communities that surround the hospital and serve the residents. The worker has to have many more "working relationships" with sources of help than does the urban worker and has to be known in many venues to effect conscientious aftercare for the patient. For many rural social workers, this immersion into the community is a very positive aspect of their work. As noted by Ginsberg (1993), "There is a special joy for many (social workers) in being well-known and recognized in the community. The social worker who is spoken to by everyone on the street, in the grocery store, and in the post office, has the special satisfaction of being an important person in the rural community" (p. 13).

SOCIAL WORKER COMMENTS

I interviewed eight rural social workers in four hospitals to explore aspects of their work. In each hospital, the social workers were detailed to either one or two floors and served various populations. Only one hospital had a social worker who was stationed on a floor within a dedicated unit. As such, the majority of these social workers defined themselves as providing general social work services, migrating from floor to floor and unit to unit. Only one social worker was not assigned the role of case management, which meant that it was not in her domain to do discharge planning. In that hospital the discharge planning was managed in a self-contained department where nonprofessional staff did the discharges with input from the social worker. All of the social workers were involved in discharge planning to one degree or another, sometimes sharing the task with nurses.

Caseloads varied from hospital to hospital and within each hospital. One hospital social worker covered the medical and surgical floors and was responsible for more than 50 patients at a time, whereas another, in a smaller hospital, had responsibility for 35 patients.

All of the social workers registered levels of frustration about their work, which mainly focused on being unable to obtain the needed resources for their patients. Whether it was equipment, home services, or placements, the social workers were unanimous in their struggle to do more with less. One social worker commented, "We are a small community here, with four nursing homes and many patients vying to get placed in one or the other of them. When there are no beds, we have to either send the patient home with what I consider inadequate supports, or leave them in the hospital. If they have to stay in the hospital, we get hell because the administration wants them out asap. We are sometimes between a rock and a hard place!"

The positive side of the work experience was reflected in comments about the personal nature of the work. Consistent with the literature, I found that the social workers felt very connected to their patients. "We are a community where everyone knows each other. I know almost everyone who enters the hospital or I know someone who knows that person. It makes the work so much more personal," said one worker. Another worker reinforced this perspective: "I know all the repeaters — those who come to the hospital several times a year — I have established a relationship with them and know them and/or members of their family. I enjoy sitting with them at their bedside and chatting and I make sure that I do that with the repeaters as often as time permits." The contrast between the urban social workers (interviewed for other chapters in this book) who knew the repeaters and the rural workers was marked. When the city social workers referred to repeaters, they often were speaking of people they knew only in the hospital setting. The rural social workers were liable to know their patients from community venues; that is, merchants, a religious organization, or school. The rural social workers see patients more frequently and seem to have more enduring relationships. This can be problematic if the patient's medical condition worsens and especially when a death occurs. As a mark of the level of connection to their patients, each social worker interviewed had attended from four to seven funerals over the past year.

Because the hospitals are smaller, the delineation of role between the nurses and social workers is not as sharp. This was mentioned by several of the social workers, not in a territorial or hostile way, but seeing the nursing department as partners in care with the social work department. "While there is some overlap between us and nursing, especially in the area of assessment and discharge, we seem to share many of the responsibilities and try to not make this an issue between us," commented a social worker, adding, "We have good collaboration between us and nursing and with the physical therapists, dietary people, and other departments. We do care rounds daily and while sometimes the personality of someone will get in the way, for the most part, we respect one another."

One social worker, who worked mostly with the psychiatric patients in a small community hospital, commented that he had previously been employed in an urban hospital and, although the resources were scant there as well, the pace and turnover rate were very high and he felt the frustration of not having any follow-up or personal connection to the patients or family members. This feeling of isolation impelled him to seek work in a rural area.

The challenge and satisfaction of rural medical social work are reflected in the comments of one social worker: "I love working where I live. I like knowing the people I serve and have them knowing me. I like it that I see the results of my work and can meet someone on the street who I saw only days ago in the hospital. Yes, it is frustrating that people live so far away and that we have to scrounge around and compete with other institutions for the resources we know we need for the patients, but the satisfactions are great and we get to live in a beautiful, uncluttered part of the world."

14

SOCIAL WORK ON THE PSYCHIATRIC UNIT

ABOUT MENTAL ILLNESS

Mental illnesses are diseases that cause disturbances in one's thinking, perception, and behavior. These disturbances can be mild, having minimal impact on one's functioning, or more severe, impairing the person's ability to think and function in a normal manner and environment. The term "mental illness" encompasses numerous psychiatric disorders that can strike anyone regardless of age, economic status, race, creed, or color. Mental illnesses affect 22.1% of Americans ages 18 and older. This averages 1 in 5 American adults — approximately 54 million — who are diagnosed with a mental disorder in a given year. Four of the ten leading causes of disability in the United States and other developed countries are mental disorders — major depression, bipolar disorder, schizophrenia, and obsessive–compulsive disorder (Murray & Lopez, 1996; National Institute of Mental Health [NIMH], 2001).

Depression and anxiety disorders are the two most common mental illnesses, affecting approximately 19 million American adults annually. Depression is more prevalent in women; approximately 12.4 million women each year, roughly twice the rate of men (6.4 million). Anxiety disorders affect approximately 19.1 million American adults ages 18 to 54, which is about 13.3% of people in this age group in a given year, with statistics for women much higher than for men. Anxiety disorders frequently co-occur with depressive disorders, eating disorders, or substance abuse. More than 2.5 million Americans suffer from schizophrenia (a psychotic illness in which the individual suffers from hallucinations and markedly disordered thinking and is often unable to function in society); this equates to about 1% of Americans, with men and women affected equally. More than 2 million people have bipolar disorder, also known as manic–depressive illness, with men and women affected equally. Approximately 3.3 million American adults ages 18 to 54, or about 2.3% of people in this age group, also exhibit obsessive–compulsive disorder (NIMH, 2001).

In the United States, mental disorders are codified using the fourth edition of the *Diagnostic and Statistical Manual of Mental Disorders* (*DSM-IV*) (American Psychiatric Association, 2000). This several-hundred-page volume lists all mental disorders and their symptoms and assigns a number (code) to the mental illness. These diagnostic codes are used throughout the insurance industry and with Medicare and Medicaid, establishing a uniform system of reporting mental disorders. All mental health professionals — psychiatrists, social workers, psychologists, and others — use the DSM.

SOCIAL WORK AND MENTAL HEALTH — THE HISTORY

With the person-in-environment perspective, it seems natural that social workers would have become central players in developing and implementing psychiatric services. In fact, "Social workers have been playing a role in the mental health service system since the early days of the profession. … During the early part of the century, psychiatric social workers were mainly involved in after-care of discharged mentally ill patients" (Aviram, 2002, p. 617). Freudian theory became popular in the United States in the 1920s and social workers grasped this theoretical framework to help anchor their work in mental health. Schools of social work established training programs based on Freudian theory and certain schools of social work became prominent in the training of psychiatric social workers. Following both world wars, returning servicemen, traumatized by their war experiences, flooded hospitals and mental health centers with both physical and psychological problems. Veterans' hospitals employed large numbers of psychiatric social workers to address the multiplicity of needs of these soldiers. Many struggled with posttraumatic stress disorders, depression, anxiety reactions, and poor impulse control over their anger; many were unable to assume the structure of their previous lives nor were they able to work (Cowles, 2003).

Social work practice in mental health expanded greatly after World War II with a push toward community prevention and treatment.

Heretofore, people with mental illness had been cared for in hospitals and institutions. The deinstitutionalization movement, an effort to transfer patients to the community for care, took off in the 1950s. This shift to the community evolved because mental hospitals were overcrowded, the costs to taxpayers had reached alarming proportions, mental health care was bureaucratically overburdened, and there was the growing conviction that the needs of the mentally ill were not being met. The community orientation to serving the needs of people with mental illness provided new venues and opportunities for social workers. With passage of the Community Mental Health Acts in the 1960s, the federal government assumed greater responsibility for larger segments of mental health services.

During the Reagan administration, the federal government's share of the funding to the states for community mental health dropped from 24% in 1976 to 2% in 1984. Most states were not able to support their local programs and thus began downsizing publicly funded services. Many social workers had to seek alternate employment and many mentally ill people were forced out of the programs that had cared for them (Cowles, 2003). As a consequence of this trend, many families had to assume the burden of caring for their mentally ill relatives. Relatives began to organize around the need for services, resulting in a strong consumer movement that is active to this day.

One of the greatest influences on mental health services over the last few decades has been the development and introduction of several classes of drugs that address psychiatric disorders. These drugs have been used to successfully treat patients with severe psychotic disorders who previously would have spent their lives in institutions. In addition, specific drugs have been developed to treat depression, anxiety, and obsessive–compulsive disorders, allowing many who would not be able to function maximally with their illnesses to be able to function adequately in society. Many are able to hold jobs, have stable family lives, and enjoy a good quality of life. Despite these advances in pharmacology, many people with mental illness still do not thrive. For these patients the primary approach to management is intervention by trained mental health professionals. This work often falls to social workers both in the community and in hospital settings (Alper & Kerson, 1997).

Only since the 1950s has coverage for mental health disorders been included as a reimbursable medical condition. From the 1950s to the 1990s, reimbursement rates fluctuated, but not to the extent that services were seriously impacted or compromised. Over the last two decades, managed care companies have taken over the insurance industry and have exerted tremendous influence over services offered. As a result, coverage for mental health services has been reduced and length of service shortened.

Social workers in hospitals who work with the mentally ill are also faced with the demands of the managed care environment and often must offer less service in severely constrained environments where length of stay and depth of services offered have to be weighed. In outpatient settings, in mental health clinics all across the United States, as an extension of the care of the hospital, managed care companies dictate medications and tenure of services as well (Aviram, 2002) and can even dictate forms of acceptable treatment (Riffe, 1998). It is not unusual for a managed care company to limit outpatient treatment based on determinations made by insurance executives rather than mental health professionals.

MENTAL ILLNESS — THE PATIENT EXPERIENCE

Persons with severe mental illness present with a variety of symptoms and behaviors that include inappropriate anxiety, disturbances of thought and perception, broad and variable range of moods, and cognitive dysfunction. Some symptoms overlap various illness categories. For example, someone with an anxiety disorder may also be depressed; a person with schizophrenia may also have symptoms of anxiety. Often these overlapping conditions make exact diagnosis and subsequent treatment more difficult.

In an adult, specific symptoms that would require psychiatric intervention and assessment include marked personality change, inability to cope with problems and daily activities, strange or grandiose ideas, excessive anxieties, prolonged depression and apathy, marked changes in eating or sleeping, abuse of alcohol or drugs, or excessive anger, hostility, or violent behavior. These symptoms may initially seem to be slight deviations of behavior, but as the illness progresses, these behaviors and symptoms become more marked and dominate the person's behavior and personality. In most psychiatric illnesses, there is a range of symptoms that warrants a descriptor of mild to major disturbance.

Anxiety, psychosis, mood disturbances, and cognitive disturbances are the most common forms of mental illness. Whereas all of us, at one time or another, have experienced anxiety, individuals with an anxiety disorder have anxious feelings and symptoms disproportionate to the circumstance, they find great difficulty in being able to control these feelings, and, in its most advanced form, the anxiety interferes with and can prohibit optimal functioning. Persons with anxiety report feelings of dread and fear, have a rapid heartbeat, feel lightheaded or dizzy, experience shortness of breath, and have muscle tension. Certain medications prove helpful to control some of the symptoms. Life is difficult for the anxiety-ridden person: they are assaulted by irrational fears and often take steps to constrict their lives to avoid anxiety-inducing situations. Unless overwhelmed by anxiety, a person would not usually be hospitalized for this condition.

People with psychosis experience disturbances of thought. The most common form of psychotic illness is schizophrenia. Schizophrenia is a chronic, severe, disabling disease of the brain. Its cause is unknown. The major symptoms of schizophrenia include hallucinations (visual or auditory), delusions, disorganized thinking and speech, and potential withdrawal into a psychotic world. Hallucinations occur when an individual experiences a sensory impression that has no basis in reality; the sensory impression is falsely experienced as real. Auditory hallucinations, for example, involve the impression that one is hearing a voice. A delusion, a false belief held by an individual despite evidence to the contrary, is another feature of psychotic illness. Paranoia, the most common form of delusion, is a belief that someone is trying to harm the individual. Delusions and hallucinations are the most commonly observed psychotic symptoms and often warrant hospitalization to keep the patient safe and to begin treatment to address the illness. Often these patients present with agitation, disorganized thoughts and behaviors, and loose or illogical thoughts, some with a flat or blunted affect, the inability to experience pleasure, poor motivation, and poor concrete thinking. Most people who are diagnosed with schizophrenia have a long-term disability associated with the disorder; they will likely be unable to hold a job, will have disturbed relationships with others, and will require medications for life to control their disordered thought patterns (U.S. Department of Health and Human Services [USDHHS], 1999). Unfortunately, these medications, although more or less effective in controlling the hallucinations and delusions, have numerous side effects including blurred vision, dry mouth, lethargy, and a stony appearance (Hershberg & Posner, 1994).

Mood disturbances manifest themselves as sustained feelings of sadness or elation. People who are persistently sad are said to have depression; those who have a sustained elevated mood are described as having mania. Depression is described along a continuum from mild to severe. People who are severely depressed are often unable to function in an active society, are handicapped and limited by their sadness and negative worldview, and cannot relate adequately to those around them. They feel persistent despair, have seriously compromised self-esteem, may not eat, experience sleep disturbances, and have general feelings of apathy and lack of motivation. Depressed people are hospitalized when their physical well-being is compromised by their mental illness and when there is a danger of suicide generated by their negativity. Medications abound for depression, and many people with chronic depression are now able to lead relatively normal lives and be engaged with others (USDHHS, 1999).

People with cognitive dysfunction are not able to perform and execute certain tasks, have limited recall ability, and generally cannot think clearly enough to manage alone or, when most seriously compromised, at all. Dementia and Alzheimer's disease are common forms of cognitive dysfunction. In each of these illnesses, attention, concentration, and intellectual functions are the most notable deficits. Those who are diagnosed with cognitive dysfunction will often be hospitalized for diagnostic evaluation and then be moved to restricted environments where supervision and care will be provided for them.

The individual with serious mental illness has to deal not only with the illness but also with related issues of stigma. "The influence of stigma encompasses stereotype, prejudice, discrimination, separation, and status loss which makes individuals with mental illness more vulnerable to social rejection, income loss, limited opportunities for employment or education, relapse, and experiencing another psychiatric disorder" (Kahng & Mowbray, 2004, p. 225). The historical antecedents for the stigmatizing of people with mental illness relate to treatment and behaviors recorded centuries ago when the mentally ill were seen as a danger to society and were taken out of society and placed in institutions to protect the public. Even as treatment for the mentally ill has become more humane and accepted, the stigma of mental illness has remained and the general public still responds with suspicion and caution in the presence of this population. Part of the explanation for this resides with the media, which perpetuates misconceptions about mental illness, sensationalizing crimes in which persons with mental illness have been involved, and generally not taking a sympathetic view of this debilitating disease. Stigma is related to self-esteem, and when persons with mental illness are treated poorly and are stigmatized, they tend to internalize these negative societal views, causing their often-fragile levels of self-esteem to plummet. The circularity of this self-defeating, self-deprecating spiral is often the cause of relapse, development of new symptomatology, and eventual hospitalization for many who struggle to keep their illness at bay.

THE FAMILY EXPERIENCE OF MENTAL ILLNESS

Over the last four decades, relatives have assumed increasing responsibility for the ongoing care of mentally ill family members. This situation has evolved due to the deinstitutionalization movement of the 1950s and the shift away from the institution or hospital to the community as the locus of care. Johnson (2000), in a review of the literature on family management of the mentally ill, concluded that, "What seems clear from the accumulated literature is that living and caring for a person with mental illness can have a tremendous impact on the family, and that the family is a potential buffer against the stressors on its mentally ill member" (p. 128).

Family members with a relative who has a mental illness are often the object of stigma and are frequently harmed by this experience. Parents are blamed for the illness of their child, siblings and spouses are blamed for not ensuring that relatives with mental illness adhere to treatment plans, and children are fearful of being contaminated by the mental illness of their parents or siblings (Corrigan & Miller, 2004).

In a study of reactions of more than 200 family members to the diagnosis of mental illness in their families, men seemed to have a more difficult time accepting the initial diagnosis of a family member's illness than did women. Fathers had an especially difficult time when the patient was their son. Families in which the mentally ill patient had had only one hospitalization were quite different than those with a pattern of hospitalization and rehospitalizations. Families who had been through the cycle of hospitalization, discharge, decompositions, crisis, and rehospitalizations did not share the optimism of the first timers. Middle and upper class families often felt embarrassed that a family member was not functioning up to standard and felt distanced from neighbors and uninformed family members. When families were asked what kept them going through the worst and most trying periods, faith, family, and obligation were identified. Despite the difficulties noted by these family members, many expressed great fondness for the ill family member, even when his or her behavior was disruptive and time consuming for the family (Johnson, 2000).

THE HOSPITAL PSYCHIATRIC SOCIAL WORKER

The priorities of psychiatric hospitalization focus on ameliorating the risk of danger to the self or others. Inpatient units are seen as short-term intensive settings that are designed to contain and resolve crises that cannot be resolved in the community. Most admissions are for people who are suicidal, homicidal, or decompensating (experiencing the rapid return of severe or psychotic symptoms) to such a degree that they cannot care for themselves nor respond to community-based interventions. The guiding principles of safety, crisis intervention, acute medication, and reevaluation of ongoing medications dominate the inpatient unit. Almost half of those with serious mental illness develop alcohol or drug abuse problems, which also have to monitored and addressed during an acute admission (USDHHS, 1999).

Social workers focus their professional interventions on trying to help individuals cope with their problems and better adjust to the particular struggles their illness imposes. Newly admitted patients to a psychiatric unit are usually disoriented due to their mental condition; additionally, they may be struggling with a sense of failure, the typical fears anyone experiences when admitted to a hospital, and a pervasive sense of anguish over what will happen and what is happening to them. Patients who have had one or more previous hospitalization may be more familiar with the experiences in the unit, but a sense of fear and failure may be present. For some, coming to a hospital may provide a sense of relief that they will finally be cared for; treated with medications, psychotherapy, or both to address their illness. Social workers are positioned to offer therapeutic intervention and work towarrd educating the patient and family about medication compliance, making efforts to reassure the patient, and developing a discharge plan that will enable the patient to be cared for in an outpatient facility or day treatment program. As in the other units in the hospital, there is the mandate to stabilize the patient and arrange for a safe and carefully planned discharge in the shortest amount of time. Social workers are part of a multidisciplinary team, consisting of nurses, psychiatrists, and psychologists, to facilitate inpatient care and discharge.

In direct work with patients, the social worker employs the basic philosophy of psychiatric rehabilitation: to teach people with serious mental illness the skills needed to function as normally as possible in the community. The goal is to increase community functioning, reduce the effect of psychiatric symptoms, and enable the mentally ill person (the consumer) to remain functional and out of the hospital. The orientation to the work is grounded in the beliefs of empowerment, competence, and recovery. The principle of empowerment encourages consumers (patients) to actively manage their psychiatric symptoms, to make choices about their treatment, and to develop a positive sense of self. A focus on competence moves the focus away from symptoms to abilities, helping people build on their existing strengths and skills, rather than stressing symptoms and deviance. The focus on recovery suggests a positive goal in place of a negative one. Rather than attempting to reduce the risk of relapse, recovery is seen as moving people to fulfilling personal goals, reinforcing that there is life after hospitalization and beyond psychiatric diagnosis. During recovery, while acknowledging the variable course of mental illness, social workers shift the emphasis of intervention toward a mindset of possibility and capability (Carpenter, 2002; Stromwall & Hurdle, 2003; Turney & Conway, 2000).

Working with families is another vital social work role in the mental health arena. Aviram (2002) comments that families want more information on the different aspects of mental illnesses. They ask for information about how best to manage the patient; they seek training and guidance on how best to deal with the burden of care of the mentally ill family member. They need help identifying and accessing community resources for their family members and themselves and want support and direction on how to advocate for their family member with mental illness. The same philosophical orientation to service is employed with families, stressing management, empowerment, and building on the strengths of the family system and resources.

SOCIAL WORKER COMMENTS

I interviewed eight social workers in three different hospitals to understand how they articulate their professional role and determine what they see as the difficulties and satisfactions of their work.

All of the social workers worked on locked units: staff and patients were locked into the unit and the only way to enter or leave was if staff unlocked the doors. Locked units are the norm on most psychiatric floors, especially because most admissions are for people with serious mental illness, who are thus at risk to others or themselves. Two of the social workers I interviewed worked on units of 18 beds; the others worked on larger units of 30 beds.

The physical configuration of the units was similar; each had a central meeting room for patients and families, with a television, couches, tables, and so forth. Patients slept in one- or two-bed rooms. During the day, the patients were encouraged, in some cases, and mandated in others, to leave their rooms and participate in the activities of the unit, which included group and individual therapy sessions, visiting with family, or supervised activity. The physical appearance of patients on each unit was also similar: patients were dressed in either street clothes or hospital issue, many looked unkempt, some talked to themselves, some raged, some sat quietly or watched television. Some patients, those who had attempted suicide, were under greater levels of surveillance and had aides with them at all times. In appearance and demeanor, the gap between staff and patient was noticeable, as was the gap between patient and visitor. Many of the patients had a "medicated" appearance: a stoniness in their facial expressions, movement that is not smooth, or glazed eyes and a somewhat vacant look.

When the social workers were asked to describe their role and function, each noted that they were responsible for running groups on the unit, mostly with patients and some with family members. Most of the social workers agreed that newly diagnosed patients require social and emotional support, psychoeducation, and help in building hope toward reintegrating into society (Miller & Mason, 2001). As such, the social workers attempt to keep the morale on the unit as upbeat as possible and work toward keeping the patients and families engaged in the treatment and patient progress. All eight social workers carried a caseload, having daily and sometimes twice daily sessions with patients and frequent meetings with family members. The social workers worked collaboratively with the psychiatrists and in some respects saw themselves as their emissaries of the physicians, working with patients to help them understand their medication requirements and the need to be compliant with the medication schedule.

It was the opinion of several of the social workers that one of the more difficult aspects of their work was trying to educate the patients of the necessity of staying with their medications and following up with therapy and treatment after they left the hospital. The balance between being optimistic with the newer patients, trying to help them so that they did not become "repeaters," and impressing upon them the necessity of follow-up was delicate. "How do you tell someone with a first episode psychotic break that they will be fine if they only take their meds when I am fairly certain that they will be back here some time in the future? I struggle with that because I know, or think I know, that they will probably not follow through, but I have to be as optimistic as possible for the sake of the patient and family."

The family work posed difficult challenges for the social workers. These challenges can be summarized as handling family responses that are very stereotypical of attitudes toward people with mental illness. Even with education about mental illness, "It is very difficult to convince a parent that he or she is not responsible for the mental illness of their child; it is very hard to remove the guilt which is imposed by society. I have seen parents weeping in my office as I try to ease their pain over their adult child's situation." The situation with families worsens over time and with readmission to the hospital: "Many of the families are burned out and sick of the revolving door of the psych unit. They need respite care for themselves, which, of course does not exist, but they almost have a respite when the family member is in the hospital and ironically don't really want the patient to return home."

Many do not return home and thus residential treatment must be found, which evoked another set of reactions from the social workers interviewed. By and large they felt that community resources were limited at best and nonexistent at worst. Because much of the social worker's time is spent arranging for aftercare for the patient, with limited resources and aftercare options, it becomes a frustrating part of their job.

The one quality each social worker identified as essential in the work is being able to convey to the patient and family that they are cared about. "So many see the mentally ill as disposable people who drain the resources of the community and hospital. I don't accept that notion and try to convey to the patient especially that he or she is a valued person and member of society," said one worker. Another worker commented, "Self-esteem is so fragile with the patients. And, until they can be stabilized and get a handle on their thoughts, they are truly not reachable. But I have seen changes in the patients from the time they are admitted, started on some medication, and within 24 hours they are helped and are more reasonable and rational. The medications are so vital to keeping them stable."

The turnaround on the units varied from 48 hours for some to days and weeks for others. Sometimes, the longer hospitalizations are a result of not having resources or places to send a patient for aftercare; lack of group homes, day treatment facilities, and so forth. Despite the inherent frustrations of the work, most of the social workers who were interviewed were upbeat about their job, liked coming to work, and found satisfaction in being able to reach into the mental illness and find the person under the diagnosis. Although the venue does not allow for much deep analytic work, most of the social workers were pleased that they could use their clinical skills with those patients who were oriented and able to relate more fully. "I love what I do," said one social worker, "I help people who are struggling and try to put them on a good track. I work with families, work that many social workers here in the hospital don't get a chance to do, and I find that very stimulating and interesting. I was offered a job in another unit and didn't give it a second thought. This is where I make a difference."

15

SOCIAL WORK IN THE PEDIATRIC UNIT

ABOUT PEDIATRIC ILLNESS

Every year, thousands of children are hospitalized with a variety of chronic and life-threatening health concerns. Families suffer with their sick children, and health care professionals work to provide both the child and family members with the most responsive care possible. Most would agree that a sick child pulls at the emotional fabric of families and engenders a sympathetic response from everyone.

In the United States, there were approximately 36 million hospital stays in 2000; about 18% of these stays (more than 6 million admissions) were for children and adolescents 17 years and younger. In hospital descriptors of care for children, there are three groupings: neonatal conditions (hospital stays for newborns and infants 30 days of age or less), pediatric illness (stays for ill children and adolescents over 30 days of age), and adolescent care (patients 13 to 18 years old). Almost two thirds of all childhood hospital stays are for newborns and neonates (babies up to 30 days old); the vast majority of these stays (95%) are for births of infants in the hospital. In 2000, children younger than 1 year comprised only 1% of the U.S. population but accounted for nearly 13% of all hospital stays. Children and adolescents 1 to 17 years old represent 24% of the population but account for 5% of hospital stays (Owens, Thompson, Elixhauser, & Ryan, 2003).

REASONS FOR HOSPITALIZATION

Five of the top ten most common diagnoses for neonates relate to respiratory problems or infections, conditions which often result from premature birth. In these cases the infant stays for a period of days or weeks until he or she is strong enough (i.e., has gained enough weight and lung capacity has reached normal levels) to leave the hospital. The most common neonatal conditions that require extension of the hospital stay or return to the hospital are conditions associated with bilirubin metabolism (jaundice), respiratory distress, infections, and congenital anomalies. Nonneonates that require hospitalization display illnesses such as pneumonia, asthma, and acute bronchitis. Often newborns with respiratory illness are kept in incubators with oxygen pumped in to help them breathe.

Infectious disease is another precipitant for hospitalization, accounting for 6 of the top 10 diagnoses for infants and 5 of the top 10 diagnoses for 3- to 5-year-olds. About 7%, or 1 in 14, of pediatric hospitalizations are for mental disorders (Owens et al., 2003).

For adolescents, injuries — including leg injuries, medication poisonings, and head injuries — are among the top reasons for hospital stays. Digestive illnesses, including gastroenteritis, are the second most common pediatric conditions. Appendectomy is the most common surgical procedure performed on children and adolescents in the hospital, occurring more than 238 times per day in the United States. By the teen years, pregnancy becomes a significant reason for hospitalization, with approximately 20 hospital stays for pregnancy per 1,000 13- to 17-year-old girls in the United States.

Within the above description of pediatric illness, units in hospitals are configured in various ways. In some hospitals, all pregnancies (adolescent or not) are seen in the gynecological unit of the hospital, whereas other hospitals treat teen mothers in a separate unit. Similarly, neonates may be seen in either a separate or aligned pediatric unit of the hospital. In some hospitals, all of these categories of care are handled together. In larger hospitals, separate units are more the standard, whereas a smaller, community hospital may have blended services.

The illness experience for the family and patient in the pediatric unit depends on the severity of the precipitating medical event and the length of stay. For many situations — routine infections, some respiratory problems, and minor injuries — the treatment is overnight or a few days at most. But for more serious conditions — surgical, chronic, or cardiac — the stay is more protracted, with stressors unique to a pediatric patient.

THE SICK CHILD

The varying dynamics in pediatric care are as extensive as the age range for this category of patient. In presenting the dynamics of pediatric hospitalizations, I will describe separately the needs and concerns of the younger child (up to age 12) and the adolescent.

The Young Child

In response to being hospitalized, the young patient experiences a variety of stressors. Being ill and thrust in an alien environment is immensely stressful for adults and can only be imagined for a young child. "In addition to physical discomfort, concern about bodily integrity, and uncertainty over the future, hospitalization involves separation from the home environment, reduced access to familiar figures, and intrusive monitoring procedures" (Kronenberger, Carter, & Thomas, 1997, p. 212). Under these trying circumstances, children are at risk for developing behavioral problems and psychological symptoms. These hospital-based behavior problems may interfere with the child's functioning and recovery and may necessitate in-hospital intervention from social work staff or psychiatry.

The greatest source of stress for the child under seven years of age is separation from parents. Children of this age are accustomed to their parents' care and protection and, when subjected to the alien environment of the hospital, they are frightened and angry that their parents have not been able to protect them from the painful events of the hospital nor return them to their home environment. The parents are often overwhelmed themselves and are uncertain of what can be done to address the concerns of their child. This combination of stress often sends the child into a depressive state, unable to understand what has happened and feeling unsafe.

The most common responses to a hospitalization include separation anxiety, regression, sadness, apathy or withdrawal, fears of the dark or health personnel, hyperactivity, aggression, and sleep disturbances (Elander, Nillson, & Lindbergh, 1986). Many of these feelings and behaviors are typical for children who are not ill, but they are exacerbated when children feel anxious. For sick childlen, they are fueled by the anxiety and fear generated by the hospital experience. A review of studies indicated that as many as 40% of children in pediatric settings exhibit depressive symptoms and 20% experience emotional as well as behavioral difficulties (Rodriguez & Boggs, 1998).

In addition, especially if the child is critically ill, invasive diagnostic procedures — CT scans, MRIs, scopes — create high levels of stress. Considering the cognitive stage of development, one would expect the younger child to experience these procedures as punishment for wrong-doing, with additional fear that surgical procedures will result in body mutilation (Melnyk & Alpert-Gillis, 1998).

Ideally, "Interventions that promote normalcy while a child is in an unfamiliar setting such as a hospital need to be incorporated into the child's care" (Kaminski, Pellino, & Wish, 2002, p. 321). For this reason, pediatric units have play areas that children are encouraged to use, and it is not uncommon to find these play areas full of children and parents. Even ill, these patients *are* children, and play is the medium of activity for them. In addition, play can enable the child to express, master, and ultimately cope better with anxieties, fears, and conflicts relating to the hospital experience (Kaminski et al.).

The hardest time for many young children is when their parents leave for the day and they are faced with the silence and aloneness of their situation. In many pediatric units, provisions are made for parents to stay in the same room with their child to address such moments. This brings with it security for the patient, but it may provoke other concerns for the parent, who is torn between caring for the ill child and external responsibilities that are being pushed aside. As a youngster, however, the moments of aloneness are often incomprehensible, and it is logical that the young child would bring a level of fantasy — including the notion of punishment — to enable their understanding of it. Young children strive to make sense of their world but do not have the level of understanding and comprehension of adults. Young children create their own internal explanations and logic. Usually a youngster's perspective is self-referential — they explain things in terms of themselves, including why things happen. Therefore, they might assume that their illness is because of something they have done.

In addition, especially for the younger patient, procedures that exclude the parents, interchanges and examination with doctors and other medical staff, and general fear of strange situations, are enough to promote anxiety and fear in the child.

The Adolescent

For the adolescent, who is at a more advanced developmental stage than the younger patient, the hospitalization experience poses difficult and more specific challenges. Compared to younger patients, adolescents have increased needs for control over their lives, have privacy concerns, and are much more involved with peers. In the hospital, adolescents, who are beginning to assert their independence, are thrust into dependency on adults, are forced to have frequent examinations, and are asked questions about their bodies that may cause embarrassment.

In addition, those social supports that might buffer these feelings — family time, visits with friends, and contact with school — are limited by the hospital regime and the reality of whatever restrictions their illness imposes. These limitations and challenges to self-esteem can complicate recovery by adding a level of depression that also has to be overcome (Gusella & Ward, 1998).

Denholm and Ferguson (1987), in their review of existing literature on the hospital experience for the adolescent, identified five basic needs of hospitalized adolescents: privacy, peer visitation and contact, mobility, independence, and educational continuity (being able to maintain school contact). These needs are especially accurate for adolescents who are hospitalized for extended periods of time. Although the review is dated, the assessment of adolescent angst is not.

In research by Gusella and Ward (1998), 69 adolescents were interviewed about their hospital stays and identified the following advantages of being in the hospital: getting healthy, having friendly staff and a pleasant stay, having readily available care, getting away from home, and having less school. Disadvantages identified by this group included loss of contact with friends, being away from home and school, loss of freedom and privacy, the food, being sick in bed, and taking medications. Interestingly absent from the list are concerns about their own well being: fear of dying, fear of getting sick again, fear of becoming sicker. Perhaps this list relates to adolescents' sense of invincibility and not being fully immersed in the adult world of concern for the future.

PEDIATRIC HOSPITALIZATIONS — THE FAMILY EXPERIENCE

The psychosocial and environmental factors of having a critically ill child can equate to a time of crisis, creating a sense of helplessness and vulnerability for parents. The emotional impact and injury to parents' self-esteem can be devastating and sometimes debilitating as they try to make sense out of a senseless situation. Practical problems also create often seemingly insurmountable hurdles, including time away from other children, separation from extended family, time away from work, and time away from home and routine. If a newborn is ill, parents often express concern that they have not had a chance to know their baby and that the baby does not know them, so there is an added sense of frustration and anguish; for the parents of an older child, or toddler, there is the potential loss of a relationship with the child and the loss of a future (Dungan, Jaquay, Reznik, & Sands, 1995). As noted by Robinson (1987), extended hospitalizations present severe and cumulative stresses for parents and family members.

Research with parents who have a seriously ill child has documented some of the struggles and experiences of hospitalization. Emotional concerns were ranked most pressing, including struggles with feelings of guilt, fears about the unstable condition of the child, uncertainty about the vulnerability of the child, and frustration at having no sense of control of the medical situation were identified by most of those interviewed. Communication problems with professionals were found to be the second most significant stressor, with changes in the family routine during the child's hospitalization the third. Finances and family disruption, concern for siblings of the ill child, and living in and visiting the hospital were also noted as difficult areas for families. Parents identified two coping strategies as most helpful: gaining information and obtaining support from hospital professionals. Family members expressed how difficult it was to hear, understand, absorb, and sort through the immense amount of information received from the medical professionals. It is difficult enough for parents to understand and make sense of their experience, but the added anguish of not comprehending some of the medicalese (medical jargon) was very stressful, leading to feelings of being overwhelmed and intimidated. Other helpful coping strategies identified were normalizing the experience (trying to see the hospitalization as part of a sequence of life events), reprioritizing (setting different standards and goals for their child and themselves as a result of the illness), obtaining support from family and friends, obtaining support from others having the same or similar experience, and relying on inner strengths and beliefs (Horn, Feldman, & Ploof, 1995).

Another stressful aspect of the hospitalization experience for parents revolves around the confusion of their role as parents. How do they enact the parent role while the child is in the hospital. In essence, when the child is hospitalized, the parents relinquish the vital role of caretaker of their child. For some parents, this creates levels of anxiety and stress that are not as apparent as some of the stressors mentioned in the Horn et al. (1995) study. Guilt about the child's illness is a compelling aspect of the underlying emotional confusion and struggle for parents. Did they wait too long to bring the child for medical care? Could they have done something to prevent this illness? Did they do something to create this terrible illness? Did they give this child bad genes that could have caused this illness? These and other questions in this vein plague the parents of a seriously or critically ill child. Another facet of role confusion resides in the parents' anguish over how they might be judged by others, including hospital professionals. Are they really good parents, or have they been negligent and will they be seen as such?

Having a sense of control over the child's situation and outcome is central for parents (Horn et al., 1995). Relinquishing the care for one's ill child to the medical team is equated to surrendering control over what happens to him or her in the hospital. However, parents must remember that control is illusory to begin with, because illness knows no bounds or reason or special categories. Trying to make sense of the senseless — why their child was stricken — emotionally undermines many parents as they grapple with having lost control over a situation.

SOCIAL WORK ROLE AND FUNCTION

The social worker on the pediatric unit is placed in a strategic position to care for both patients and family members. From the social work perspective, services are delivered from a family-centered orientation and there is constant dialogue between family members and medical staff, that the parents have a voice in decision making about their child and the care he or she receives (Miceli & Clark, 2004). Consistent with the social work systems orientation, the patient is the sick child *and* the family members who care for him or her.

Because the social worker has day-to-day familiarity with the medical care team and the hospital systems, he or she is able to facilitate interaction among patients, family members, and medical professionals (Bergman & Fritz, 1982). With this orientation and position, the social worker engages the parents in brief treatment to help them deal with the present stage of illness and to prepare for home and, if necessary, future hospitalizations. In addition, "The social worker facilitates the expression of feelings, provides and/or helps the patient and family to seek appropriate information, encourages their active involvement in the diagnostic process, suggests resources that might be useful, and helps them to understand and accept the diagnosis. Perhaps, most importantly, the social worker encourages the maintenance of self-esteem and emotional integrity of the patient and family" (Mailick, 1990, p. 107).

Dungan et al. (1995) describe some of the challenges faced by social work staff on the pediatric unit: containing the crisis, enabling the mastery of tasks, differentiating between past and current sources of stress, validating the family's efforts, being sensitive to cross-cultural issues, tolerating strong affect (emotions usually run high), and supporting bereaved parents as needed. In efforts to contain the crisis of the hospitalization and illness, the social worker has to balance the needed emotional expression of feelings for the parents and family with the need to help the family to continue functioning. If parents are too overwhelmed by their feelings of frustration, lack of control, and so forth, they may not be emotionally available to handle their sick child and his or her needs for comfort and support. In an effort to enable the mastery of tasks, the social worker must be attuned to the feelings of vulnerability and helplessness the parents are experiencing and try to find ways parents can feel empowered either through tasks or via information acquisition. During crisis, preexisting emotional or relationship issues tend to surface, when the emotional overload of the present reminds the parents of previous unresolved problems and feelings. The social worker attempts to keep the family in the present, but when this cannot be accomplished, brief counseling with the social worker may prove helpful. As part of validating the family's efforts, the social worker can reinforce that the parents should have no regrets, that they are with the child in love, and that they are not being judged by staff.

Cross-cultural issues are always present in a hospital setting, and the social worker needs to both be informed about specific cultural beliefs and practices and be respectful of them and even advocate to other staff members to be tolerant when rituals are different from the dominant culture. Pediatric social workers are challenged daily to accept a wide range of emotional situations that are being experienced and played out by children and their family members. Suffering and emotional expressions are common on a pediatric unit with sick and vulnerable children going through very difficult and often painful experiences. There is something about the vulnerability of children that touches many social workers; to do this work, social workers must know what level of emotionality they can tolerate and have outlets for their own well-being in order to be effective on their unit. Moreover, sitting with children and family members who are experiencing anguish and sadness requires that social workers have great patience, skill, and understanding not only of the patient and family member but also of themselves. Death is frequent on the pediatric unit; some social workers have daily encounters with families whose child has died. Fundamental bereavement counseling skills have to be part of the social worker's repertoire (Dungan et al., 1995).

Based on the above description of social worker role and function, pediatric social workers (and especially pediatric social workers in pediatric critical care areas) are advised to identify and collaborate with colleagues to share the emotional impact of the work, to understand and accept their own vulnerabilities and emotional areas, and to accept their own impotence and powerlessness in the face of illness.

SOCIAL WORKER COMMENTS

Eighteen social workers in four venues were interviewed to inform the work on the pediatric unit. Six of the social workers worked with infants in the neonatal unit and twelve worked on a general pediatric floor with children from several months old through adolescence.

Neonatal Social Workers

Neonatal age range on the units was differentially defined among the social workers, ranging from newborn to 18 months. Caseloads varied from 15 to 50 cases at a given time. The variety of medical situations was broad, ranging from respiratory to cardiac problems, bleeding disorders, digestive problems, and failure-to-thrive situations. Many babies on the neonatal unit are seriously below a safe birth weight and need the extra and intensive care of the unit.

Generally, the social workers identified support to parents as their major and daily responsibility. Because the patients are very young, interaction with them is limited, but parent interaction was constant, though varied. In one hospital, child life workers were specifically detailed to work with the infants, freeing the social work staff to devote as much time as needed to parental concerns and problems. Interventions regarding concrete and emotional concerns were the primary areas of work for the social workers. Concrete concerns included covering medication and treatment costs, insurance issues, and housing if the family needed to be near the hospital for a critically ill infant. Parent education was a primary focus of work — explaining to parents what to expect on the neonatal unit, translating some of the medical jargon, and explaining medical procedures and protocols. One social worker explained that parents do not get as much information as they need from the nurses, because nursing is often focused only on the physical condition of the baby. As such, parents may be afraid to ask the nurses some of their questions. In these cases, the social worker can serve as the bridge between the complexity of the medical work and the parents' need for information from the medical staff.

For infants who are critically ill, one social work task is to help the parents deal with the probable death of their infant. The death of a newborn is very difficult; so much expectation accompanies a new life. Helping parents deal with the loss of that potential life and the loss of that relationship becomes the focus of the work. Death is a constant on the neonatal unit. "The death of an infant," commented one social worker, "affects everyone on the unit. Support staff and especially the other families are hit hard and everyone feels vulnerable." One worker described the situation when a death is sudden versus an anticipated death: "In the event of sudden death, the infant is taken into a private room and the parents are encouraged to be with the baby, to hold him or her, and to await the arrival of the funeral home personnel. In the event of an anticipated dying, the infant and family are kept together in a private room where they await the moment of death. The parents can hold and be with the baby as he or she is dying. Often we will make a plaster casting of the hands and feet of the infant for the family to have. We will make a memory box of items used by the baby, take pictures, and help plan a memorial with the family." The poignancy and sensitivity of these moments can only be imagined, and the social workers initiating these postdeath observances have to handle not only the emotions of the family but their own emotions as well.

The presence and actuality of death are draining for most of the social workers. One worker stated that she has "no time for feelings. I go into mode and do the drill I know I have to with the parents. Even so, it is hard and I don't want to feel too much; otherwise I will lose my boundaries and flounder."

On the other end of the spectrum, the social workers identified with the remarkable resiliency of the infant body and the evidence of a "will to live" that is seen in many of the infants. "My greatest joy," commented a social worker, "is saying goodbye to a family when they have had a critically small or ill child and the child has recovered adequately to be able to go home. We had a baby here who weighed one pound when she was born and she stayed with us for months. We hated to say goodbye to the baby and the family when she was finally able to leave the hospital. It was like losing a good friend, and we had all become quite close to this family. This is the miracle of life and it makes all the effort and stress of our job worthwhile."

General Pediatrics

"We do everything," declared one social worker, "We work with the kids, with the parents, we advocate with insurance companies, we do discharge planning and make all the arrangement for that, and we sometimes have to support the staff as well as each other! Every once in a while we have to deal with the police if we suspect child abuse or neglect. We are everywhere on the unit!" This multitask description was echoed by the other 11 social workers, each describing multiple roles and responsibilities they are expected to perform in the articulation of their work. The general feeling from the interviewed workers was that they assume a crisis orientation to their work, especially with those children who are brought to the hospital unexpectedly. An example of an unexpected admission is a child experiencing his or her first asthma attack, a child who is injured, or a child having a first encounter with an as yet, undiagnosed illness. These situations require the social worker to be available to help the family negotiate the hospital systems and help them deal with the numerous reactions that first-time hospitalizations provoke. "Most parents — and their children, for that matter — are very nervous, not sure of what has happened or is happening. For these families, we go into intro mode and help acquaint them with hospital routine and make them as comfortable as possible under very difficult circumstances" explained one worker. She continued, "The children also need support and company and attention. Many of them have never been in a hospital before and the machines and equipment are scary at a time when they don't feel at all well. So I always try to spend as much time as possible, sometimes just sitting with a child, sometimes holding the little ones."

For the returning child of a family with whom the social worker is familiar, different dynamics between worker and family ensue. These families are familiar with the routine of the unit, so social worker orientation is not essential. However, the patient's return usually signifies a more serious level of illness and that creates a greater need for emotional support and outreach on the part of the social worker.

As in other hospital units, the impact of managed care necessitates shorter hospitalizations; therefore, discharge planning is a large part of the work of the social worker. In one instance, a worker lamented that so much of the time is spent arranging a safe discharge that social work skills sometimes are not needed other than for advocacy and negotiation with insurance companies.

Another worker mentioned that she occasionally is "the recipient of the anger from the parents or family of the child. Sometimes it is about the care, the food, the nurses, etc., but I have learned over the years, that this anger is about the frustration they feel over having a sick child and feeling impotent about what is happening to their kid. I try to rechannel these feelings but sometimes the parents just need to let off steam; it is not about their feelings toward me but about the anger at what has happened in their lives."

In discussing how death is handled on their unit, several of the social workers felt that it was one of the harder parts of their job. In some cases, however, it is seen "as a blessing, especially if there is no chance that the child will ever live a 'normal' life. We see so much illness and deformity that some deaths are very acceptable and are even welcomed, not by the parents but by the staff. In one way, it puts closure on the failure of nature, of medicine, and the medical world. In essence, we bury the worst mistakes that have been created." Staying with the family through the death ordeal is a common part of the work and is expected of the social work staff. Some hospitals have support groups for parents and family of the sick child as well as bereavement groups. Every social worker interviewed spoke in favor of these groups and wanted this service expanded on their individual unit.

One social worker clarified what is compelling about the work: "After all is said and done, the patients are children. What that means for me," she continued, "is that I will see a very sick child, yet this kid wants to play with other children. I will see the child in the playroom, just being a kid. It is this resiliency that keeps me going, this striving to be a regular kid. I give my all for that to go on."

16

THE INTERFACE OF MEDICINE
AND SOCIAL WORK

As described in this volume, the variety, trajectory, and complexity of medical conditions are astounding. Despite this, in many instances the medical profession has been able to make significant strides in the management of illness and disease. Generally, people in the United States are living longer and enjoying a better quality of life, being maintained and sustained despite serious medical conditions. Functioning in the era of managed care, social workers employed in hospitals serve a vital function as members of the interdisciplinary team and as the liaison between patients and the multiple systems in which they are thrust when hospitalized. To be effective in their role, social workers must be knowledgeable about the client population and the problems they present, aware of the organization constraints and functioning, familiar with community resources and supports, and comfortable with counseling approaches and intervention modalities (Cowles, 2000). In sum, the social worker is positioned between the patient and the medical environment. It is at this interface that the work is done. This volume has attempted to bridge the interface, illuminating both the medical and social work sides of the equation.

Social work efforts within the hospital setting continue to use a biopsychosocial approach. This was confirmed by the comments of the social workers interviewed, who often noted that a lot of their efforts go beyond immediate patient care and extend to the forces in the patient's environment that contribute to and may exacerbate the patient's condition and functioning. An additional approach to social work services, perhaps driven by the necessity for evidence-based practice, is the International Classification of Impairments, Disabilities, and Handicaps (ICIDH), which provides an orientation to practice based on functionality, in addition to health status. With this orientation, social workers are directed to classify a patient's condition on both a physical and functional level. In addition, they evaluate environmental factors that interact with all the components of functioning. The information social workers consider when doing a patient evaluation — diagnosis and functioning — provides a broader base from which to gather a meaningful picture of the patient, allowing for more in-depth decision making about patient care and aftercare arrangements (Fred, 2005). This approach was also confirmed by the social worker interviews.

Perhaps it is a mindset that draws one to hospital social work, a predilection to want to be helpful to those who are ill or in pain. Perhaps, it is personal history that moves one to be able to see difficult situations and find rewards that others could not see. Whatever the motivation, one cannot help but be impressed by the devotion and commitment noted in the social workers interviewed for this book.

Hospital social work is not for everyone. Bearing witness to pain and suffering of others is difficult; being in an atmosphere where death is a given and a constant is emotionally draining. The work is demanding, stressful, and, at times, emotionally charged. However, I hope the reader has gained an appreciation and awareness of the rewards of and the possibility for effective and meaningful social work practice with both patients and their caregivers and families. Almost every social worker interviewed spoke positively of their work, feeling a sense of accomplishment on a regular basis. The medical establishment will always need the services of social workers to augment care and interact with patients and caregivers. Social workers are often the soul of the hospital, providing support, understanding, and caring at a person-to-person level.

REFERENCES

Ai, A., Peterson, C., Dunkle, R., Saunders, D., Bolling, S., & Buchtel, H. (1997). How gender affects psychological adjustment one year after coronary artery bypass graft surgery. *Women & Health, 26*(4), 45–65.

Allen, J. (1990). Physical and psychosocial outcomes after coronary artery bypass graft surgery: Review of the literature. *Heart & Lung, 19*, 49–55.

Alper, S., & Kerson, T. S. (1997). "Would you abandon your child?" An inpatient psychiatric staff confront change, a difficult case — and each other. In T. S. Kerson (Ed.), *Social work in healthcare settings* (2nd ed., pp. 445–461). New York: Haworth Press.

American Burn Association. (2002). *Burn incidence and treatment in the United States fact sheet.* Chicago: Author.

American Cancer Society. (2004). *Cancer facts & figures 2004.* Atlanta, GA: Author.

American Heart Association. (2004). *Heart disease and stroke statistics — 2004 update.* Dallas, TX: Author.

American Hospital Association. (1984). *Discharge planning guidelines.* Chicago: Author.

American Hospital Association. (2005). *AHA hospital statistics.* Chicago: Author.

American Psychiatric Association. (2000). *Diagnostic and statistical manual of mental disorders* (4th ed.). Washington, DC: Author.

Andrykowski, M., Carpenter, J., & Munn, R. (2003). Psychosocial sequelae of cancer diagnosis and treatment. In L. Schein, H. Bernard, H. Spitz, & P. Muskin (Eds.), *Psychosocial treatment for medical conditions — principles and techniques* (pp. 79–131). New York: Brunner-Routledge.

Aviram, A. (2002). The changing role of the social worker in the mental health system. *Social Work in Health Care, 35*(1/2), 615–632.

Babcock, J. (1998a). Discharge planning in acute care. In D. Aronstein & B. Thompson (Eds.), *HIV and social work* (pp. 89–100). New York: Harrington Park Press.

Babcock, J. (1998b). Involving family and significant others in acute care. In D. Aronstein & B. Thompson (Eds.), *HIV and social work* (pp. 101–108). New York: Harrington Park Press.

Bacon, L. (1987). Lessons of AIDS: Racism, homophobia are the real epidemic. *Listen Real Loud, 8*(2), 5–7.

Barakat, L., Kazak, A., Meadows, A., Casey, R., & Stuber, M. (1997). Families surviving cancer: A comparison of posttraumatic stress symptoms with families of healthy children. *Journal of Pediatric Psychology, 22*, 843–859.

Bartlett, H. (1975). Ida M. Cannon: Pioneer in medical social work. *Social Service Review, 49*(2), 208–229.

Beder, J. (1997). Withdrawal from dialysis. *Dialysis and Transplantation, 26*(8), 535–540.

Beder, J. (1999). Evaluation research on the effectiveness of social work intervention on dialysis patients: The first three months. *Social Work in Health Care, 30*(1), 15–30.

Bennahum, D. A. (2003). The historical development of hospice and palliative care. In W. Forman, J. Kitzes, R. Anderson, & D. Sheehan (Eds.), *Hospice and palliative care* (pp. 1–12). Boston: Jones and Bartlett.

Ben-Zur, H., Rappaport, B., Ammar, R., & Uretzky, G. (2000). Coping strategies, life style changes, and pessimism after open-heart surgery. *Health & Social Work, 25*(3), 201–209.

Bergman, A., & Fritz, G. (1982). Psychiatric and social work collaboration in a pediatric chronic illness hospital. *Social Work in Health Care, 7*(1), 45–55.

Berkman, B., & Volland, P. (1997). Health care practice overview. In R. Edwards (Ed.), *Encyclopedia of social work* (19th ed., pp. 143–149). Washington, DC: NASW Press.

Berkow, R. (1987). End stage renal disease. In R. Berkow (Ed.), *The Merck manual* (pp. 1566–1582). Rahway, NJ: Merck.

Bernstein, N. R. (1982). Burn patients' use of autohypnosis: Making a painful experience bearable. *Clinics in Plastic Surgery, 9*, 337–346.

Bernstein, N. R. (1988). Coping with disfigurement. In N. Bernstein, A. Brelau, & J. Graham (Eds.), *Coping strategies for burn survivors and their families* (pp. 3–16). New York: Praeger.

Blakeney, P., Herndon, D. N., Desai, M. H., Beard, S., & Wales-Seale, P. (1988). Long-term psychosocial adjustment following burn injury. *Journal of Burn Care Rehabilitation, 9*(6), 661–664.

Blanchard, C. G., Albrecht, T. L., Ruckdeschel, J., Grant, J. C., & Hemmick, M. (1995). The role of social support in adaptation to cancer and to survival. *Journal of Psychosocial Oncology, 13*(2), 75–95.

Blotcky, A., Raczynski, J., Gurwitch, R., & Smith, K. (1985). Family influences on hopelessness among children early in the cancer experience. *Journal of Pediatric Psychology, 10*(4), 479–493.

Blum, D. (1993). Social work services for adult cancer patients and their families. In N. Stearns, M. Lauria, J. Hermann, & P. Fogelberg (Eds.), *Oncology social work* (pp. 101–129). Atlanta, GA: American Cancer Society.

Blumenfield, S., Bennett, C., & Rehr, H. (1998). Discharge planning: A key function. In H. Rehr, G. Rosenberg, & S. Blumenfield (Eds.), *Creative social work in health care* (pp. 83–91). New York: Springer.

Bohnengel, A. (1983). Coping with kidney transplantation. *Perspectives, 5*, 5–16.

Boschen, K. (1996). Correlates of life satisfaction, residential satisfaction, and locus of control among adults with spinal cord injuries. *Rehabilitation Counseling Bulletin, 39*, 230–243.

Bradford, A. (1999). Rebuild: An orthopedic trauma support group and community outreach program. *Health & Social Work, 24*(4), 307–312.

Bright, M. (1994). Social work practice with organ transplant patients. In M. Holosko & P. Taylor (Eds.), *Social work practice in health care settings* (2nd ed., pp. 441–452). Toronto: Canadian Scholars' Press.

Bristow, D., & Herrick, C. (2002). Emergency departments: The roles of the nurse care manager and the social worker. *Continuing Care, 21*(2), 28–29.

Brown, M. (1996, February 2–4). Never let the patient smell fear. *USA Weekend*, pp. 4–6.

Campbell, A. (1998). Family caregivers: Caring for ESRD partners. *Advances in Renal Replacement Therapy, 5*(2), 98–108.

Caplan, L. (2000). *Caplan's stroke: A clinical approach* (3rd ed.). Boston: Butterworth-Heinemann.

Carlson, L., Bultz, B., Speca, M., & St. Pierre, M. (2000a). Partners of cancer patients: Part I. Impact, adjustment, and coping across the illness trajectory. *Journal of Psychosocial Oncology, 18*(2), 39–62.

Carlson, L., Bultz, B., Speca, M., & St. Pierre, M. (2000b). Partners of cancer patients: Part II. Psychosocial interventions and suggestions for improvement. *Journal of Psychosocial Oncology, 18*(3), 33–43.

Carpenter, J. (2002). Mental health recovery paradigm: Implications for social work. *Health & Social Work, 27*(2), 86–94.

Carter, A. H., & Petro, J. A. (1998). *Rising from the flames: The experience of the severely burned.* Philadelphia: University of Pennsylvania Press.

Cates, J., Graham, L., Boeglin, D., & Tielker, S. (1990). The effect of AIDS on the family system. *Families in Society, 71*, 195–201.

Centers for Disease Control. (1999). Division of Injury Control, Center for Environmental Health and Injury Control. Retrieved September 2004, from http://www.web-app.cdc.gove/cgi-bin/broker.exe.

Centers for Disease Control. (2003). *HIV/AIDS surveillance report: HIV infection and AIDS in the United States, 2003.* Washington, DC: Author.

Centers for Disease Control. (2004a). Burns. Retrieved September 8, 2004, from http://cdc.gov.

Centers for Disease Control. (2004b). Traumatic brain injury. Retrieved November 21, 2004, from http://www.cdc.gov/node.do/id.

Chandra, V., Szklo, M., Goldberg, R., & Tonascia, J. (1983). The impact of marital status on survival after myocardial infarction: A population based study. *American Journal of Epidemiology, 117*, 320–325.

Chase, B. W., Cornille, T., & English, R. (2000). Life satisfaction among persons with spinal cord injuries. *Journal of Rehabilitation, 66*(3), 14–20.

Chesler, M., & Barbarin, O. (1987). *Childhood cancer and the family: Meeting the challenge of stress and support.* New York: Brunner/Mazel.

Christ, G., & Wiener, L. (1987). Psychosocial issues in AIDS. *Social Work in Health Care, 13*(1), 6–14.

Cincotta, N. (1993). Special programs for children with cancer and their families. In N. Stearns, M. Lauria, J. Hermann, & P. Fogelberg (Eds.), *Oncology social work* (pp. 257–268). Atlanta, GA: American Cancer Society.

Contrada, R., Goyal, T., Cather, C., Rafalson, L., Idler, E., & Krause, T. (2004). Psychosocial factors in outcomes of heart surgery: The impact of religious involvement and depressive symptoms. *Health Psychology, 23*(3), 227–238.

Corcoran, K. (1997). Managed care: Implications for social work. In R. Edwards (Ed.), *Encyclopedia of social work, supplement* (pp. 191–200). Washington, DC: NASW Press.

Cordoba, C., Fobair, P., & Callan, D. (1993). Common issues facing adults with cancer. In N. Stearns, M. Lauria, J. Hermann, & P. Fogelberg (Eds.), *Oncology social work* (pp. 43–77). Atlanta, GA: American Cancer Society.

Corrigan, P., & Miller, F. (2004). Shame, blame, and contamination: A review of the impact of mental illness stigma on family members. *Journal of Mental Health, 13*(6), 537–548.

Coward, R., & Dwyer, J. (1993). The health and well-being of rural elders. In L. Ginsberg (Ed.), *Social work in rural communities* (pp. 164–182). Alexandria, VA: Council on Social Work Education.

Cowles, L. (2000). *Social work in the health field.* New York: Haworth Press.

Cowles, L. (2003). *Social work in the health field* (2nd ed.). New York: Haworth Press.

Crewe, N. M., & Krause, J. S. (1991). An eleven-year follow-up of adjustment to spinal cord injury. *Rehabilitation Psychology, 35*, 205–210.

Cunningham, J., Chan, F., Jones, J., Kramnetz, B., Stoll, J., & Calabresa, J. (1999). Brain injury rehabilitation: A primer for case managers. In F. Chan & M. Leahy (Eds.), *Health care and disability management* (pp. 475–526). Lake Zurich, IL: Vocational Consultants Press.

Curran, J. W. (1983). AIDS — two years later. *New England Journal of Medicine, 309*, 609–611.

Cwikel, J., & Behar, L. (1999a). Organizing social work services with adult cancer patients: Integrating empirical research. *Social Work in Health Care, 28*(3), 55–76.

Cwikel, J., & Behar, L. (1999b). Social work with adult cancer patients: A vote-count review of intervention research. *Social Work in Health Care, 29*(2), 39–67.

Danks, R. (2003). Burn management. *Journal of Emergency Medical Services, 28*(5), 118–141.

Davidson, K. (1990). Evolving social work roles in health care: The case of discharge planning. In K. Davidson & S. Clarke (Eds.), *Social work in health care* (Vol. 2, pp. 181–194). New York: Haworth Press.

Davitt, J., & Kaye, L. (1996). Supporting patient autonomy: Decision making in home health care. *Social Work, 41*(1), 41–50.

Degeneffe, C. (2001). Family caregiving and traumatic brain injury. *Health and Social Work, 26*(5), 257–268.

Denholm, C. J., & Ferguson, R. V. (1987). Strategies to promote the developmental needs of hospitalized adolescents. *Children's Health Care, 23,* 925–937.

DeOreo, P. B. (1997). Hemodialysis patient-assisted functional health status predicts continued survival, hospitalization, and dialysis-attendance compliance. *American Journal of Kidney Diseases, 30*(2), 204–212.

Derevensky, J., Tsanos, A., & Handman, M. (1998). Children with cancer: An examination of their coping and adaptive behavior. *Journal of Psychosocial Oncology, 16*(1), 37–61.

Dhooper, S. (1990). Family coping with the crisis of heart attack. In K. Davidson & S. Clarke (Eds.), *Social work in health care* (Vol. 2, pp. 225–244). New York: Haworth Press.

Dhooper, S. (1994). *Social work and transplantation of human organs.* Westport, CT: Praeger.

Dobroff, J., Dolinko, A., Lichtiger, E., Uribarri, J., & Epstein, I. (2001). Dialysis patient characteristics and outcomes: The complexity of social work practice with the end stage renal disease population. *Social Work in Health Care, 33,* 105–128.

Dungan, S., Jaquay, T., Resnik, K., & Sands, E. (1995). Pediatric critical care social work: Clinical practice with parents of critically ill children. *Social Work in Health Care, 21*(1), 69–80.

Dziegielewski, S. (2004). The many faces of social work practice. In S. Dziegielewski (Ed.), *The changing face of health care social work* (2nd ed., pp. 48–71). New York: Springer.

Dziegielewski, S., & Duncklee, D. E. (2004). Emergency room social work. In S. Dziegielewski (Ed.), *The changing face of health care social work* (2nd ed., pp. 323–337). New York: Springer.

Dziegielewski, S., & Kalinoski, A. (2004). Case management and discharge planning. In S. Dziegielewski (Ed.), *The changing face of health care social work* (2nd ed., pp. 338–349). New York: Springer.

Edinburg, G., & Cottler, J. (1997). Managed care. In R. Edwards (Ed.), *Encyclopedia of social work* (pp. 1635–1642). Washington, DC: NASW Press.

Egan, M., & Kadushin, G. (1995). Competitive allies: Rural nurses' and social workers' perceptions of the social work role in the hospital setting. *Social work in health care, 20*(3), 1–23.

Egan, M., & Kadushin, G. (1999). The social worker in the emerging field of home care: Professional activities and ethical concerns. *Health & Social Work, 24*(1), 43–56.

Eide, A., & Roysamb, E. (2002). The relationship between level of disability, psychological problems, social activity, and social networks. *Rehabilitation Psychology, 47*(2), 165–183.

Elander, G., Nillson, A., & Lindbergh, T. (1986). Behavior in 4 year olds who have experienced hospitalization and day care. *American Journal of Orthopsychiatry, 56,* 612–616.

Eustler, N. E., & Martinez, J. M. (2003). The interdisciplinary team. In W. Forman, J. Kitzes, R. Anderson, & D. Sheehan (Eds.), *Hospice and palliative care* (pp. 13–34). Boston: Jones & Bartlett.

Evangelista, L., Doering, L., & Dracup, K. (2003). Meaning and life purpose: The perspectives of post-transplant women. *Heart & Lung, 32,* 250–257.

Ey, S., Compas, B., Epping-Jordan, J., & Worsham, N. (1998). Stress responses and psychological adjustment in patients with cancer and their spouses. *Journal of Psychosocial Oncology, 16*(2), 59–77.

Fearnow-Kenney, M., & Kliewer, W. (2000). Threat appraisal and adjustment among children with cancer. *Journal of Psychosocial Oncology, 18*(3), 1–17.

Fesko, S. (2001). Disclosure of HIV status in the workplace: Considerations and strategies. *Health & Social Work, 26*(4), 235–241.

Figueiras, M., & Weinman, J. (2003). Do similar patient and spouse perceptions of myocardial infarction predict recovery? *Psychology and Health, 18*(2), 201–216.

Fischer, M. (2003). Psychosocial evaluation interview protocol for living related and living unrelated kidney donors. *Social Work in Health Care, 38*(1), 39–61.

Flaherty, S. (2004). *The role of the social worker in a physical medicine and rehabilitation setting.* East Meadow, NY: Nassau City Medical Center.

Fleury, J., Kimbrell, L., & Kruszewski, M. (1995). Life after a cardiac event: Women's experience in healing. *Heart & Lung, 24,* 474–482.

Frank, A., Auslander, G., & Weissgarten, J. (2003). Quality of life of patients with end stage renal disease at various stages of the illness. *Social Work in Health Care, 38*(2), 1–27.

Frank, N., Blount, R., & Brown, R. (1997). Attributions, coping, and adjustment in children with cancer. *Journal of Pediatric Psychology, 22*(4), 563–576.

Fred, S. (2005). Focus shifts from disease to functioning. *NASW News, 50*(6).

Fuhrer, M. J. (1996). The subjective well-being of people with spinal cord injury: Relationship to impairment, disability, and handicap. *Topics in Spinal Cord Injury Rehabilitation, 1*(4), 56–71.

Furr, L. A. (1998). Psychosocial aspects of serious renal disease and dialysis: A review of the literature. *Social Work in Health Care, 27*(3), 97–118.

Furstenberg, A. L., & Olson, M. (1984). Social work and AIDS. *Social Work in Health Care, 9*(4), 45–61.

Gant, L. (1998). Essential facts every social worker needs to know. In D. Aronstein & B. Thompson (Eds.), *HIV and social work: A practitioner's guide* (pp. 3–25). New York: Harrington Park Press.

Gibelman, M. (2002). Social work in an era of managed care. In A. Roberts & G. Greene (Eds.), *Social workers' desk reference* (pp. 16–23). New York: Oxford Press.

Gier, M., Levick, M., & Blanzia, P. (1988). Stress reduction with heart transplant patients and their families: A multidisciplinary approach. *Journal of Heart Transplantation, 7,* 342–347.

Gil, S., & Gilbar, O. (2001). Hopelessness among cancer patients. *Journal of Psychosocial Oncology, 19*(1), 21–33.

Gilboa, D. (2001). Long-term psychosocial adjustment after burn injury. *Burns, 27,* 335–341.

Gillinov, M. (2002). Coronary artery bypass surgery. In E. Topol (Ed.), *Textbook of cardiovascular medicine* (2nd ed., pp. 1695–1714). Philadelphia: Lippincott Williams and Wilkins.

Gilson, S. F., Bricout, J. C., & Baskind, F. (1998). Listening to the voices of individuals with disabilities. *Families and Society, 79*(2), 188–196.

Ginsberg, L. (1993). Introduction: An overview of rural social work. In L. Ginsberg (Ed.), *Social work in rural communities* (2nd ed., pp. 2–17). Alexandria, VA: Council on Social Work Education.

Goffman, E. (1963). *Stigma: Notes on the management of spoiled identity.* New York: Simon & Schuster.

Goggin, K., Catley, D., Brisco, S., Engelson, E., Rabkin, J., & Kotler, D. (2001). A female perspective on living with HIV disease. *Health & Social Work, 26*(2), 80–90.

Goldbeck, L. (2001). Parental coping with the diagnosis of childhood cancer: Gender effects, dissimilarity within couples and quality of life. *Psycho-Oncology, 10*, 325–335.

Grant, J. C., Elliot, T., Newman-Giber, J., & Bartolucci, A. (2001). Social problem-solving abilities, social support, and adjustment among family caregivers of individuals with a stroke. *Rehabilitation Psychology, 46*(1), 44–57.

Grassi, L., Roberto, R., & Laura, S. (1998). Coping style and psychosocial-related variables in HIV-infected patients. *Psychosomatics, 39*, 350–359.

Gusella, J., & Ward, A. (1998). The experience of hospitalized adolescents: How well do we meet their developmental needs? *Children's Health Care, 27*(2), 131–145.

Hailey, B., Moss, S., Street, R., Gersh, A., Calabrese, A., & Campbell, C. (2001). Mental health services in an outpatient dialysis practice. *Dialysis and Transplantation, 30*(1), 732–739.

Hammer, D., & Kerson, T. S. (1997). Discharge planning in a community hospital: A patient whose symptoms the system could not manage. In T. S. K. Associates (Ed.), *Social work in health settings: Practice in context* (pp. 227–241). New York: Haworth Press.

Hampton, N. Z. (2004). Subjective well being among people with spinal cord injuries: The role of self-efficacy, perceived social support, and perceived health. *Rehabilitation Counseling Bulletin, 48*(1), 31–38.

Hart, G. (1981). Spinal cord injury: Impact on clients' significant others. *Rehabilitation Nursing, 6*, 11–15.

Healy, J. (1981). Emergency rooms and psychosocial services. *Health & Social Work, 6*(1), 36–43.

Hepworth, D., Rooney, R., & Larsen, J. (2002). *Direct social work practice* (6th ed.). Pacific Grove, CA: Brooks/Cole.

Herschel, J., & Vaitones, V. (2004). *Oncology social worker: A crucial member of the oncology team.* Philadelphia: Association of Oncology Social Workers.

Hershberg, S., & Posner, C. (1994). Social work practice in a psychiatric ambulatory care setting. In M. Holosko & P. Taylor (Eds.), *Social work practice in health care settings* (pp. 307–322). Toronto: Canadian Scholars' Press.

Holland, J., & Lewis, S. (2000). *The human side of cancer.* New York: Harper Collins.

Holland, L., & Rogich, L. E. (1980). Dealing with grief in the emergency room. *Health & Social Work, 5*(2), 12–17.

Holtom, P. (1992). Medical issues in HIV-related illness. In H. Land (Ed.), *A complete guide to psychosocial intervention* (pp. 263–280). Milwaukee, WI: Family Service Association.

Horn, J., Feldman, H., & Ploof, D. (1995). Parent and professional perceptions about stress and coping strategies during a child's lengthy hospitalization. *Social Work in Health Care, 21*(1), 107–127.

Hosack, K., & Rocchio, C. (1995). Serving families of persons with severe brain injury in an era of managed care. *Journal of Head Trauma Rehabilitation, 10*(2), 57–65.

Iglehart, A. (1990). Discharge planning: Professional perspective versus organizational effects. *Health & Social Work, 15*(4), 301–309.

Johnson, E. (2000). Differences among families coping with serious mental illness: A qualitative analysis. *American Journal of Orthopsychiatry, 70*(1), 126–134.

Jones, J., & Egan, M. (2000). The transplant experience of liver recipients: Ethical issues and practice implications. *Social Work in Health Care, 31*(2), 65–88.

Kadushin, G. (1999). Barriers to social support and support received from their families of origin among gay men with HIV/AIDS. *Health & Social Work, 24*(3), 198–209.

Kadushin, G., & Kulys, R. (1993). Discharge planning revisited: What do social workers actually do in discharge planning? *Social Work, 38*(6), 713–726.

Kahng, S. K., & Mowbray, C. (2004). Factors influencing self-esteem among individuals with severe mental illness: Implications for social work. *Social Work Research, 28*(4), 225–236.

Kaminski, M., Pellino, T., & Wish, J. (2002). Play and pets: The physical and emotional impact of child-life and pet therapy on hospitalized children. *Children's Health Care, 31*(4), 321–335.

Kaplan, L., Tomaszewski, E., & Gorin, S. (2004). Current trends and the future of HIV/AIDS services: A social work perspective. *Health & Social Work, 29*(2), 153–161.

Karter, M. J. (2001). *Fire loss in the United States during 2000.* Quincy, MA: National Fire Protection Association, Fire Analysis and Research Division.

Kazak, A., Alderfer, M., Streisand, R., Simms, S., Rourke, M., Barakat, L., et al. (2004). Treatment of post-traumatic stress symptoms in adolescent survivors of childhood cancer and their families: A randomized clinical trial. *Journal of Family Psychology, 18*(3), 493–504.

Keller, C. (1991). Seeking normalcy: The experience of coronary artery bypass surgery. *Research on Nursing Health, 14,* 173–178.

Kilbourn, K., & Durning, P. (2003). Oncology and psycho-oncology. In S. Llewelyn & P. Kennedy (Eds.), *Handbook of clinical health psychology.* Sussex, UK: John Wiley & Sons.

Kimmel, P., Peterson, R., Weihs, K., & Summers, S. (1995). Behavioral compliance with dialysis prescription in hemodialysis patients. *Journal of the American Society of Nephrology, 5*(10), 1826–1834.

King, K., Reis, H., Porter, L., & Norsen, L. (1993). Social support and long-term recovery from coronary artery surgery: Effects on patients and spouses. *Health Psychology, 12*(1), 56–63.

Klang, B., Bjorvell, H., Berglund, J., Sundstedt, C., & Clyne, N. (1998). Pre-dialysis patient education: Effects on functioning and well-being in uremic patients. *Journal of Advanced Nursing, 28*(1), 36–44.

Kleve, L., & Robinson, E. (1999). A survey of psychological need amongst adult burn-injured patients. *Burns, 25,* 575–579.

Koocher, G. (1986). Psychosocial issues during the acute treatment of pediatric cancer. *Cancer, 58,* 468–472.

Koocher, G., & Pollin, I. (2001). Preventive psychosocial intervention in cancer. In A. Baum & B. Andersen (Eds.), *Psychosocial interventions for cancer* (pp. 363–374). Washington, DC: American Psychological Association.

Kornblith, A. B., Anderson, J., Cella, D., Tross, S., Zuckerman, E., Cherin, E., et al. (1992). Comparison of psychosocial adaptation and sexual function of survivors of advanced Hodgkin's disease treated by MOPP, ABVD, or MOPP alternating with ABVD. *Cancer, 70,* 2508–2516.

Krause, J. S., & Dawis, R. (1992). Prediction of life satisfaction after spinal cord injury: A four year longitudinal approach. *Rehabilitation Psychology, 37,* 49–59.

Kreutzer, J., Serio, C., & Berquist, S. (1994). Family needs after brain injury: A quantitative analysis. *Journal of Head Trauma Rehabilitation, 9,* 104–115.

Kronenberger, W., Carter, B., & Thomas, D. (1997). Assessment behavior problems in pediatric settings: Development of the pediatric inpatient behavior scale. *Children's Health Care, 26*(4), 211–232.

Kübler-Ross, E. (1969). *On death and dying.* New York: Macmillan.

Kulik, J., & Mahler, H. (1989). Social support and recovery from surgery. *Health Psychology, 8,* 221–238.

Kulik, J., & Mahler, H. (1993). Emotional support as a moderator of adjustment and compliance after coronary artery bypass surgery: A longitudinal study. *Journal of Behavioral Medicine, 16*(1), 45–63.

Kupst, M. J., Natta, M., Richardson, C., Schulman, J. L., Lavigne, J., & Das, L. (1995). Family coping with pediatric leukemia. *Journal of Pediatric Psychology, 20*(5), 601–618.

Kupst, M. J., & Schulman, J. L. (1988). Long-term coping with pediatric leukemia: A six-year follow-up study. *Journal of Pediatric Psychology, 13*(1), 17–22.

Land, H. (1992). Stress and coping in AIDS caregivers: Partners, friends, and family members. In H. Land (Ed.), *A complete guide to psychosocial intervention* (pp. 199–214). Milwaukee, WI: Family Service Association.

Lang, P., & Mitrowski, C. (1981). Supportive and concrete services for teenage oncology patients. *Health & Social Work, 6*(4), 42–45.

Lee, T. (2004). *Harvard heart letter — wishing you a speedy recovery.* Boston: Harvard Medical School.

Livneh, H., & Antonak, R. F. (1997). *Psychosocial adaptation to chronic illness and disability.* Austin, TX: PRO-ED.

Livneh, H., & Wilson, L. (2003). Coping strategies as predictors and mediators of disability-related variables and psychosocial adaptation: An exploratory investigation. *Rehabilitation Counseling Bulletin, 46*(4), 194–202.

Lohmann, R. (1997). Managed care: A review of recent research. In R. Edwards (Ed.), *Encyclopedia of social work, supplement* (pp. 200–213). Washington, DC: NASW Press.

Lopes, A., Albert, J. M., Young, E. et al. (2004). Screening for depression in hemodialysis patients: Associations with diagonsis, treatment, and outcomes in the DOPPS. *Kidney International, 66*(5), 2047–2053.

Lynn-McHale, D., Corsetta, A., & Brady-Avis, E. (1997). Preoperative ICU tours: Are they helpful? *American Journal of Critical Care, 6,* 106–115.

MacDonald, D. (1991). Hospice social work: A search for identity. *Health and Social Work, 16*(4), 274–279.

MacLean-Brine, D. (1994). Social work practice in a women's health care centre. In M. Holosko & P. Taylor (Eds.), *Social work practice in health care settings* (2nd ed., pp. 193–213). Toronto: Canadian Scholars' Press.

Mahler, H., & Kulik, J. (2002). Effects of a videotape information interventions for spouses on spouse distress and patient recovery from surgery. *Health Psychology, 21*(5), 427–437.

Mailick, M. (1990). The impact of severe illness on the individual and family. In K. Davidson & S. Clarke (Eds.), *Social work in health care* (pp. 101–114). New York: Haworth Press.

Matthews, D. (2003). *AIDS sourcebook* (3rd ed.). Detroit, MI: Omnigraphics.

Mazzella, A. (2004). Psychosocial factors in treating the depressed renal patient. *Journal of Nephrology Social Work, 23,* 40–47.

McDonnell, A. (1986). *Quality hospice care. Administration, organization, and models.* Owings Mills, MD: Rand Communications.

McKinley, M. (2000). Missed treatments: How to help patients change problem behavior. *Nephrology News & Issues, 14*(12), 16–20.

McLeod, E., Bywaters, P., & Cooke, M. (2003). Social work in accident and emergency departments: A better deal for older patients' health? *British Journal of Social Work, 33,* 787–802.

Meade, M., Taylor, L., Kreutzer, J., Marwitz, J., & Vera, T. (2004). A preliminary study of acute family needs after spinal cord injury: Analysis and implications. *Rehabilitation Psychology, 49*(2), 150–155.

Melnyk, B., & Alpert-Gillis, L. (1998). The cope program: A strategy to improve outcomes of critically ill young children and their parents. *Pediatric Nursing, 24*(6), 521–527.

Miceli, P., & Clark, P. (2004). Your patient — my child. *Journal of Nursing Care, 20*(1), 43–53.

Mick, S., & Morlock, L. (1990). America's rural hospitals: A selective review of 1980s research. *Journal of Rural Health, 6*(4), 437–466.

Miller, J. M. (2000). *Coping with chronic illness. Overcoming powerlessness* (3rd ed.). Philadelphia: F. A. Davis.

Miller, R., & Mason, S. (2001). Using group therapy to enhance treatment compliance in first episode schizophrenia. *Social Work with Groups, 24*(1), 37–51.

Mingardi, G., Cornalba, L., Cortinovis, E. et al. (1999). Health-related quality of life in dialysis patients: A report from an Italian study using the SF-36 health survey. *Nephrology Dialysis Transplantation, 14*(6), 1503–1510.

Moser, D., & Dracup, K. (1996). Is anxiety early after myocardial infarction associated with subsequent ischemic and arrhythmic events? *Journal of Psychosomatic Medicine, 58,* 395–401.

Murray, C., & Lopez, A. (1996). *The global burden of disease: A comprehensive assessment of mortality and disability from diseases, injuries, and risk factors in 1990 and projected to 2020.* Cambridge, MA: Harvard University Press.

Nacman, M. (1990). Social work in health settings: A historical review. In K. Davidson & S. Clarke (Eds.), *Social work in health care* (pp. 7–22). New York: Haworth Press.

Naierman, N. (2003). Debunking the myths of hospice. In R. Baird & S. Rosenbaum (Ed.), *Caring for the dying* (pp. 25–33). Amherst, NY: Prometheus Books.

National Health Service (UK). (1998). Cardiac rehabilitation. *Effective Health Care, 4*(4), 1–12.

National Institute of Mental Health. (2001). *The numbers count: Mental Disorders in America* (NIH Publication No. 01-4584). Washington, DC: U.S. Department of Health and Human Services.

National Kidney Foundation. (1995). *Dialysis.* New York: Author.

National Kidney Foundation. (1997). *Kidney transplant: A new lease on life.* New York: Author.

National Kidney Foundation. (2002). *Professional advocacy for the nephrology social worker.* New York: Author.

National Spinal Cord Injury Association. (2004). National spinal cord injury association fact sheet #2. Retrieved November 17, 2004, from http://wwwmakoa.org/nscia/fact02.html.

Northouse, L. L., Dorris, G., & Charon-Moore, C. (1995). Factors affecting couples' adjustment to recurrent breast cancer. *Social Science and Medicine, 41,* 69–76.

Nosek, M., & Hughes, R. (2003). Psychosocial issues of women with physical disabilities. *Rehabilitation Counseling Bulletin, 46*(4), 224–232.

Noyes, R., & Andreasen, N. J. C. (1971). The psychological reaction to severe burns. *Psychosomatics, 12,* 416–422.

Oldridge, N., Radowski, B., & Gottleib, M. (1992). Use of outpatient cardiac rehabilitation services: Factors associated with attendance. *Journal of Cardiopulmonary Rehabilitation, 12*(25), 25–31.

Organ Procurement and Transplantation Network. (2004). Organ procurement and transplantation. Retrieved December 13, 2004, from www.optn.org/latestData/rptData.asp.

Orr, D. A., Reznikoff, M. S., & Smith, G. M. (1989). Body image, self-esteem, and depression in burn injured adolescents and young adults. *Journal of Burn Care Rehabilitation, 10,* 454–461.

Owens, P. L., Thompson, J., Elixhauser, A., & Ryan, K. (2003). *Care of children and adolescents in US Hospitals.* Rockville, MD: Agency for Healthcare Research and Quality.

Pallua, N., Kunsebeck, H.W., & Noah, E. (2003). Psychosocial adjustments 5 years after burn injury. *Burns, 29,* 142–152.

Palmer, S., & Glass, T. (2003). Family function and stroke recovery: A review. *Rehabilitation Psychology, 48*(4), 255–265.

Paris, W., Hutkin-Slade, L., Calhoun-Wilson, G., & Oehlert, W. (1999). Social work services on an organ transplantation program: A preliminary cost-benefit analysis. *Research on Social Work Practice, 9*(2), 201–212.

Patenaude, A., & Last, B. (2001). Cancer and children: Where are we coming from? Where are we going? *Psycho-Oncology, 10,* 281–283.

Patterson, L., & Dorfman, L. (2002). Family support for hospice caregivers. *American Journal of Hospice and Palliative Care, 19*(5), 315–323.

Pedersen, S., Middel, B., & Larsen, M. (2003). Posttraumatic stress disorder in first-time myocardial infarction patients. *Heart & Lung, 32*(5), 300–307.

Peleg-Oren, N., Sherer, M., & Soskolne, V. (2003). Effect of gender on the social and psychological adjustment of cancer patients. *Social Work in Health Care, 37*(3), 17–34.

Pizzo, P. (1993). The medical diagnosis and treatment of childhood cancer. In N. Stearns, M. Lauria, J. Hermann, & P. Fogelberg (Eds.), *Oncology social work* (pp. 177–198). Atlanta, GA: American Cancer Society.

Ponto, J., & Berg, W. (1992). Social work services in the emergency department: A cost-benefit analysis of an extended coverage program. *Health & Social Work, 17*(1), 66–73.

Pryor, J., Reeder, G., & Landau, S. (1999). A social-psychological analysis of HIV-related stigma. *American Behavioral Scientist, 42*(7), 1193–1212.

Purk, J., & Richardson, R. (1994). Older adult stroke patients and their spousal caregivers. *Families in Society, 75*(10), 608–620.

Rankin, S. (2002). Women recovering from acute myocardial infarction: Psychosocial and physical functioning outcomes for 12 months after acute myocardial infarction. *Heart & Lung, 31*(6), 399–410.

Reese, D., & Sontag, M. (2001). Successful interpersonal collaboration on the hospice team. *Health & Social Work, 26*(3), 167–174.

Rehr, H. (1998). Health care and the social work connection. In H. Rehr, G. Rosenberg, & S. Blumenfield (Eds.), *Creative social work in health care* (pp. 7–19). New York: Springer.

Rehr, H., Blumenfield, S., & Rosenberg, G. (1998). Collaboration and consultation: Key social work roles in health care. In H. Rehr, G. Rosenberg, & S. Blumenfield (Eds.), *Creative social work in health care* (pp. 93–99). New York: Springer.

Richman, J. (1995). Hospice. In R. L. Edwards & J. G. Hopps (Eds.), *Encyclopedia of social work* (Vol. 2, pp. 1358–1365). Washington, DC: NASW Press.

Riffe, H. (1998). The managed care experience: The social worker's perspective. *Social Work in Health Care, 28*(2), 1–9.

Robinson, C. (1987). Roadblocks to family-centered care when a chronically ill child is hospitalized. *Maternal Child Nursing Journal, 16*(2), 181–193.

Rock, B. (2002). Social work in health care for the 21st century: The biopsychosocial model. In A. R. Roberts & G. J. Greene (Eds.), *Social workers' desk reference* (pp. 10–15). New York: Oxford University Press.

Rodriguez, C., & Boggs, S. (1998). Assessment of behavioral distress and depression in a pediatric population. *Children's Health Care, 27*(3), 157–170.

Rose, A. (1998). Back to the future: Survival, uncertainty, and hope. In D. Aronstein & B. Thompson (Eds.), *HIV and social work* (pp. 65–72). New York: Harrington Park Press.

Rosen, L. (1999). Common psychological factors in the treatment of end stage renal disease. *Journal of Nephrology Social Work, 19,* 69–71.

Rosenthal, D. (1993). The nature of adult cancer: Medical diagnosis and treatment. In N. Stearns, M. Lauria, J. Hermann, & P. Fogelberg (Eds.), *Oncology Social Work.* Atlanta, GA: American Cancer Society, 19–40.

Ross, J. (1993). Understanding the family experience with childhood cancer. In N. Stearns, M. Lauria, J. Hermann, & P. Fogelberg (Eds.), *Oncology social work* (pp. 199–236). Atlanta, GA: American Cancer Society.

Rossi, L., Vila, V., Zago, M., & Ferreira, E. (2005). The stigma of burns. *Burns 31*(1), 37–44.

Rowlands, A. (2001). Ability or disability? Strengths-based practice in the area of traumatic brain injury. *Families in Society, 82*(3), 273–286.

Rusnack, B., Schaefer, S. M., & Moxley, D. (1988). "Safe passage": Social work roles and functions in hospice care. *Social Work in Health Care, 13*(3), 3–19.

Rusnack, B., Schaefer, S. M., & Moxley, D. (1991). Hospice: Social work's response to a new form of social caring. *Social Work in Health Care, 15*(2), 95–119.

Sales, E., Schultz, R., & Biegel, D. (1992). Psychosocial impact of cancer on the family: A review of the literature. *Journal of Psychosocial Oncology, 9*(4), 1–18.

Sanger, M., Copeland, D., & Davidson, E. (1991). Psychosocial adjustment among pediatric cancer patients: A multidimensional assessment. *Journal of Pediatric Oncology, 16*(4), 463–474.

Sanner, M. (2003). Transplant recipients' conceptions of three key phenomena in transplantation: The organ donation, the organ donor, and the organ transplant. *Clinical Transplantation, 17*, 391–400.

Schneider, R. (2004). Fatigue among caregivers of chronic renal failure patients: A principal component analysis. *Journal of Nephrology Social Work, 23*, 68–74.

Schnoll, R., Knowles, J., & Harlow, L. (2002). Correlates of adjustment among cancer survivors. *Journal of Psychosocial Oncology, 20*(1), 37–59.

Schott, T., & Bandura, B. (1988). Wives of heart attack patients: The stress of caring. In R. Anderson & M. Bury (Eds.), *Living with chronic illness* (pp. 117–136). London: Unwin Hyman.

Shapiro, J., & Shumaker, S. (1988). Differences in emotional well-being and communication styles between mothers and fathers of pediatric cancer patients. *Psycho-Oncology, 5*, 121–131.

Sharpe, L. (1991). Discharge planning: Before the fact. *Discharge Planning Update. 11*(4), 3–5.

Shields, G., Schondel, C., Barnhart, L., Fitzpatrick, V., Sidell, N., Adams, P., et al. (1995). Social work in pediatric oncology: A family needs assessment. *Social Work in Health Care, 21*(1), 39–54.

Sloper, T., Larcombe, I., & Charlton, A. (1994). Psychosocial adjustment of five-year survivors of childhood cancer. *Journal of Cancer Education, 9*(3), 163–169.

Smirnow, V. (1998). Depression. *Dialysis and Transplantation, 24*(2), 104–106.

Smith M., Hong, B., & Robinson, A. (1985). Diagnosis of depression in patients with end-stage renal disease. *American Journal of Medicine, 79*, 160–165.

Smith, S., & Soliday, E. (2001). The effects of parental chronic kidney disease on the family. *Journal of Nephrology Social Work, 21*, 29–37.

Soskis, C. (1985). *Social work in the emergency room*. New York: Springer.

Sowell, R. L. (1997). Reconstruction case management. *Journal of the Association of Nurses in AIDS, 8*(6), 43–45.

Spiegel, D., & Diamond, S. (2001). Psychosocial interventions in cancer: Group therapy techniques. In A. Baum & B. Anderson (Eds.), *Psychosocial interventions for cancer* (pp. 215–233). Washington, DC: American Psychological Association.

Stanton, G. M. (1984). A needs assessment of significant others following the patient's spinal cord injury. *Journal of Neurosurgical Nursing, 16*, 253–256.

Sternberg, C. (1992). AIDS in hospital and acute-care settings: The social work perspective. In H. Land (Ed.), *A complete guide to psychosocial intervention* (pp. 39–49). Milwaukee, WI: Family Service Association.

Stewart, R. S. (1983). Psychiatric issues in renal dialysis and transplantation. *Hospital and Community Psychiatry, 34*(7), 623–628.

Stewart, J. (2003). "Getting used to it": Children finding the ordinary and routine in the uncertain context of cancer. *Qualitative Health Journal, 13*(3), 394–407.

Stovall, A. (1993). Social work services for the child and family. In N. Stearns, M. Lauria, J. Hermann, & P. Fogelberg (Eds.), *Oncology social work* (pp. 237–255). Atlanta, GA: American Cancer Society.

Stromwall, L., & Hurdle, D. (2003). Psychiatric rehabilitation: An empowerment-based approach to mental health services. *Health & Social Work, 28*(3), 206–213.

Summers, L. (1993). Limited access: Health care for the rural poor, executive summary, 1991. In L. Ginsberg (Ed.), *Social work in rural communities* (2nd ed., pp. 230–243). Alexandria, VA: Council on Social Work Education.

Summers, T. (1991). Psychosocial support of the burned patient. *Critical Care Nursing Clinics of North America, 3*(2), 237–244.

Suszycki, L. H. (1986). Social work groups on a heart transplant program. *Journal of Heart Transplantation, 5,* 166–170.

Suzuki, L., & Kato, P. (2003). Psychosocial support for patients in pediatric oncology: The influence of parents, schools, peers, and technology. *Journal of Pediatric Oncology Nursing, 20*(4), 159–174.

Szromba, C. (1998). Education for pre-dialysis patients: A continuing challenge. *ANNA, 25*(1), 80–82.

Taal, L., & Faber, A. (1998). Posttraumatic stress and maladjustment among adult burn survivors 1–2 years postburn. *Burns, 24,* 399–405.

Taylor, S. E. (1995). *Health psychology.* New York: McGraw-Hill.

Tazelaar, S. L., Prieto, M., Lake, K. D., & Emery, R. (1992). Heart transplantation in high-risk psychosocial patients. *Journal of Heart and Lung Transplantation, 11,* 207.

Tempereau, C. E., Grossman, A. R., & Brones, M. F. (1989). Loss of will to live in patients with burns. *Journal of Burn Care Rehabilitation, 10,* 464–468.

Thompson, B. (2003). Lazarus phenomena: An exploratory study of gay men living with HIV. *Social Work in Health Care, 37*(1), 87–114.

Thompson, D., & Meddis, R. (1990). Wives' responses to counseling early after myocardial infarction. *Journal of Psychosomatic Research, 6,* 249–258.

Thompson, S., Galbraith, M., Thomas, C., Swan, J., & Vrungos, S. (2002). Caregivers of stroke patient family members: Behavioral and attitudinal indicators of overprotective care. *Psychology and Health, 17*(3), 297–312.

Thornton, A., & Battistel, L. (2001). Working with burn survivors: A social work approach. *Australian Social Work, 54*(3), 93–103.

Turney, H., & Conway, P. (2000). Managed mental health care: Implications for social work practice and social work education. *Journal of Family Social Work, 5*(1), 5–19.

UNAIDS/WHO. (2003). *AIDS epidemic update.* Geneva, Switzerland: Author.

United States renal data system report. (2003). Bethesda, MD: National Institutes of Health.

Urbina, A., & Jones, K. (2004). Crystal methamphetamine, its analogues, and HIV infection: Medical and psychiatric aspects of a new epidemic. *Infectious Diseases, 38,* 890–894.

U.S. Department of Health and Human Services. (1999). *Mental health: A report of the surgeon general.* Rockville, MD: Author.

USRD. (1998). *USRD 1998 annual data report.* Bethesda, MD: National Institutes of Health.

Van Dongen-Melman, J. E., Pruyn, J., DeGroot, A., Kooy, H., Hahlren, K., & Verhulst, F. (1995). Late psychosocial consequences for parents of children who survived cancer. *Journal of Pediatric Psychology, 20,* 567–586.

Van Dongen-Melman, J. E., & Saunders-Woudstra, J. A. (1986). Psychosocial aspects of childhood cancer: A review of the literature. *Journal of Child Psychology and Psychiatry, 27,* 145–180.

Van Horn, E., Fleury, J., & Moore, S. (2002). Family interventions during the trajectory of recovery from cardiac event: An integrative literature review. *Heart & Lung, 31*(3), 186–198.

van Wormer, C., & Boes, M. (1997). Humor in the emergency room: A social work perspective. *Health & Social Work, 22*(2), 87–92.

Vess, J., Moreland, J., Schwebel, A., & Kraut, E. (1988). Psychosocial needs of cancer patients: Learning from patients and their spouses. *Journal of Psychosocial Oncology, 6*(1/2), 31–51.

Weaver, F., Guihan, M., Pape, T., Legro, S., & Collins, E. (2001). Creating a research agenda in SCI based on provider and consumer input. *Spinal Cord Injuries Psychosocial Process, 14*(2), 77–88.

Wells, P. (1993). Preparing for sudden death: Social work in the emergency room. *Social Work, 38*(3), 339–343.

Williams, E. E., & Griffiths, T. A. (1991). Psychological consequences of burn injury. *Burns, 17,* 478–480.

Williams, N., Davey, M., & Klock-Powell, K. (2003). Rising from the ashes: Stories of recovery, adaptation, and resiliency in burn survivors. *Social Work in Health Care, 36*(4), 53–77.

Wisely, J. A., & Tarrier, N. (2001). A survey of the need for psychological input in a follow-up service for adult burn-injured patients. *Burns, 27,* 801–807.

Wolfson, J. C. (2004, December 24). Giving a gift of life. *Newsday,* pp. A40–A41.

York, R., Denton, R., & Moran, J. (1989). Rural and urban social work: Is there a difference? *Journal of Contemporary Social Work,* 201–209.

Zabora, J. (1998). Screening procedures for psychosocial issues. In J. C. Holland (Ed.), *Psycho-oncology* (pp. 653–661). New York: Oxford University Press.

Zebrack, B., & Chesler, M. (2000). Managed care: The new context for social work in health care — Implications for survivors of childhood cancer and their families. *Social Work in Health Care, 31*(2), 89–103.

Zebrack, B., & Chesler, M. (2002). Quality of life in childhood cancer survivors. *Psycho-Oncology, 11,* 132–141.

Zebrack, B., Chesler, M., Orbuch, T., & Parry, C. (2002). Mothers of survivors of childhood cancer: Their worries and concern. *Journal of Psychosocial Oncology, 20*(2), 1–25.

Zilberfein, F., Hutson, C., Snyder, S., & Epstein, I. (2001). Social work practice with pre- and post-liver transplant patients: A retrospective self-study. *Social Work in Health Care, 33*(3/4), 91–104.

INDEX

A

Active listening, 51, 77, 93
Adolescent patients, 166–167
Ai, A., 37
AIDS (acquired immunodeficiency
    syndrome), *see* HIV/AIDS
Alzheimer's disease, 156
American Burn Association, 124
American Cancer Society (ACS), 81–82
American Heart Association (AMA), 109
American Hospital Association, 10, 146
Antonak, R. F., 116
Assessment, 93
Aviram, A., 159

B

Babcock, J., 104
Bandura, B., 39
Barakat, L., 74
Barbarin, O., 74
Barnard, Christian, 58
Behar, L., 91
Bellevue Hospital, 2
Biegel, D., 88
Biopsychosocial approach, 4, 8, 173
Blum, D., 90
Boes, M., 136
Brady-Avis, E., 41
Bristow, D., 135
Burn centers, 123
Burns, 123–124
    children as victims, 133–134
    degree and size of, 123–124

family experience, 128–129, 131
    forensic burns, 131–132
    pain management, 127–128
    patient experience, 125–126
    phases of recovery, 126–127
    stigma of burn victim, 125
    total body surface area (TBSA), 124
Burn unit social worker, 123–134
    children as patients, 133–134
    comments of, 132–134
    interventions of, 130
    short-/long-term role, 132
    supportive counseling, 130
Bypass surgery, patient experience, 36–37

C

Cabot, Richard C., 1–4, 8
Campbell, A., 28
Cancer, 81–83; *see also* Oncology social work
    caregiver experience, 88–89
    chemotherapy, 84
    immunotheraphy, 84
    patient experience, 84–86
    psychosocial considerations, 86–88
    radiation treatments, 83
    treatment options, 83–84
Cannon, Ida, 2–4, 8
Cardiac care social worker, 33–44
    bypass surgery, 36–37
    comments of, 41–44
    coronary heart disease, 33–34
    family/caregiver experience, 38–39